Implementing and Overseeing Electronic Voting and Counting Technologies

Lead Authors

Ben Goldsmith
Holly Ruthrauff

Copyright © 2013 International Foundation for Electoral Systems and National Democratic Institute for International Affairs.

All rights reserved.

Permission Statement: No part of this publication may be reproduced in any form or by any means, electronic or mechanical, including photocopying, recording, or by any information storage and retrieval system without the written permission of IFES.

Requests for permission should include the following information:

- A description of the material for which permission to copy is desired.
- The purpose for which the copied material will be used and the manner in which it will be used.
- Your name, title, company or organization name, telephone number, fax number, e-mail address and mailing address.

Please send all requests for permission to:

International Foundation for Electoral Systems
1850 K Street, NW, Fifth Floor
Washington, D.C. 20006
Email: editor@ifes.org
Fax: 202.350.6701

National Democratic Institute for International Affairs
455 Massachusetts Avenue NW, 8th Floor
Washington, D.C. 20001
Email: kgest@ndi.org
Fax: 888.875.2887

Disclaimer: The author's views expressed in this publication do not necessarily reflect the views of the International Foundation for Electoral Systems, the National Democratic Institute and the U.S. Agency for International Development.

ISBN: 978-0-9910142-0-0

ABOUT IFES

The International Foundation for Electoral Systems (IFES) supports citizens' right to participate in free and fair elections. Our independent expertise strengthens electoral systems and builds local capacity to deliver sustainable solutions.

As the global leader in democracy promotion, we advance good governance and democratic rights by:

- Providing technical assistance to election officials
- Empowering the underrepresented to participate in the political process
- Applying field-based research to improve the electoral cycle

Since 1987, IFES has worked in over 135 countries – from developing democracies, to mature democracies. For more information, visit www.IFES.org.

ABOUT NDI

The National Democratic Institute (NDI) is a nonprofit, nonpartisan, nongovernmental organization that responds to the aspirations of people around the world to live in democratic societies that recognize and promote basic human rights.

Since its founding in 1983, NDI and its local partners have worked to support and strengthen democratic institutions and practices by strengthening political parties, civic organizations and parliaments, safeguarding elections, and promoting citizen participation, openness and accountability in government.

With staff members and volunteer political practitioners from more than 100 nations, NDI brings together individuals and groups to share ideas, knowledge, experiences and expertise. Partners receive broad exposure to best practices in international democratic development that can be adapted to the needs of their own countries. NDI's multinational approach reinforces the message that while there is no single democratic model, certain core principles are shared by all democracies.

The Institute's work upholds the principles enshrined in the Universal Declaration of Human Rights. It also promotes the development of institutionalized channels of communications among citizens, political institutions and elected officials, and strengthens their ability to improve the quality of life for all citizens. For more information about NDI, please visit www.ndi.org.

ACKNOWLEDGMENTS

As a growing number of countries at various stages of development consider the use of electronic technologies in electoral processes, they face opportunities and challenges. This Guide was prepared by IFES and NDI to help election authorities, civil society, political parties and other stakeholders engage in inclusive, transparent and accountable decisionmaking, implementation and oversight of electronic voting and counting technologies. It is also intended to help inform international and local democracy and governance support communities in designing and implementing effective electoral assistance programs in countries adopting or considering the use of electronic technologies.

The Guide is the product of close collaboration between IFES and NDI, each with complementary areas of expertise. It reflects IFES' 25 years of experience – in over 135 countries – of strengthening electoral systems and building local capacity to deliver sustainable electoral solutions by providing technical assistance to election officials; empowering the underrepresented to participate in political processes; and applying field-based research to improve the electoral cycle. It also draws from NDI's 30 years of experience in international election observation and in supporting the efforts of political parties and nonpartisan citizen election monitoring groups in more than 125 countries to promote electoral integrity and popular political participation.

Ben Goldsmith, IFES Electoral Technology Advisor, and Holly Ruthrauff, formerly with NDI's Elections and Political Processes team, were the authors of the Guide. Ben primarily concentrated on issues related to the design and implementation of electronic technologies, while Holly focused mainly on issues related to the oversight of such technologies. Ben has 15 years of experience advising and managing election administration projects in post conflict and developing democracies. Ben has helped to conduct elections and provided technical assistance in various countries including Afghanistan, Bosnia, Iraq, Kosovo, Kenya and the United Kingdom. He is an expert on electronic voting and has advised electoral officials in several countries on the design and use of these technologies. He is the author of Electronic Voting & Counting Technologies: A Guide to Conducting Feasibility Studies and was the lead IFES researcher on the evaluation of various facets of the internet voting pilot in Norway. Holly has more than 15 years of experience with electoral assistance and observation. She has organized observer missions, developed more than 10 publications and handbooks for both international and domestic observers, and provided technical assistance to domestic observer efforts around the world through her work at NDI, Election Reform International Services (ERIS) and the Organization for Security and Co-operation in Europe's Office for Democratic Institutions and Human Rights (OSCE/ODIHR).

Rakesh Sharma, IFES Director of Applied Research, and Michael McNulty, NDI Senior Program Manager in Elections and Political Processes, were the editors of the Guide and managers of its publication. Rakesh and Michael also drafted elements of the Guide. Pat Merloe, NDI Senior Associate and Director of Electoral Programs, provided guidance and editing throughout the drafting process. NDI Program Assistant Sunila Chilukuri and IFES Research Coordinator Ayesha Chugh supported the editors and played important roles in text revisions and additions.

NDI's Michael McNulty and IFES' George Carmona conducted the Philippines case study and drafted the report. The Brazil case study was conducted and drafted by NDI consultant Ambassador Ecaterine Siradze-Delaunay and IFES consultant F. Daniel Hidalgo. The Netherlands case study was researched and drafted by IFES consultant Susanne Caarls and Guide co-author Holly Ruthrauff.

IFES and NDI express appreciation for the valuable recommendations provided, in their personal capacities, by noted electronic voting and counting technologies experts Vladimir Pran, Democracy Reporting International; Jonathan Stonestreet; Rokey Suleman; Ole Holtved; Ronan McDermott, and Mike Yard.

The writing, editing, production and publication of this Guide were made possible by a grant from the United States Agency for International Development (USAID). We hope that those who use this Guide will contact IFES and NDI with any comments, suggestions and requests.

William R. Sweeney, Jr., President & CEO, IFES and
Kenneth Wollack, President, NDI

Implementing and Overseeing Electronic Voting and Counting Technologies

LIST OF ACRONYMS

Center for People Empowerment in Governance	CenPEG
Council of Europe	CoE
COMELEC Advisory Council	CAC
Commission on Elections	COMELEC
Direct Recording Electronic	DRE
Electronic Ballot Printer	EBP
Election Commission of Pakistan	ECP
Election Management Body	EMB
Electronic Voting Machines	EVM
Frequently Asked Questions	FAQ
Help America Vote Act	HAVA
Information and Communications Technology	ICT
Information Technology	IT
International Foundation for Electoral Systems	IFES
International Republican Institute	IRI
International Standards Organization	ISO

Internet Service Provider	ISP
La Oficina Nacional de Procesos Electorales	ONPE
National Citizens' Movements for Free Elections	NAMFREL
National Democratic Institute	NDI
National Software Reference Library	NSRL
Nederlandse Apparatenfabriek NV	NEDAP
New Voting Technologies	NVT
Ordem dos Advogados do Brasil	OAM
Organization for Security and Cooperation in Europe	OSCE
Organization of American States	OAS
Optical Character Recognition	OCR
Optical Mark Recognition	OMR
Parish Pastoral Council for Responsible Voting	PPCRV
Precinct Count Optical Scan	PCOS
Request for Proposals	RFP
Technical Guidelines Development Committee	TGDC
Toegepast Natuurwetenschappelijk Onderzoek	TNO
Tribunal Superior Eleitoral	TSE
U.S. Election Assistance Commission	EAC
Voluntary Voting System Guidelines	VVSG
Voter-Verified Paper Audit Trail	VVPAT
Web Accessibility Initiative	WAI

HOW TO USE THIS MANUAL

This manual has been designed to provide a critical source of information on electronic voting and counting technologies for specialists in Democracy & Governance, as well as Election Management Bodies (EMBs), civil society organizations (CSOs), political parties and other key stakeholders engaged in electoral processes around the world. The manual provides a guide to the challenges, opportunities and considerations involved in decision-making, design and implementation of the technologies to assist EMBs as they move through the process or seek to understand it better, as well as to help other stakeholders, including civil society and electoral contestants, understand how to engage in and monitor these processes.

IFES and NDI have designed the manual to provide both a brief primer as well as detailed exposition on the key issues related to electronic voting and counting. As such, the manual is adaptable for use by readers at different levels of engagement with these technologies. The guide below indicates how two different types of readers can use this manual.

FOR READERS INTERESTED ONLY IN A BRIEF PRIMER ON ELECTRONIC VOTING AND COUNTING TECHNOLOGIES

- The Overview chapter (Chapter 1) provides a brief introduction to the main issues involved in the effective design, implementation and oversight of these technologies. The chapter has been written to provide enough coverage of these issues so that the reader can gain a solid understanding of these issues without the need to read the detailed descriptions of each issue. For readers that would like to explore a particular issue or process in more depth, each issue covered in Chapter 1 has footnotes that guide the reader to specific subsections and page numbers of Chapter 2 that address the issue in more detail.

- Chapter 2 addresses the key issues in much more depth by outlining in a chronological manner the processes of deciding on, designing, implementing and observing electronic voting or counting projects. While it is more detailed than Chapter 1, the general reader can still use two specific design elements of this chapter to quickly gain a general understanding of the most important points, as explained below.

    1. Each of the key issues related to electronic voting and counting is addressed in subsections in Chapter 2. For each subsection, a summary of the discussion in this subsection is provided in brief text that is formatted as below:

        ### DECISION IN PRINCIPLE

        The decision-in-principle stage of the decision-making process is vitally important, as it helps to establish the parameters for the consideration of electronic voting and counting technologies. This stage involves several essential steps:

2. Additionally, at the end of each subsection, a list of key considerations is provided for both EMBs and oversight groups. This quick reference list can be used by EMBs, oversight groups, or a general audience to identify the questions that should be considered for the issue highlighted in the preceding subsection. This checklist is formatted as below:

> **KEY CONSIDERATIONS:**
> **CHALLENGES AND RECOUNTS**
>
> **FOR IMPLEMENTING BODIES**
>
> ☑ Does the legal framework clearly define who can lodge a challenge against the results, to which body the challenge should be lodged, in what circumstances an investigation will be conducted and in what situation a recount of the results will occur?

FOR READERS INTERESTED IN A MORE DETAILED UNDERSTANDING

- Chapter 2 addresses each of the key issues related to electronic voting and counting technologies in much more depth than Chapter 1. Each of the key issues related to electronic voting and counting is addressed in sub-sections in Chapter 2.

- For EMBs and oversight groups engaged in the implementation or oversight of these technologies, there is a checklist of important questions that should be considered by both EMBs and oversight groups for the issues addressed in each of the Chapter 2 subsections (please see Example 2 above). EMBs and oversight groups can use these checklists to ensure that they are considering the significant aspects of each phase of the decisionmaking, design, implementation and evaluation of electronic voting and counting technology projects.

- Chapter 2 also provides text boxes with brief case studies of how a particular issue related to electronic voting and counting technologies was addressed in practice. These case studies provide the reader with practical examples and lessons learned that can help inform their thinking on key issues.

- Appendices 1 – 3 contain detailed cases studies on the use of electronic voting and/or counting technologies in the Philippines, Netherlands, and Brazil. These case studies provide descriptive narratives on how these countries addressed many of the issues detailed in the manual. These case studies also give the reader an appreciation of the challenges and complexity involved in the design, implementation and monitoring of e-voting and counting technologies, as well as the many lesson learned that have emerged from these three countries' experiences.

- Appendix 4 provides a list of additional resources on electronic voting and counting technologies.

CONTENTS

CHAPTER 1
OVERVIEW OF ELECTRONIC VOTING AND COUNTING TECHNOLOGIES — 19

Framework for the Guide and Overview Section 20
Weighing the Benefits and Challenges 21
Electronic Voting 23
Electronic Counting 25
Common Electronic Voting and Counting Technologies 25
Electronic Voting and Counting Around the World 29
Key Electronic Voting and Counting Considerations 32

CHAPTER 2
IMPLEMENTING AND OVERSEEING ELECTRONIC VOTING AND COUNTING PROJECTS — 73

2.1 MAKING A DECISION ON E-VOTING OR E-COUNTING — 75

Decision in Principle 77
    Key Considerations: Decision in Principle 87

Pilot Projects 88
    Key Considerations: Pilot Projects 93

Decision on Adoption 95
    Key Considerations: Decision on Adoption 99

2.2 BUILDING THE SYSTEM FOR E-VOTING OR E-COUNTING   101

Standards for Implementation 101
    Key Considerations: Standards for Implementation 105

Legal and Procedural Framework 106
    Key Considerations: Legal and Procedural Framework 114

Design Requirements 116
    Key Considerations: Design Requirements 122

Procurement, Production and Delivery 124
    Key Considerations: Procurement, Production and Delivery .. 132

Security Mechanisms 134
    Key Considerations: Security Mechanisms 145

Recruitment and Training of Personnel 147
    Key Considerations: Recruitment and Training of Personnel 150

2.3 IMPLEMENTING ELECTRONIC VOTING OR ELECTRONIC COUNTING IN AN ELECTION   153

Project and Risk Management 153
    Key Considerations: Project and Risk Management 160

Voter Education and Information 162
    Key Considerations: Voter Education and Information 168

Software and Hardware Maintenance, Storage and Update 170
    Key Considerations: Software/Hardware Maintenance,
    Storage and Update 172

Testing, Source Code Review and Certification 173
    Key Considerations: Testing, Source Code Review
    and Certification.. 182

Election Day (Setup, Testing, Security, Troubleshooting) 183
    Key Considerations: Election Day (Set-up, Testing, Security,
    Troubleshooting) 192

Tabulation.. 194
    Key Considerations: Tabulation 198

Challenges and Recounts.. 199
    Key Considerations: Challenges and Recounts 203

Post-Election Audits 205
    Key Considerations: Post-election Audits..................................... 210

Evaluation of system 211
    Key Considerations: Evaluation of System 216

Internet Voting... 218
    Key Considerations: Internet Voting 226

CONCLUDING REMARKS   229

ANNEXES   233

CASE STUDY REPORT ON BRAZIL ELECTRONIC VOTING, 1996 TO PRESENT   235

CASE STUDY REPORT ON ELECTRONIC VOTING IN THE NETHERLANDS	259
CASE STUDY REPORT ON THE PHILIPPINES 2010 ELECTIONS	275
IMPLEMENTING AND OVERSEEING ELECTRONIC VOTING AND COUNTING TECHNOLOGIES: RESOURCE ANNEX	307

CHAPTER 1
OVERVIEW OF ELECTRONIC VOTING AND COUNTING TECHNOLOGIES

Traditional electoral procedures involving casting and hand counting paper ballots have come to dominate elections since their introduction in the mid-19th century. Technology increasingly offers new mechanisms for conducting traditionally-manual processes, and elections are no exception. There are many different technologies that can be used to support the electoral process. This guide will focus on electronic technologies that assist voting and the subsequent counting of votes.

The current discourse on these technologies includes such terms as electronic voting machines, e-voting, e-enabled elections, new voting technologies (NVT), remote voting, precinct count optical scanning (PCOS), and e-counting. This array of terminology relates to different technological solutions. The field of election technologies concerning voting and counting is developing, and the conceptual framework is still emerging. Therefore, it is easy to find the same terms being used in different ways in different countries or regions, which can create confusion.

When discussing electronic voting, two separate, but sometimes related technologies are generally referred to – electronic voting and electronic counting. The traditional paper-based voting system consists of a voter manually marking the paper ballot and then the ballot being counted by hand by election officials. In elections using electronic voting or counting technologies, one or both of these processes are automated electronically.

FRAMEWORK FOR THE GUIDE AND OVERVIEW SECTION

This guide and the overview section will focus on the most commonly-used electronic voting and counting technologies: namely, non-remote EVMs used in the supervised environment of the polling station and electronic counting machines. Much that is discussed in the guide and overview is also relevant for remote electronic voting from unsupervised environments. However, the use of such remote voting technologies presents complex challenges in implementation. This is especially the case for remote voter identification and authentication, audit mechanisms, data secrecy and security. At the same time, the logistics of implementing remote voting may be much simpler than for non-remote voting.

The overview section of this guide is meant to be useful for election administrators, electoral stakeholders, including oversight actors and those in the donor community who might be considering the merits of introducing electronic voting and/or counting technologies in a country. It is important to note that electronic voting and counting technologies can create new and important stakeholder groups in the electoral process. These groups include technology vendors, who often play a very important role in the election, certification bodies, academia and IT experts. All of these groups may play a key role in providing, checking or overseeing the use of new technologies.

This overview provides an introduction to the key considerations and themes to be assessed when contemplating the use of electronic voting and counting technologies – issues that will be explored in more detail in the next section of the manual. These include practical considerations related to the use of electronic voting and counting technologies, such as the legality of using such technology under existing legal frameworks; timeline for consideration and implementation; sustainability of the technology; integrity of elections using this technology; trust in the technologies; and the security of the technologies and data. Key issues also include normative aspects of the electoral process, such as inclusiveness, transparency, accountability and ballot secrecy in elections when using electronic voting and counting technologies. Finally, a section is included that attempts to summarize what can be characterized as emerging electoral standards related to the use of electronic voting and counting technologies.

Consideration of the use of electronic voting or counting technologies is an incredibly complex topic. In highlighting the many issues that need to be assessed when considering the use of these technologies, it is hoped the overview will provide electoral stakeholders with the tools needed to give electronic voting and counting technologies the due consideration they deserve.

WEIGHING THE BENEFITS AND CHALLENGES

The increasing adoption of these new technologies in some regions comes in part from the recognition that technology may offer benefits over traditional methods of voting and counting. Such benefits may include:

- eliminating the cost and logistics involved with paper ballots; improved voter identification mechanisms;
- improved accessibility to voting;
- easy conduct of complex elections; increase in voter turnout;

- eliminating invalid ballots;
- faster, more accurate and standardized counting of ballots; and
- prevention of certain forms of fraud.[1]

However, the use of new technologies brings new challenges. These challenges may include:

- lack of transparency;
- negative impact on confidence in the process;
- confusion for the illiterate or uneducated voters on process;
- need to conduct widespread voter education, how to use it and its impact on the process;
- difficulties in auditing results;
- secrecy of the ballot;
- security of the voting and counting process;
- cost of introducing and maintaining the technology over the lifecycle of the equipment;
- potentially losing control over the process to outside technology vendors; recruitment of staff with specialized IT skills;
- added complexity in the electoral process and the ability of the EMB to deal adequately with this complexity; and
- consequences in the event of equipment or system malfunction.

In addition to these challenges, it is also vitally important that electronic voting and counting systems are implemented in such a way as to not violate core electoral standards.

The challenges need to be carefully considered and balanced against anticipated benefits when deciding whether to use such technologies for elections.

---

[1] While the use of electronic voting and counting technologies can serve to prevent some kinds of fraud, it also opens up the possibility for new kinds of fraud. The use of these technologies should certainly not be seen as the means by which fraud is eliminated entirely from the electoral process.

The relevance of each of these possible advantages and disadvantages will vary from country to country, as will the challenges and issues presented by the existing system being used for elections. Therefore, there is no one answer on the appropriateness of using election technologies. Rather, each electoral jurisdiction will need to fully assess possible advantages and disadvantages to see whether using such technologies is beneficial.

Because the decisions on these matters will profoundly affect voters' confidence in electoral results, the assessment should be made through a broadly consultative process and be based on equally broad consensus. Without such inclusive and transparent deliberations, suspicions that often exist in competitive political environments may undermine the decision to use electronic voting or counting systems, and erode the legitimacy of the electoral process.

ELECTRONIC VOTING

In electronic voting, an electronic device is used by the voter to make and record their ballot choice. The choice is either recorded on the machine itself, or the machine produces a token on which the choices are recorded. The token is then placed in a ballot box (internal or external to the machine). The token can be a printout of the ballot choice, or the ballot choice can be recorded on another medium. For example, in Belgium a magnetic card has been used for this purpose. Electronic voting devices include voting machines placed in polling stations (sometimes referred to as direct recording electronic (DRE) voting machines), SMS voting and Internet voting.

There are two other distinctions (Figure 1) to be made when it comes to electronic voting machines, which are also important in implementation:
- Remote and non-remote voting machines
- Supervised and unsupervised environments

FIGURE 1 – KEY DISTINCTIONS FOR IMPLEMENTATION OF ELECTRONIC VOTING

- Remote Voting: An electronic device used to cast a vote, and then transmits the ballot choice across a communication channel. The ballot choice is then recorded in a central location, e.g. Internet voting and SMS voting.

- Non-Remote Voting Machines: An electronic device used to cast a vote, which records the ballot choice made on a local medium, e.g. the machine itself or a printed ballot.

- Supervised Environments: A voting machine used in a location where election staff is present to manage the voting process, such as a polling station.

- Unsupervised Environments: A voting device used in a location where no election staff is present to manage the voting process, such as any computer the voter uses for Internet voting.

It is possible to combine remote voting with supervised environments, for example, Internet voting computers set up in polling stations. This allows polling staff to verify the identity of voters by using voter lists before allowing them to vote, and to ensure secrecy of the vote – two significant challenges with other forms of remote voting.

ELECTRONIC COUNTING

Electronic counting involves the use of a device to count votes cast. The most common such counting machines use scanning technologies, such as optical mark recognition (OMR) or optical character recognition (OCR), to count ballots that have been completed manually by voters. This broad category of technologies also includes punch card counting machines and electronic ballot boxes used to count electronic records on tokens produced by electronic voting machines.

Electronic voting and electronic counting technologies, while representing different stages of the electoral process, can be combined, as is done by the DRE voting machine. It not only enables the voter to make his or her ballot choices, but also records them directly on the machine and produces results on the machine at the end of the voting process.

It is not mandatory, however, to combine the technologies. It is possible to have electronic voting without electronic counting and electronic counting without electronic voting. It is also possible to have voting and counting on entirely different devices, whereby a voting machine is used to produce tokens with the ballot choices made and a separate counting device tallies the votes recorded on these tokens.

COMMON ELECTRONIC VOTING AND COUNTING TECHNOLOGIES

There are many different electronic voting and counting technologies being used globally. The variety of technologies used makes it difficult to easily categorize them. The most common types of technologies are identified are as follows:

DIRECT RECORDING ELECTRONIC (DRE) SYSTEM

Often referred to as electronic voting machines (EVMs), DRE systems use a keyboard, touch-screen, mouse, pen or other electronic device to allow a voter to record his or her vote electronically. DREs are used in non-remote, supervised locations (polling stations). The DRE system captures the voter's choices and stores an electronic record of their vote in the machine. The data captured by each individual DRE unit is then transmitted by either electronic means (i.e., Internet, cellular network or memory card) or manually (i.e., by printing the results from each machine and tabulating them) to capture the total number of votes cast for specific parties or candidates. DRE systems may or may not produce a paper record to allow the voter to verify their voting choices. This paper record, also called a voter verified paper audit trail (VVPAT), has been implemented in multiple ways in different countries.

DREs with VVPATs are perceived to have an advantage over DREs without VVPATs, because paper trails provide greater transparency to the voter, which can engender greater trust. DRE voting without VVPATs, which is a form of "black box voting," does not provide sufficient means for voters and stakeholders to verify votes have been accurately recorded. DREs with VVPAT provide election management bodies (EMBs) and those who provide oversight with the potential to audit the results or conduct a meaningful recount. However, DREs with VVPATs also introduce greater technological complexity into the process, which may result in greater challenges for EMBs in terms of reliability of the machine, training for staff and sustainability of the overall system.

DREs can be confusing for voters who are not familiar or comfortable with information technology (IT). However, in some contexts, voters may benefit from a streamlined presentation of ballots on DREs in complicated voting systems – with or without VVPAT – where a paper ballot design may lead to a significant number of spoilt and invalid ballots. It is important to note that ballot design may be a challenge no matter which voting system is used.

ELECTRONIC BALLOT PRINTERS (EBPS)

EBPs are similar to DREs, in that the voter uses a DRE-type interface for the act of making voting choices. However, unlike DREs, an EBP does not store vote data. Instead, it prints out a paper receipt or produces a token containing the voting choice(s). The voter then takes this receipt or token and places it into the ballot box, which may be electronic and automatically count the vote.

EBPs are considered easier to understand and more user-friendly for the voter than DREs, as they split the actions of marking the voter's choice and casting the ballot in the same way a voter marks and casts a ballot in traditional paper voting. The first machine (ballot printer) only marks the voter's choice, but does not record the vote, while the second machine (ballot scanner or "electronic ballot box") only records and tallies the votes. Like the DREs with a VVPAT, the voter can verify their vote, either on a printed paper ballot or by inserting the ballot token into another voting machine. There is the possibility of a recount of the paper receipt or token if the electronic results are challenged or audited. However, because they involve two separate machines, EBP systems may entail higher costs, require greater IT capacity from EMBs and encounter more challenges to ensuring sustainability than other systems.

OPTICAL MARK RECOGNITION (OMR)

OMR counting machines combine aspects of paper ballot voting with electronic counting. The voter uses a pen or pencil to mark his or her choices (usually by filling in an oval or connecting an arrow) on a special machine-readable paper ballot. The ballot is then read by an OMR machine that tallies votes using the marks made by the voter. There are two methods used to tally votes using an OMR system. The tallying can be done at the polling station with the voter feeding the ballot into the machine, or votes can be tallied at a central/regional counting facility where votes from more than one polling station are counted.

OMR systems provide greater ability for recounts than DREs without VVPAT. Generally, OMR systems cost less than DREs and may put less strain on EMBs in terms of sustainability of the systems. On the other hand, these systems entail significant focus on details such as ballot design, type of ink used, paper stock thickness and other factors that may inhibit the ability of OMR machines to accurately count votes. OMR machines are always used in a supervised, non-remote location.

INTERNET VOTING SYSTEM

In an Internet voting system, the voter casts his or her vote using a computer with access to the Internet. Internet voting generally takes place in an unsupervised, remote location, from any computer that has Internet access, such as a voter's home or work. It can also take place in supervised, non-remote locations if, for example, electoral authorities provide Internet kiosks at polling stations.

Convenience and greater access are the two key benefits cited for a move to Internet voting. In terms of access, Internet voting is perceived to provide access to specific populations that may have difficulty in voting at polling stations, e.g. persons with disabilities and eligible voters living outside a country. However, Internet voting from unsupervised locations requires voting systems to place a greater emphasis on voter authentication to avoid impersonation, and also elicits concerns about the secrecy of the ballot. Internet voting also raises security concerns with regard to hacking into the system or other ways of corrupting data. Similar to DREs without VVPAT, Internet voting also raises questions about verifiability, may not allow recounts and presents challenges for adjudication of electoral complaints. Finally, transparency in Internet voting systems may be compromised to an even greater extent than with DREs. Such challenges are not beyond solution, but to date remain significant.

ELECTRONIC VOTING AND COUNTING AROUND THE WORLD

This guide will use the terminology "electronic voting and counting technologies." As already demonstrated, there are a wide range of technology options covered by electronic voting and counting technologies. Suppliers also implement technologies in different ways, creating a confusing array of alternatives available to EMBs within and between these two broad categories. The variety of offered technologies might be one factor that has led to very different experiences in countries, which have used or attempted to use electronic voting and counting technologies.

Voting technologies have a surprisingly long history. In the United States, mechanical lever voting machines were first used for elections in 1892 and were commonly used in U.S. elections until the 1990s. Electronic technologies began to appear in the 1960s with punch card counting machines. In the following decades, technologies such as DRE voting machines, ballot scanning machines and Internet voting began to appear. The U.S. was at the forefront of adopting many of these technologies. Through the 1990s and the first decade of the new millennium, an increasing number of countries around the world also started to adopt these technologies.

Recent research has shown that 31 countries around the world have used non remote electronic voting machines for binding political elections at some point.[2] Some of these countries have experimented with EVMs and then decided not to continue with their use, in some cases after using them for many years. EVMs are being used in 20 countries, with six of these countries still piloting the technology. Globally, very different trends are seen in different

---

2 Esteve, Jordi Barrat I, Ben Goldsmith and John Turner. International Experience with E-Voting. Norwegian E-Vote Project. IFES, June 2012.

FIGURE 2: MAP OF GLOBAL NON-REMOTE ELECTRONIC VOTING EXPERIENCE

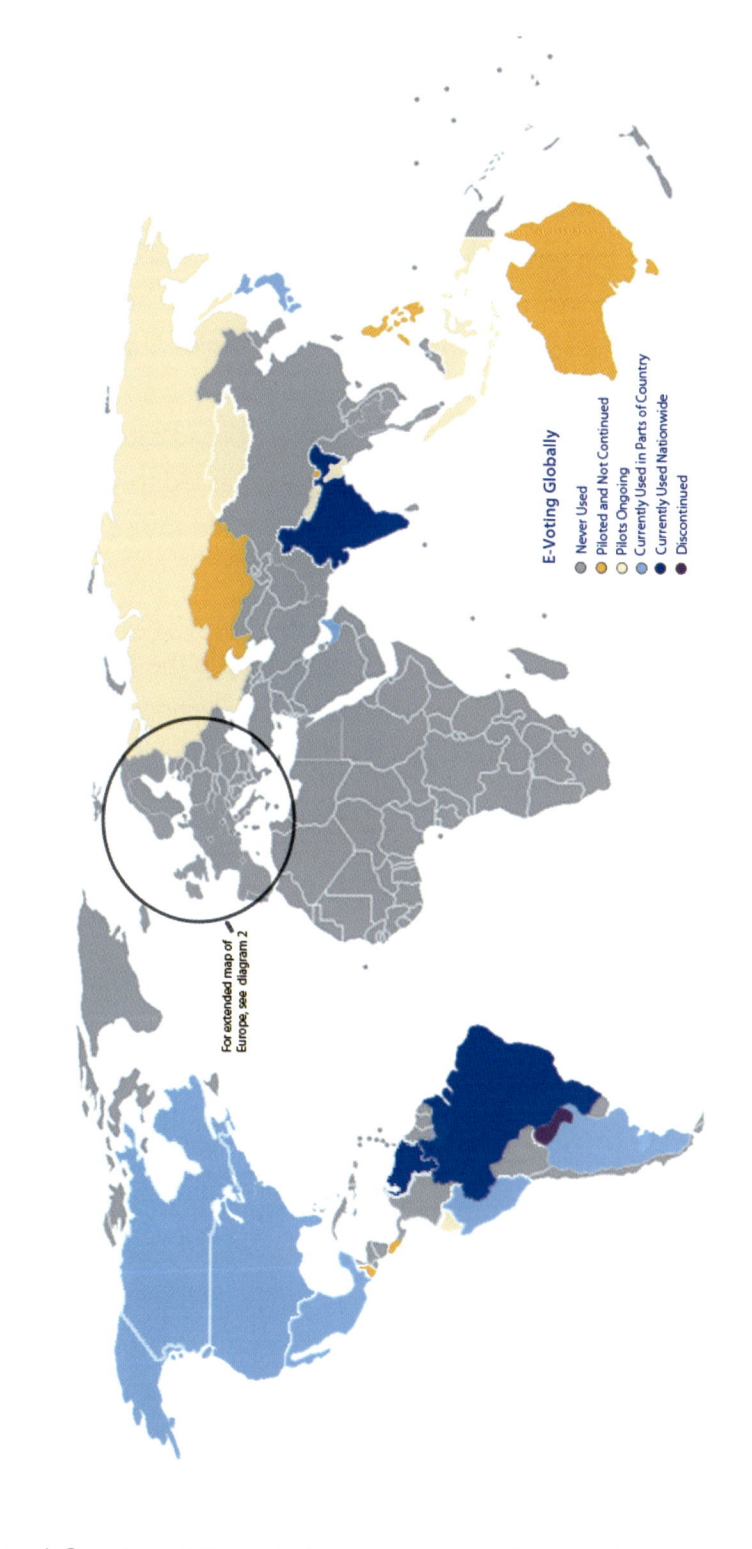

30 Chapter 1 Overview of Electronic Voting and Counting Technologies

regions. Europe and North America can be seen as moving away from the use of EVMs, while South America and Asia show increasing interest in using electronic voting technologies. Unfortunately, no similar research is available for the global use of electronic counting technologies.

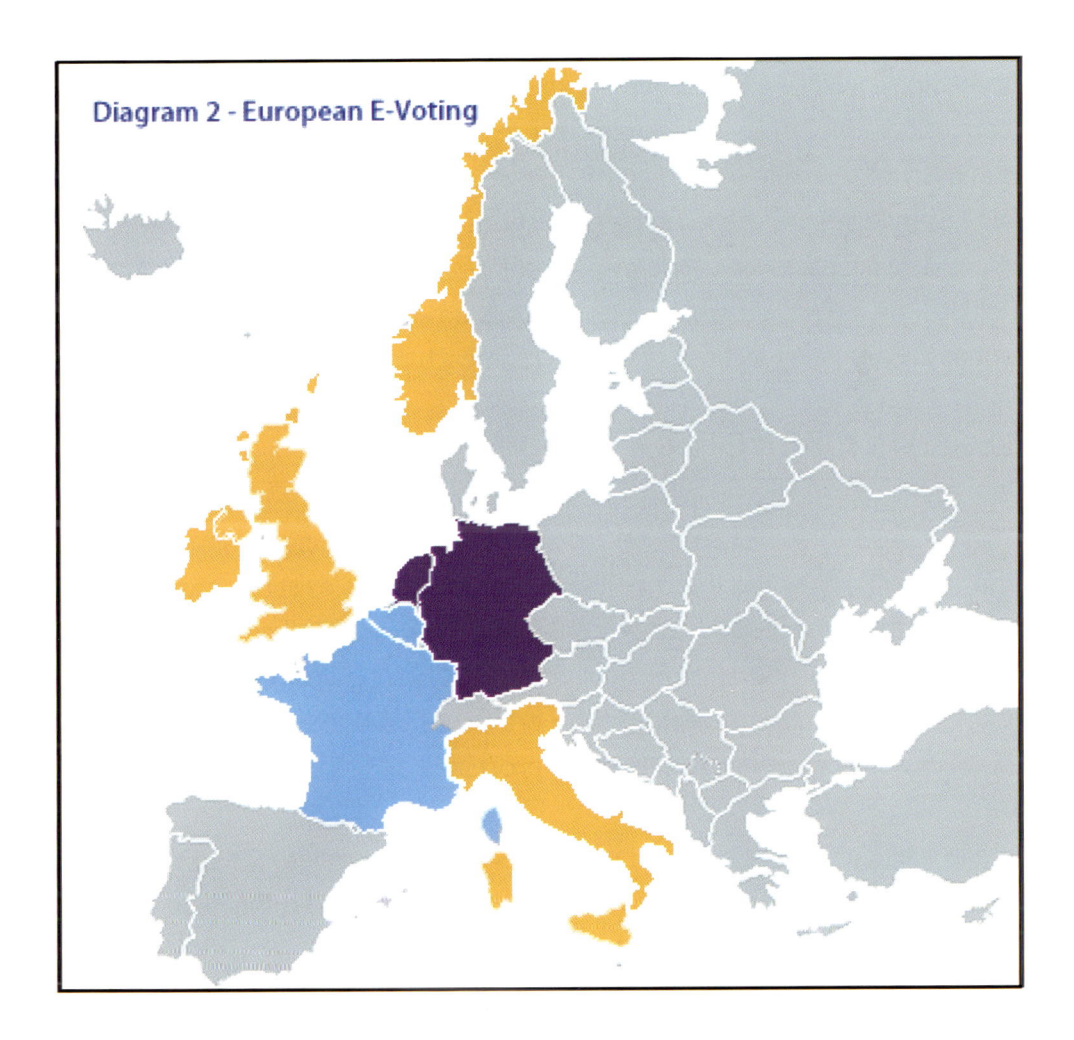

Diagram 2 - European E-Voting

KEY ELECTRONIC VOTING AND COUNTING CONSIDERATIONS

As outlined previously, there are an increasing number of countries around the world that have implemented or piloted electronic voting and counting technologies. While each country's experience is different, there are some common themes that surface across these experiences. This section provides a summary of thematic issues that often arise when electronic voting and counting technologies are used. The considerations identified here are explored in more detail in part two of the manual, but it is hoped the following discussion will provide a basic understanding of each issue and the challenges electronic voting and counting technologies present in each regard.

LEGALITY OF E-VOTING[3]

When considering the use of electronic voting and counting technologies, the compatibility of these technologies with a country's existing constitutional and legal framework needs to be considered very carefully. The use of these technologies may not only be contradictory to existing provisions in the legal framework, but may require additional provisions be drafted to cover the ways in which technologies impact electoral processes.

It may well be that the existing legal framework makes reference to physical ballot boxes and ballot box seals, to actual ballot papers and the ways in which ballots are counted and adjudicated. All of these processes can occur with an electronic voting or counting machine, but in a different way.

---

3 For more detailed information on this topic, please refer to the following sections in Part 2: Decision in Principle, pgs. 77-81; Legal and Procedural Framework, pgs. 106-113.

Therefore, the electoral legal framework needs to be reviewed to determine whether the use of electronic voting or counting technologies is in compliance with the law. It is highly likely that if only paper balloting has been used in the past, then the laws will have been written in such a way as to preclude the use of these technologies. Parts of the legislation requiring amendment will need to be identified, and suitable amendments will need to be passed before a trial or full use of electronic voting and counting technologies can be implemented. The consequence of not doing so could be to invalidate any election held with electronic voting or counting technology.

However, rather than simply addressing electoral framework issues that might be inconsistent with using electronic voting or counting technologies, it would be advisable to conduct a comprehensive review of relevant legislation to ensure all aspects of using electronic technologies in a country's elections are lawful and appropriately regulated. The review could also cover issues such as transparency mechanisms, security mechanisms, certification requirements, audit requirements and procedures for challenging results generated by electronic voting or counting machines. It may also be relevant to review other legislation that might not be directly related to elections, such as laws dealing with information technology; administrative and criminal codes; data security and protection; procurement; and the issue of government contracts. Such legislation may have an impact on the legal framework for using electronic voting or counting technologies, or may require an amendment to permit their use.

A balance needs to be established in drafting legislation to enable electronic voting or counting. A similar level of detail to paper based voting should be included in this legislation. Those drafting the legislation must also ensure the EMB has sufficient flexibility to respond to changes in technology and the way in which it is implemented. The EMB needs to be aware that, not only will legislation and regulations be required for proper implementation of electronic voting or counting technologies, but procedures and protocols for internal use and management are also vital.

If legal changes are required to use electronic voting or counting technologies, it is prudent to start the process of making legal amendments as early as possible, as the process may be lengthy. This will allow sufficient time to develop or amend legislation in a manner inclusive of citizens and political contestants.

At least as important as revising the law substantively is the process by which it is addressed. An open and inclusive process for deliberating any legal amendments concerning these issues is vital to winning public confidence and reaching an agreement with potential electoral contestants on the new rules of the electoral competition. The importance of a transparent and inclusive approach cannot be overstated.

TIMEFRAME[4]

The timeframe for consideration and possible adoption of electronic voting and counting technologies is an issue that needs to be carefully considered. It is easy to underestimate the time that proper consideration and implementation can take, even for a pilot project. A full assessment of electoral requirements; availability of technologies; and identifying benefits and challenges of using such technologies can take many months. Once suitable technologies are identified, they must be procured – ideally and initially on a small scale – for a pilot. When pilots are held, a full and thorough evaluation of the process must be conducted before any plans or decisions are made for further implementation.

Legislation and regulations need to be drafted and passed, which in many countries could take months or even longer. Consultations should take place in the ini-

---

[4] For more detailed information on this topic, please refer to the following section in Part 2: Project and Risk Management, pgs. 153-161.

tial stages and throughout the process with stakeholders regarding whether the technology should be implemented and, if so, in what form. Technology suppliers need adequate time to develop and deliver equipment and systems, including testing and certification of desired systems. Election officials need to be trained and voter education needs to be conducted on use of the technologies.

The complexity involved in implementation of such technology projects also means that even where comprehensive project plans and timelines are developed, there should be flexibility within the timeline to cope with unforeseen problems and challenges. Such complications often occur. Unlike other technology implementation projects, there is little room for delaying the completion date where elections are concerned. The election must take place on a certain date, and if the technology is not ready, it presents a serious problem.

EMBs considering the use of electronic voting or counting technologies need to be fully aware of these time challenges and plan accordingly. In most cases, the timeline for proper implementation of such technologies is likely to be measured in years rather than months, even for pilots.

SUSTAINABILITY[5]

Electronic voting and counting systems result in implementing elections in very different ways than traditional paper-based systems. These differences may have many benefits to offer in the conduct of elections, but they can also carry many disadvantages. The importance attached to the benefits vis-à-vis the challenges of using such technologies will vary from country to country. These country-specific circumstances will have a significant impact on the overall feasibility and desirability of using electronic voting and counting technologies.

---

5 For more detailed information on this topic, please refer to the following sections in Part 2: Decision in Principle, pgs. 77-81; and Recruitment and Training of Personnel, pgs. 147-151.

Even if the use of such technology is both technically feasible and desirable, it needs to be sustainable in the long run. There are a number of contributing factors to the long-term sustainability of implementing electronic voting and counting, including financial aspects, project management and staffing arrangements.

The implementation of electronic voting or counting systems is usually an expensive exercise. Estimating the full cost of implementing the systems is not as easy as it may first seem, and the costs involved go far beyond just the procurement of voting or counting machines. Such additional costs include ongoing supplier support for contracts; management facilities for central/local tabulation of results; special booths/stands for voting machines; securing environmentally-controlled storage; maintenance and repair; replacement for expired equipment; consumables, such as ink cartridges and paper; testing and certification; specialized staff/technicians required to configure; testing and support for the technology; and voter and stakeholder education costs.

While a significant component of these costs is involved in the initial investment, there are many ongoing costs that need to be covered. A full appreciation of the costs involved over the life cycle of the electronic voting and counting machines needs to be factored into the estimate of financial sustainability for the technology. This is especially the case where a donor might be assisting a country in piloting or implementing a voting or counting system. The EMB needs to be confident it can provide the finances to continue implementation of the technology in absence of donor support.

From a project management perspective, the implementation of an electronic voting and counting technology project is complex, even if only for a small pilot project. The EMB will need to coordinate a range of tasks to implement the project, including procurement, logistics, procedural development, training, voter education, testing and IT configuration and support.

Not only will implementing the technology require special project management skills, it will require sufficient resources. The temptation to add management responsibilities to existing staff duties must be avoided, or the implementation of the technology will be at risk for poor management and could prove unsuccessful.

Another aspect of managing a technology project of this nature is that the transition from one system (e.g. paper-based elections) to another (e.g. electronic voting) needs to be executed effectively. Staff at all levels of the EMB, including polling and counting staff, will need to be properly trained in the new system and adequate support provided as they begin to use the technology. Political parties, candidates, media and observers will need to be educated about how the electronic voting or counting technology works, and the opportunities they have for oversight. Finally, and most importantly, voters will have to be informed about the use of technology and the ways in which it will affect their interaction with the electoral process.

The use of electronic voting and counting technologies also changes the skill sets required by some EMB and temporary staff conducting polling and counting. If polling and counting staff are to be able to set up voting or counting machines and deal with common problems encountered with these machines, then it may make it significantly more difficult in some places to recruit sufficiently qualified staff. Technical staff will also need to be hired by the EMB to provide support for less common faults with the technology. To be useful on Election Day, technical staff should be deployed nationwide to respond quickly to problems. Such resources may be difficult to recruit in some places.

Suppliers of electronic voting or counting technologies may be willing to assist with the challenge of recruiting qualified technical staff by providing staff themselves. When such assistance is provided by a supplier, the EMB must be careful that it does not effectively cede control of key parts of the electoral process to the supplier (addressed below in the section on accountability). While this support may often be provided in the interest of implementing the project successfully, it represents an abdication of responsibility on the part of the EMB and creates an unhealthy dependency on the supplier. It also indicates a lack of sustainability in the use of the voting or counting technology. This lack of sustainability is not insurmountable, but it must be recognized and addressed.

All of these challenges to sustainability need to be carefully deliberated by any EMB and other stakeholders involved in making important public policy decisions concerning the use of these technologies.

INCLUSIVENESS[6]

Elections should be as inclusive as possible, for voters and contestants alike. Inclusiveness is closely linked to the right to vote and the right to run for office, as well as the obligation of governments to facilitate these rights. There should be no discrimination toward any group in regard to voting rights or their implementation. An inclusive election process is also one that is based on open, broad consultation with stakeholders.

Innovations offered by electronic voting and counting can create opportunities for a more inclusive election process. Increased accessibility is one of the arguments in favor of the adoption of such technologies. Certain groups of voters struggle to participate in traditional elections. For example, voters with disabilities may only be able to vote with assistance, which can violate their right to a secret ballot. Electronic voting machines can be designed with features to assist voters with disabilities to cast ballots unaided, enabling a country to better meet international electoral standards. For instance, voting machines may be designed with audio explanations to

---

6 For more detailed information on this topic, please refer to the following sections in Part 2: Decision in Principle, pgs. 77-81; Design Requirements, pgs. 116-123; and Voter Education/Information, pgs. 162-169.

allow blind voters to vote unaided; font size can be adjusted for the visually impaired; and sip/puff solutions can be used for voters with limited or no motor capacity.

Electronic voting machines may also facilitate the provision of ballots in other languages, with little additional cost, which may enfranchise linguistic minorities. Remote Internet voting may increase participation among military personnel and other voters living abroad.

At the same time, implementation of new voting or counting technologies should not exclude any group of voters or inhibit their participation in any way. Certain groups of voters, such as elderly, illiterate, rural or low income voters, may be unaccustomed to using computers or other electronic devices and may be initially reluctant to vote or cast their ballots electronically. Such considerations must be factored into both the design of the technology and related public outreach to ensure maximum usability of the equipment, particularly among groups that may be unfamiliar with electronic technologies.

Unintended disenfranchisement and potential erosion of trust in the election process has to be weighed against the potential for inclusion of certain groups and other possible benefits. That calculus is a matter of importance to all citizens, and is why sometimes seemingly technical considerations in this arena are actually public policy issues that require broad participation. The opinions and concerns of stakeholders (political parties, civil society and voters), must be central to decisions about whether and how to employ electronic voting or counting technologies. In addition, they should have an opportunity to monitor the processes for procuring the proposed equipment, including testing, certification, deployment and evaluation of its performance. This type of involvement will help build an understanding of the technologies, the likely benefits and a realistic assessment of the challenges.

If there is political consensus behind the decision to adopt electronic technologies, the potential for successful implementation is much higher. On the other hand, a decision to move ahead with such technologies in the face of significant opposition or lack of involvement is very risky, and could ultimately result in the failure of the project.

The accessibility and usability of proposed technologies should remain important considerations throughout the decision making process. Civil society organizations representing particular groups, such as persons with disabilities, illiterate or linguistic minorities should be consulted at regular intervals and be invited to test the equipment with these specific interests in mind. Pilot tests of equipment should also take issues of accessibility and usability into account.

Another aspect of inclusiveness is the need to provide voter information and education on new voting and counting technologies, so voters understand and feel confident using the equipment. Specific voter education campaigns should also be designed to target certain disadvantaged groups, explaining features that may facilitate their participation. As much as possible, voters should have the opportunity to try the technology before using it on Election Day.

Observer groups should give attention to issues of inclusiveness when observing a country that adopted electronic voting or counting technologies. Those groups should collect data on Election Day that demonstrates the extent to which certain populations experience difficulties when using the technology. Post-election survey data and focus groups can also provide valuable information about voter experiences using new technology for the first time.

TRANSPARENCY[7]

Transparency is a key principle for credible elections. A transparent election process is one in which each step is open to scrutiny by stakeholders (political parties, election observers and voters alike), who are able to independently verify the process is conducted according to procedures and no irregularities have occurred. Providing transparency in an election helps establish trust and public confidence in the process, as voters have a means to verify the results are an accurate reflection of the will of the people.

Electronic voting and counting technologies pose a challenge to ensuring transparency, since many visually-verifiable steps in a traditional election (such as how ballots were marked) are automated inside a machine and, therefore, cannot be seen by the voter and others. In such circumstances, particular efforts must be made to provide transparency in each step of the process.

A degree of transparency can be afforded through the design of the voting and counting technology. For instance, a VVPAT produces a paper record that can be checked by the voter to make sure the vote is accurately recorded. A paper record also provides the possibility of an auditable process. End-to-end verification systems allow a check to be conducted that all votes have been accurately recorded and tabulated.

Equally important to the transparency of Election Day is the transparency of the development of the technology itself. The procurement, development, testing and certification of voting and counting equipment should be carried out transparently, so stakeholders are confident the machines meet relevant requirements, function properly and have the necessary security features in place.

---

7 For more detailed information on this topic, please refer to the following subsections in Part 2: Pilot Project, pgs. 88-93; Legal and Procedural Framework, pgs. 106-113; Procurement, Production, and Delivery, pgs. 124-133; Security Mechanisms, pgs. 134-145; Voter Education, pgs. 162-169; and Testing, Source Code Review and Certification, pgs. 173-181.

Stakeholders may have limited capacity to make use of these transparency mechanisms and may have to adapt their expertise to fully use them. The EMB can help observers in this regard by educating them on the electronic voting or counting system being used and how they can effectively observe it.

Certain mechanisms for providing transparency, such as the use of open source code, may be controversial, as vendors may be reluctant to disclose source code citing protection of intellectual property and the security of technologies. Irrespective of these interests, however, all software and hardware should be made available for independent review.

Electoral contestants and election observers have a critical role to play in ensuring the transparency of an election process. It is not possible for everyone to understand e-voting and counting systems. Thus, voters rely on others who have the capacity to understand these processes. It is therefore essential that stakeholders, including election observers and party/candidate agents, have access to the process.[8]

To carry out their role effectively, such monitors must be given sufficient access both in law and practice to make an informed assessment. This may require that additional points of observation be created in the electoral process. With traditional paper-based voting and manual counting, observers focus on the voting and counting process itself. Electronic voting and counting technologies entail a number of other activities, some critical to the integrity of the process, that can be observed, but which take place well in advance of Election Day. Such activities include the testing and certification of the systems and the installation of software on voting or counting machines. Those observing elections need to make additional efforts to monitor these processes, which take place outside of the normal window of election observation.

---

8 For more detail on this point see Council of Europe (2011) Guidelines on transparency of e-enabled elections, available at www.coe.int.

Observers and party/candidate agents must also have access to relevant documentation about the procurement, development, testing and certification of equipment. It is critical they are able to observe during each stage of the process, from the initial decision making about whether to use electronic voting, to the final announcement of results. The transparency of various stages of the process should be a key consideration in the observers' overall assessment of the election.

The ability of observers and party/candidate agents to fulfill their roles is more challenging in an election that uses electronic voting and counting technologies. Observers must be properly trained to understand and report on the processes they observe. Watching voters use an electronic voting machine is unlikely to provide the information necessary to effectively assess the voting process. They should, therefore, become knowledgeable about the specific technologies that have been adopted and should be prepared to evaluate the testing and auditing of the voting and counting equipment, as well as the documentation of the process.

Since election observers and party/candidate agents may not have the expertise needed to understand certain aspects of electronic voting and counting technologies, organizations and parties may need to hire personnel specifically with an information and communications technology (ICT) background. They may also decide they are unable to assess certain aspects of the process and, if so, should disclose in their reporting which parts of the process they have and have not been able to observe effectively and take this into account in their overall assessment of electoral integrity.

The complex nature of electronic voting and counting technologies may also require ICT experts to provide independent oversight of such technologies, especially regarding the review of software and hardware. Professional ICT groups and academic communities can play a useful role in assessing electronic voting, either in partnership with election observer groups or independently. While the EMB should not exclude organizations that are skeptical about the benefits of electronic voting or counting technologies, they should be aware of any such organizational agendas.

FIGURE 3 – VERIFIABILITY[9]

System verifiability or auditability is becoming an increasingly important feature for electronic voting systems. Electronic counting systems have a natural audit trail of the (often paper) ballot, so additional verifiability mechanisms are less important for such systems. With DRE voting machines, and also with remote electronic voting, there is no obvious way for the voter to be sure their ballot choices have been recorded or counted accurately.

This lack of transparency was one of the main motivations for the development of the aforementioned VVPAT. Electronic voting machines with a VVPAT store the voter's ballot choices electronically but also on a paper record, often within the voting machine. This allows the voter to check that their ballot choices have been recorded accurately on the paper record. Electronic results produced by the electronic voting machine can then be checked against paper records,

---

[9] For more detailed information on verifiability, please refer to the following subsection in Part 2: Design Requirements, pgs. 116-123.

verified by the voter, to ensure the electronic result reflects the voter's choices.

However, use of VVPAT solutions is not without complications, especially with respect to the internal printer. Other schemes have been developed to provide the voter with some form of receipt so they can individually check that the vote has been received and counted accurately. This transparency has to be accomplished without violating the secrecy of the vote, which is a challenge.

End-to-end verifiable systems provide mechanisms for any oversight body to check that votes are received as cast, recorded as received and counted as recorded (i.e., all stages of the process function correctly and accurately). The voter will have some role in this verifiability, as only they know how they intended to cast their vote. Some end-to-end voting schemes provide the voter with a code they can use to check, after Election Day, that their vote has been included in the count with the correct value. Other schemes limit the role of the voter to checking the vote was received and recorded accurately, and provide other independently-verifiable proof that recorded votes are counted accurately.

INTEGRITY[10]

One of the fundamental principles elections must comply with is that they must accurately reflect the will of the voters. The integrity of the electoral process also has implications for other related issues, as discussed later in the section on trust.

The integrity of the process when using electronic voting and counting technologies is a particular challenge because of the nature of these technologies. With traditional paper balloting and hand counting, the entire process is not only clearly visible to those observing it, but it is also easily understandable to the average voter. The ballot box can be shown to be empty at the start of voting by polling staff, then sealed, observed in the polling station to ensure that only legitimate voters are putting in ballots, and at the end of voting the seal can be broken and the ballots counted in full view of observers. This overall transparency and simplicity of the process makes it relatively easy to observe the process and identify errors in the system if and when they occur. While political party and candidate agents, observers and the media perform a monitoring function, they also carry out a verification function to ascertain whether the process leads to an accurate reflection of the will of the voters.

This basic transparency is lacking for electronic voting and electronic counting, especially for electronic voting. The complexity of electronic voting tends to be beyond the understanding of the vast majority of voters. The technologies have what are known as "black box" components that take inputs from voters and produce outputs in a way that cannot be observed and verified by external observers or easily checked by election administrators. This is a potential problem from a transparency, trust and integrity perspective.

---

[10] For more detailed information on this topic, please refer to the following sections in Part 2: Election Day, (Set-Up, Testing, Security, Troubleshooting), pgs. 183-193; Tabulation, pgs. 194-197; Challenges and Recounts, pgs. 199-203; and Internet Voting, pgs. 218-227.

Those advocating against the use of electronic voting and counting technologies in the United States have long argued black box voting should not be accepted or trusted. They argue there is absolutely no basis on which to accept or trust these voting and counting technologies.[11] Examples of voting and counting machines making significant errors in the results they generate have been provided, and the worry is that there are many more discrepancies taking place that are not identified because they are not as egregious and obvious or are impossible to identify because the necessary audit mechanisms are not in place.

As a result, additional and varied measures are required to provide the same level of assurance that an electronic voting or counting process is actually delivering an election that reflects the will of the voters. Additional measures may include transparency mechanisms; testing and certification regimes; authentication mechanisms; and audit mechanisms:

- **Transparency** – is a crucial tool to ensure the integrity of electronic voting and counting technologies. While ensuring voting and counting technologies are transparent does not alone guarantee that technologies will generate accurate results, it does provide the space and tools to do so. Making electronic voting and counting processes transparent allows the EMB and stakeholders the opportunities to monitor critical elements of the process and ensure that errors, accidental or otherwise, are not made in these aspects of the electoral process. The previous section details steps that can be taken to improve transparency in the process of introducing and implementing electronic voting and counting technologies. Steps range from access to system documentation and source code for electoral stakeholders, to additional points of observation for observers.

---

[11] See Harris, B. (2004) Black Box Voting and www.verifiedvoting.org.

FIGURE 4: NEW STAGES OF OBSERVATION – EXAMPLES FOR AN ELECTRONIC VOTING MACHINE

The introduction of electronic voting or counting technologies produces a number of new points at which oversight of the process can and should take place. These points of oversight will vary depending on the technology introduced and the specific vendor system being implemented. Examples of additional observation points for an electronic voting machine system are provided here:

- **Certification** – it is unlikely certification of the electronic voting machine system would be fully open to observation; if possible, such observation would probably be impractical due to the length of time this process can take. However, documentation about the process should be available and reviewed by observers.

- **Source Code Review** – the source code should be made available for scrutiny, although this will obviously require party/candidate agents and observers with specialized IT skills.

- **Testing** – the EMB will need to conduct its own regime of testing, regardless of whether the electronic voting machines are formally certified, and observers should consider observing this testing. Party/candidate agents and observers should also review documentation on testing.

- **Storage and Distribution** – arrangements for the storage of electronic voting machines between elections may be observed and an assessment of the security arrangements made. The procedure for handover, transportation and local storage immediately prior to the election may also be monitored.

- **Machine Configuration** – prior to the election, the electronic voting machines will need to be configured for the election being conducted. This configuration process is critical and should be monitored. This may involve observing that proper procedures are followed, as well as using mechanisms to prove that the loaded version of the software is the tested and approved version.

- **Voter Education Efforts** – voters will need to be informed in advance about the use of electronic voting machines, especially if they are being used for the first time. Party/candidate agents and observers should monitor and assess the efforts made by the EMB to educate voters.

- **Training for Polling Staff** – it is important that polling staff are properly trained in the use of electronic voting machines, new administrative and security procedures and what to do if there is a problem with the machines. Party/candidate agents and observers should monitor this training process and determine whether sufficient efforts have been made to prepare polling staff for the use of electronic voting machines.

- **Electronic Voting Helpdesk** – it is likely that implementation of an electronic voting machine system will include the establishment of a help desk for reporting and resolving problems encountered while using the voting machines during voting. Oversight of this help desk function is also important.

- **Audit of VVPAT** – the manual count of paper records produced by an electronic voting machine is a vital mechanism for ensuring that the machine functions correctly, but also for building trust in the electronic voting machine. This process must be open to observation and, accordingly, should be observed.

- **Testing[12] and Certification[13]** – given the lack of transparency of electronic voting and counting processes compared to paper balloting, it is essential that election administrators make efforts to build confidence in voting or counting machines, ensuring they work properly before they are used. This testing needs to not only ensure the systems developed meet the requirements specified by the EMB, but also that they meet the requirements of the environment.

  These tests are essential so the EMB can use electronic voting and counting technologies with confidence. It is important to note that these various tests take time and money to conduct, and an

---

12 For more detailed information on the topic of testing, please refer to the following sections in Part 2: Pilot Project, pgs. 88-93; Legal and Procedural Framework, pgs. 106-113; Design Requirements, pgs. 116-123; Testing, Source Code Review and Certification, pgs. 173-181; and Election Day, pgs. 183-193.

13 For more detailed information on the topic of certification, please refer to the following sections in Part 2: Legal and Procedural Frameworks, pgs. 106-113; and Testing, Source Code Review and Certification, pgs. 173-181.

appropriate amount of time needs to be allocated for these testing processes. The testing itself and reports analyzing results of the testing should be reviewed by electoral contestants and observers to ensure public confidence.

FIGURE 5: TYPES OF TESTING

The Council of Europe's E-Voting Handbook[14] identifies six types of testing EMBs should conduct:

- **Acceptance Testing** – this method of testing software that tests the functionality of an application performed on a system (for example software, batches of manufactured mechanical parts, or batches of chemical products) prior to its delivery.

- **Performance Testing** – this testing determines the speed or effectiveness of a computer, network, software program or device. This process can involve quantitative tests done in a laboratory, such as measuring the response time or the number of millions of instructions per second (MIPS) at which system functions. Qualitative attributes such as reliability, scalability and interoperability may also be evaluated. Performance testing is often done in conjunction with stress testing.

---

14 Caarls, S. (2010) E-voting Handbook: Key steps in the implementation of e-enabled elections, Strasbourg: Council of Europe

- **Stress Testing** – this testing determines the stability of a given system or entity. It involves testing beyond normal operational capacity, often to breaking point, in order to observe the results. Stress testing may have a more specific meaning in certain industries, such as fatigue testing for materials.

- **Security Testing** – this process determines if an information system protects data and maintains functionality as intended. The six basic security concepts that need to be covered by security testing are: confidentiality, integrity, authentication, authorization, availability and non-repudiation.

- **Usability Testing** – this technique evaluates a product by testing it on users. It can be seen as an irreplaceable usability practice, since it gives direct input on how real users use the system.

- **Review of Source Code** – this systematic examination of computer source code aims to find and rectify mistakes overlooked in the initial development phase, improving both the overall quality of the software and the developers' skills.[15]

---

15 CoE (2010), pp.34-35.

In addition, some countries choose to have electronic voting and counting technologies certified prior to use.[16] Certification serves a similar purpose as testing, but it should be conducted by a body independent of the EMB, political parties, government and suppliers. Ideally, the certification process is conducted in an open, transparent manner builds confidence in the operation of the voting or counting technology. Certification should be done by a source that is widely accepted by stakeholders as independent and competent.

The U.S. Election Assistance Commission's *Voting System Testing and Certification Program Manual* defines certification as, "the process by which the Election Assistance Commission, through testing and evaluation conducted by an accredited Voting System Testing Laboratory, validates that a voting system meets the requirements set forth in existing voting system testing standards…and performs according to the Manufacturer's specifications for the system."[17]

The Council of Europe's *Certification of E-voting Systems* considers certification as, "a process of confirmation that an e-voting system is in compliance with prescribed requirements and standards and that it at least includes provisions to ascertain the correct functioning of the system. This can be done through measures ranging from testing and auditing through to formal certification. The end result is a report and/or a certificate."

---

16 Council of Europe (2011), Certification of e-voting systems: Guidelines for developing processes that confirm compliance with prescribed requirements and standards, Strasbourg: Council of Europe, pp. 2-3.
17 U.S. Election Assistance Commission (2011), Voting System Testing and Certification Program Manual. Washington, DC, p. 17.

The Council of Europe continues, "Certification can be applied in different ways. Solutions chosen by a member State may include certification of a single e-voting system for nationwide use, it can opt to certify multiple systems, provisionally certify an e-voting system, or only test one or several parts, i.e. component testing. Member States may choose those measures described in the present guidelines that correspond with their particular voting system, bearing in mind the need to ensure that the voting procedures respond to possible threats and risks while being in line with international commitments."

Certification has an important role to play in ensuring electronic voting and counting systems comply with requirements and standards, but it also plays a vital role in establishing trust among key stakeholders. The independence and competence of certifying institution(s) is fundamental to this trust building role.

- **Authentication**[18] – it makes little sense to spend time testing and certifying an electronic voting or counting system if there is subsequently no check that this is the actual system being used for the election. Authentication can be done through digitally signing the version of software that is tested and approved. Mechanisms can then be established so the digital signature of installed software can be checked by those observing the election.

    Likewise, when electronic data passes from one stage of the process to another, for example if voting/results data from the polling station is passed to the tabulation process (often done through portable electronic media, such as a memory stick), the validity of the data received for tabulation needs to be verified. Otherwise, it would be

---

18 For more detailed information on this topic, please refer to the following sections in Part 2: Procurement, Production and Delivery, pgs. 124-133; and Internet Voting, pgs. 218-227.

easy to substitute false data into the process. This issue can also be dealt with through the use of digital signatures for data. This means only results data with an authentic digital signature would be accepted by the tabulation system. All such results transfers require verifiable safeguards that are observable by party/candidate agents and election monitors in order to maintain confidence in this highly-sensitive aspect of elections.

- **Audit**[19] – the ability to verify the operation and audit the results of an electronic voting or counting system is an emerging standard for electronic voting and counting technologies. While electronic counting solutions have a natural audit trail in the ballot that is fed into the counting machine, electronic voting solutions do not inherently have this feature. It can easily be added to electronic voting systems though. The most common way is through the use of a VVPAT, which was discussed in the section on transparency. The VVPAT is a paper record of the choices made on the voting machine, which can be checked by the voter to ensure the same electronic choices were made. The voter does not keep this paper record.

    However the audit trail is provided, it is critical that it is used to check the accuracy of the electronic voting or counting process whether or not election results are contested. A random sample of audit trails should be routinely checked against electronic results produced by electronic voting or counting machines to ensure there are no differences between the electronic and audit trail results. This is important not just for the present but for future elections that may be closely fought and where even small discrepancies may be critical. Conducting the audit in a public manner will provide an additional

---

[19] For more detailed information on this topic, please refer to the following sections in Part 2: Legal and Procedural Frameworks, pgs. 106-113; Testing, Source Code Review and Certification, pgs. 173-181; and Challenges and Recounts, pgs. 199-203; and Internet Voting, pgs. 218-227.

check on the integrity of the system and help build confidence and trust in the system. Such an audit provides an important check on the accuracy of the results. Without this audit of the paper trail, the value of the VVPAT is undermined.

TRUST[20]

Trust is a vital component of the democratic process, and trust in the election process is critical for acceptance of electoral outcomes by the public, political actors and other electoral stakeholders. It is not only important for the integrity of the electoral process that voters and other electoral stakeholders trust the process to accurately reflect votes cast, but also for these actors to trust EMBs have executed their responsibilities in a manner that safeguards the integrity of the process. While delivering elections that reflect the will of the voters is of critical importance for EMBs to generate trust, it is also important for EMBs to engage electoral stakeholders throughout the process and be responsive to their concerns and needs so trust is maintained over time.

This is especially important when electronic voting and counting technologies are being introduced into the electoral process. The inherent opaqueness of these technologies when compared to paper-based ballots, as well as the relative lack of familiarity with these technologies among most stakeholders should compel EMBs to ensure the design and implementation process is open and generates confidence. Failure to do so may lead to experiences where strong electoral systems with foundations of trust are forced to backtrack on electronic voting because electoral authorities did not engage stakeholders throughout the process and lost the support needed to move forward with electronic voting. Where there is not a tradition of strong, trusted electoral

---

20 For more detailed information on this topic, please refer to the following sections in Part 2: Decision in Principle, pgs. 77-81; Procurement, Production and Delivery, pgs. 124-133; Project and Risk Management, pgs. 153-161; Voter Education/ Information, pgs. 162-169; Post-Election Audits, pgs. 205-209; and Internet Voting, pgs. 218-227.

administration, the consequences of failing to establish confidence in electronic voting and counting technologies could be even more severe. Trust in the electoral process is a hard-won commodity that can quickly dissipate if errors are found. It is essential that EMBs take the steps necessary to further and maintain trust with the introduction of electronic voting and counting technologies.

As discussed, transparency is a key factor in generating public and stakeholder trust in the electoral process, but it is a difficult measure to provide for electronic voting systems where the casting and counting of ballots is not visible. EMBs can use a number of concrete steps to foster transparency in the process of design and implementation of electronic voting and counting systems, but the basic underlying stance for EMBs should be to have a process that is open and engages electoral stakeholders every step of the way. Given the complexity of electronic voting and counting systems, it is important that EMBs provide stakeholders with information about the technologies and the process through which these technologies will be implemented. Some steps EMBs can take to elicit trust through transparency have already been discussed above.

In addition to providing access to independent experts and stakeholders to test the technology to be used in a particular election, EMBs can also embrace transparency by making stakeholders a key part of the evaluation process while the choice of technology is being evaluated for adoption, as well as after an election. EMBs should engage informed stakeholders in these evaluations where the performance of electronic voting and counting systems is tested against either standards established for traditional, paper-based systems or emerging standards (e.g. the Council of Europe's e-voting recommendations) for electronic voting systems.

Voters are the end client for any voting system. Prudent EMBs should ensure voters are informed about changes in the way they cast their vote, and that at least some voters have a chance to try the technology out so that any usability issues can be identified early and addressed. Voter education programs that communicate the essential characteristics of the electronic voting system should be disseminated far and wide before the first use of these technologies so voters are not caught off-guard when voting. Demonstrations of voting technology through mock and pilot elections should be deployed so electoral authorities can ascertain whether voter education or other voter sensitization programs need to address specific issues in preparing voters for the introduction of the electronic voting technology.

SECRECY[21]

The secrecy of the vote is seen as one of the fundamental principles required in the conduct of democratic elections. Failure to secure the secrecy of the vote opens the possibility for voters to prove how they have voted, facilitating voter coercion and vote buying. Both of these practices undermine the free expression of the will of the voter and the possibility for election results to reflect the will of the voters.

If implemented properly, the paper-based system of voting effectively protects the secrecy of the vote. In the case of electronic counting, the same protections that currently exist for the hand counting of paper ballots should be applied. Electronic voting, however, introduces a number of additional ways secrecy can be violated. Voting machines record the choices cast on them by voters, and these votes may be recorded in the order in which they are cast with a timestamp. This means if someone knows the order in which voters cast their ballots on a voting machine or the time at which a voter cast their ballot and has access to the record of voting on the machine, they could determine the choices made by each voter.

---

21 For more detailed information on this topic, please refer to the following sections in Part 2: Legal and Procedural Frameworks, pgs. 106-113; Procurement, Production, and Delivery, pgs. 124-133; Security Mechanisms, pgs. 134-145; Election Day (Set-Up, Testing, Security, Troubleshooting) pgs: 183-193; and Internet Voting, pgs: 218-227.

Appropriate procedures restricting access to logged transactions on the voting machine would reduce this threat to the secrecy of the vote. In countries that have experienced authoritarian trends, these issues are likely to generate suspicions among citizens concerning breaches of ballot secrecy, and extra steps may be required to establish public confidence.

Other developments with electronic voting machines are increasing the threat to the secrecy of the vote. While the VVPAT is a vital tool in building confidence in the use of electronic voting machines and in providing an audit mechanism, it can also be implemented in such a way as to undermine the secrecy of the vote. Some VVPAT systems have a roll of paper on which the voter's choices are printed. As the choices are printed sequentially, this can be used with the order in which voters cast their ballots on the voting machine to determine the content of each person's vote. Access to the paper audit trail cannot be restricted in the same way as with electronic records on voting machines, since the audit trail is meant to be taken out and checked against the electronic record of the voting machine.

However, not all VVPAT systems function in this way. Some voting machine paper audit trails operate a cut-and-drop system where the printed vote is cut from the roll of paper and drops into an internal ballot box within the voting machine. This ensures that audit records are randomized in the same way as placing a paper ballot into a physical ballot box.

A potential, final challenge to the secrecy of the vote from electronic voting machines comes from the most recent developments with voting machines, whereby the machines also conduct voter identification. Most voting machines still rely on a physical process for voter identification and authentication, with polling staff checking voter names against a voter list separate from the voting machine. This means voter identification data and vote data are held in completely separate processes (the former through a manual process and the latter through an electronic process), which are never linked in any way, making it impossible to link voting data to the voter.

More recent voting machines are also fulfilling the function of voter identification and authentication. This identification can be by simply entering an ID number or passcode for the voter, or it can be through the voting machine scanning a biometric attribute of the voter and identifying them from a list of approved voters. Clearly, when the voting machine identifies the voter, it possesses both pieces of information required to break the secrecy of the vote and could retain the link between the two.

Technical solutions are readily available to ensure it is not possible to link voter data with the value of their vote. However, EMBs will need to adequately address concerns by stakeholders that this link is still maintained and that the secrecy of the vote is not violated.

While challenges related to the secrecy of the vote with electronic voting machines can be resolved, it is important that electoral stakeholders are cognizant of them and take all necessary steps to ensure the secrecy of the vote when considering the use of voting machines. At the same time, observers should evaluate whether any aspect of the process might challenge this fundamental principle.

ACCOUNTABILITY[22]

Elections are the primary means by which voters hold those elected to office accountable. While elections create an accountability mechanism, there must also

---

22 For more detailed information on this topic, please refer to the following sections in Part 2: Design Requirements, pgs. 116-123; Procurement, Production and Delivery (EMB-Vendor Relations), pgs. 124-133; Recruitment and Training of Personnel, pgs. 147-151; Project and Risk Management, pgs. 153-161; Challenges and Recounts, pgs. 199-203; Post-election Audits, pgs. 205-209; Evaluation of System, pgs. 211-217; and Internet Voting, pgs 218-227.

be accountability within an election process if it is to be genuine.[23] Accountability in an election process ensures those who conduct elections do so in compliance with the election legislation and relevant procedures, and in a manner that promotes the integrity of the process.

Generally, elections are conducted by EMBs. Within EMBs it is critical that responsibilities are clearly defined, including who has authorization to take specific actions or decisions. Officials at all levels of election administration must be responsible for their actions and decisions, and must be held accountable should they fail in their duties. Disciplinary measures and penalties must be defined for such instances, including the possibility of criminal liability for serious offenses.

The principle of accountability remains the same for elections that include electronic voting and counting, but is more complicated than traditional paper-based systems in several respects. First, because the consequences of some actions taken by officials may not be visible (since they take place within a machine), it is particularly important that each action taken is properly recorded. Second, because many aspects of implementing electronic voting and counting systems require highly-specialized skills (e.g., configuration, installation and maintenance), it may be a challenge for EMBs to identify staff that can perform such tasks. Third, because of the technical nature of the process, it is common that suppliers of the technology assist the EMB and fulfill some responsibilities of the EMB.

While it is preferable for an EMB to have in-house capacity to maintain its election equipment, it might not be possible to identify staff with needed specific, technical skills. In any case, technology vendors will inevitably be involved to a certain degree in the setup, use and maintenance of the equipment they supply.

---

23 Merloe, P. (2008) Promoting Legal Frameworks for Elections: An NDI Guide for Developing Election Laws and Legal Commentaries, pp. 17-21.

However, the EMB needs to remain in control of the relationship with the vendor and ensure the relationship does not violate its own responsibility to be in charge of implementing the electoral process. Any role for the vendor must be clearly defined so the EMB remains in control of the process at all times, and remains accountable should a problem arise.

Vendors of election technology have a different set of concerns than election officials. Their primary concern is to make money by delivering their products and services according to the contract they have concluded with the EMB. Vendors may not be aware of such constraints as election deadlines or legal requirements that must be met. It is the responsibility of the election officials to ensure the process meets deadlines and legal requirements, and liaise closely with vendors to make sure these criteria are met. The procurement process also must lead to contractual requirements that include firm deadlines for delivery that correspond to the electoral calendar, including sufficient time to remedy deficiencies in vendor performance, and sufficient penalties to deter non-performance. The vendor should not be in a position to take any action affecting the functionality of the equipment without the express authorization of the EMB. Any actions taken by the vendor should be carefully monitored and recorded.

EMBs can take steps to increase their own accountability in a number of ways. They can hold regular public consultations to present information on their recent activities and answer any complaints. This is especially necessary in a situation where new technologies are implemented that may not be broadly understood by the public or electoral contestants. EMBs can also allow political parties, election observers and the media the opportunity to attend their meetings where policies are being formulated, particularly in regard to the introduction and use of new election technologies. It is also common for EMBs to publish a report following an election that considers how the election was conducted and may provide recommendations for improvements in the future.

EMBs may be held accountable by a variety of institutions. It is good practice for electronic voting and counting systems to be certified by an independent authority, before they are approved for use, to verify they meet the necessary requirements. Audits can be conducted at regular intervals to verify that the equipment in use is the same that has been certified.

In many countries, parliamentary committees play an important oversight role, holding hearings to review the effectiveness and impartiality of EMBs. In countries with electronic voting and counting, a parliament may appoint specific independent committees with technical competence to evaluate the implementation of the technologies. For example, in Belgium, Parliament appoints an independent College of Experts that has the responsibility to review the integrity of voting and counting technologies throughout the election cycle.

Accountability can also be strengthened through the conduct of audits. On Election Day, voting and counting machines should be audited in a sample of polling stations to determine whether votes have been accurately recorded by the machines. An independent body can also conduct an overall audit of the technology after Election Day to verify that each step of the election process has been properly carried out.

Political parties, the media and citizen election observers also hold EMBs accountable by monitoring their activities and bringing any violations to the attention of the public, as well as the relevant authorities through complaints and appeals procedures. In countries with electronic voting and counting, political parties and citizen observers may need to develop specific skills to detect any violations and collect the necessary evidence to file a complaint.

SECURITY[24]

The security of the electoral process is critical for all elections. There are always points at which those wishing to manipulate the system could attempt to manipulate vote data. System security is especially important for electronic voting and counting systems, which may introduce new vulnerabilities into an election process. These vulnerabilities include external security threats to the security of the system, as well as internal threats of manipulation by those with official access to the system. These technologies are inherently less transparent than paper ballots, where all steps in the voting and counting process are observable. If electronic voting and counting systems are to be trusted by electoral stakeholders, it is important that the security challenges presented by the use of the technology are understood. Mechanisms must be in place to mitigate these security challenges, and any security breaches should be easily identified.

The security of electronic voting and counting systems has become an increasingly important public issue. Early systems were implemented with very few, if any, security mechanisms or checks and balances to ensure that they accurately recorded and reported on votes cast. The 2000 U.S. presidential election can be seen as a global turning point in terms of the scrutiny that technology-based electoral systems were subjected. While technology was certainly not the only problem in that election, it clearly showed that technology, even if well-established, was fallible; checks and balances were essential if voters and contestants were to trust the results generated by technology. This lesson later manifested itself across many aspects of electronic voting and counting, including a much greater scrutiny of the physical security of electronic voting and counting machines and investigations into the possibility of infiltrating the code which runs the systems.

---

24 For more detailed information on this topic, please refer to the following sections in Part 2: Procedural and Legal Frameworks, pgs. 106-113; Procurement, Production and Delivery, pgs. 124-133; Security Mechanisms, pgs. 134-145; Project and Risk Management, pgs. 153-161; Election Day (Set-Up, Testing, Security, Troubleshooting), pgs. 183-193; and Internet Voting, pgs. 218-227.

Electronic voting and counting machines and results systems did not fare well under this additional scrutiny. Despite the denial of suppliers and often election administrators, numerous security flaws were found in electronic voting and counting machines by IT security experts in several countries (such as the U.S., the Netherlands and Germany), some with well-established systems of electronic voting and counting. Such cases weaken public confidence in the integrity of electronic voting and counting machines and demonstrate the need for increased vigilance against emerging security risks.

It is clear the issue of physical and logistical security of voting and counting machines and associated communication networks are keen concerns for electoral stakeholders that are important for the integrity of elections. Voting machine suppliers and election administrators have had to increase the measures implemented to ensure this security is achieved, both in terms of voting machine design and in terms of control procedures relating to access to electronic voting machines and systems. The problem is that, as technological solutions ensure system security is improved, so are the ways in which systems can be hacked and manipulated.

As a result, one of the key ways in which these security concerns have been mitigated is through the development of effective audit mechanisms for electronic voting machines, such as the VVPAT. This ensures that, when audit trails are routinely checked, even when a security breach occurs, it can be detected.

EMERGING ELECTRONIC VOTING STANDARDS

Electoral standards based on public international law are well-elaborated in documents issued by intergovernmental organizations such as the United Nations; the African Union; the Commonwealth; the Council of Europe; including its European Commission for Democracy through Law (the Venice Commission); the European Union; the Organization of American States (OAS);

the Organization for Security and Cooperation in Europe (OSCE); and other bodies. These sources illustrate a common understanding of the content of international electoral standards, drawing directly from the wording of Article 21 of the Universal Declaration of Human Rights, Article 25 of the International Covenant on Civil and Political Rights (ICCPR), other articles in those documents related to the exercise of rights that are essential to democratic elections, and other human rights treaties, declarations and instruments. A number of rulings by international tribunals concerning genuine elections and writings of highly-qualified legal experts advance electoral standards in harmony with those sources of law, and the generally-accepted practices of states conducting elections reflect them as well.

The core of these international electoral standards can be defined as the right of citizens, without discrimination, to take part in government and public affairs, directly or indirectly through freely chosen representatives, by exercising their right to vote and to be elected at genuine periodic elections, which shall be by universal and equal suffrage, held by secret ballot and guaranteeing the free expression of the will of the electors. This combines with the right to seek, receive and impart information (i.e., the freedom of expression) about the nature of electoral processes, forming the basis for electoral transparency.[25]

These international electoral standards frame the conditions for using any tools to secure genuine elections, including electronic voting and counting. Because these new technologies for voting and counting fundamentally change the way many components of the electoral process are conducted, the standards demand corresponding new techniques to safeguard electoral integrity and earn public trust in their use. As a result, there have been initiatives in recent years to evolve these international electoral standards in order to cope with the challenges of using voting and counting technologies. The Council of Europe's

---

[25] P. Merloe, "Human Rights – The Basis for Inclusiveness, Transparency, Accountability and Public Confidence in Elections," in International Election Principles: Democracy & the Rule of Law (JH Young, ed., ABA 2009), pp. 3, 18-20.

2004 *Recommendation on Legal, Operational and Technical Standards for E-voting* did much to set the agenda for this adoption of existing standards for electronic voting and counting technologies. The Council of Europe followed up this document with several other publications, including documents on transparency and certification of e-voting systems.[26] The OSCE's Office for Democratic Institutions and Human Rights, the OAS, the Carter Center and NDI have approached the issue of standards for electronic voting and counting technologies from the perspective of observing or monitoring elections in which these technologies are used. IFES and International IDEA have also sought to provide guidelines and standards for the implementation of electronic voting and counting technologies by EMBs.

In analyzing the publications by the organizations listed above, it is clear that some trends are emerging in the recommendations about the conduct of elections using electronic voting and counting technologies. Common themes can be seen in the following areas:

- **Transparency** – as much of the process as possible should be transparent and verifiable. Effective access should be provided for party/candidate agents and observers in a manner that does not obstruct the electoral process.

- **Public Confidence** – closely related to and relying heavily upon transparency is the requirement that voters understand and have confidence in the electronic voting or counting technology being used. Public confidence requires that stakeholders are: involved in the processes of deciding whether to introduce electronic voting and counting technologies and considering the type of system to be introduced; provided information so they understand the technologies

---

26 "E-voting Handbook: Key steps in the implementation of e-enabled elections", "Guidelines on certification of e-voting processes" and "Guidelines on transparency of e-enabled elections", www.coe.int/t/dgap/democracy/Activities/GGIS/E-voting/Default_en.asp

being used; given the opportunity to take part in simulations of the systems that take place; allowed to monitor testing, certification and auditing and review findings; and informed well in advance about the introduction, timeline and how to participate.

- **Usability** – electronic voting and counting technologies must be easy to understand and use. Stakeholders should be involved in the design of electronic voting and counting technologies and in public testing. Further, electronic voting and counting technologies should endeavor to maximize the accessibility of the voting system for persons with disabilities and minority language groups, and must not disenfranchise others. They must also afford voters the possibility to review and amend their vote before confirmation of their choice.

- **System Certification** – electronic voting and counting technologies must be certified by a qualified, independent body before their use and periodically thereafter. This ensures the use of such electronic technologies continues to meet the requirements of the electoral jurisdiction as well as the technical specifications for the system. Further, the certification process should be conducted in a transparent manner providing electoral stakeholders access to information on the process and earning public confidence.

- **System Testing** – any electronic voting or counting system should be subjected to a comprehensive range of testing before it is approved for use by an EMB. This testing should take place transparently and with access for electoral competitors and observers.

- **System Security** – the opportunities for systematic manipulation of the results mean that system security needs to be taken seriously. Security measures need to ensure that data cannot be lost in the event of a breakdown; only authorized voters can use an electronic voting or counting system; system configuration and results generated can be authenticated; and, only authorized persons are allowed to access electronic voting, counting and results management functionality, although party/candidate agents and observers should be able to monitor the integrity of that functionality. Any intervention that affects the system while electronic voting and/or counting is taking place should be carried out in teams of two, be reported on and be monitored by the electoral authority, party/candidate agents and observers. Attempts to hack into electronic voting and counting machines or the election management system into which results are received need to be detected, reported and protected against.

- **Auditability and Recounts** – electronic voting and counting technologies must be auditable so it is possible to determine whether they operated correctly. It must be possible to conduct a recount. Such recounts must involve accurate and monitored manual recounts of votes cast electronically (e.g., with the paper record representing the basis for legal determination of the vote cast) and not merely be a repetition of the electronic result already provided.

- **Verifiability** – it must also be possible to assure voters their votes are being counted as cast while also ensuring that secrecy of the vote is not compromised. This requires that electronic voting systems create an audit trail which is verifiable. It should provide the voter with a token or code with which to perform the verification. However, the token or code must not allow the voter to prove to others how they have cast their vote. The most common solution to this for in-person electronic voting machines is through the production of a VVPAT, and this solution is emerging as a standard in this regard. It should be noted that a VVPAT is not appropriate for unsupervised remote electronic voting (e.g. Internet voting, text message voting etc.) as there would be nothing to stop a voter from removing the paper record of the vote, and making vote buying and voter coercion possible.

- **Mandatory Audit of Results** – the existence of an audit trail for electronic voting and counting systems achieves little if it is not used to verify that electronic results and the audit trail deliver the same result. A mandatory audit of the results generated by electronic voting or counting technologies should be required by law and take place for a statistically significant random sample of ballots whether or not results are subject to a dispute.

- **Secrecy of the Ballot** – the use of electronic voting and counting technologies must comply with the need for secrecy of the ballot. This requirement is not a new standard, but it is one that is made more difficult by electronic voting and counting technologies. This is especially the case for remote electronic voting systems, where voters have to first identify themselves and vote electronically using the same interface.

- **Accountability in Vendor Relations** – the EMB needs to remain in control of the relationship with the vendor and ensure the relationship does not violate its own responsibility to be in charge of implementing the electoral process. Any role for the vendor must be clearly defined so the EMB remains in control of the process at all times and remains accountable, should a problem arise.

- **Incremental Implementation** – whenever electronic voting and counting technologies are introduced, they should be done so in an incremental manner and should start with less important elections. This will allow public understanding and trust to develop in the new system, and provide time to deal with problems and resistance.

It is too early to say international standards are fully evolved concerning the use of electronic voting and counting technologies. Nevertheless, trends can be seen in emerging electoral standards concerning their adoption. As a means to maintain electoral integrity, these trends in emerging standards should be carefully considered when the adoption of any new technology is deliberated and employed.

CHAPTER 2
IMPLEMENTING AND OVERSEEING ELECTRONIC VOTING AND COUNTING PROJECTS

This part of the manual takes the reader through the processes of implementing and observing electronic voting or counting projects, and is divided into three main sections discussed chronologically below. These sections address:

1. the decision-making process for adopting electronic voting or counting solutions;
2. building the electronic voting or counting solution; and
3. implementing the technology for an election.

The first section covers the needs assessment and decision in principle as to whether technologies exist that meet these needs, piloting these technologies, and the final decision on adoption based on a full assessment of pilots conducted.

The second section, focused on building the system, looks at issues such as the applicable standards with which electronic voting or counting must comply, the revision of the legal framework to properly regulate the use of electronic voting or counting technologies, the design and procurement of the new technologies, staff training and security requirements for the technology.

Finally, the third section outlines challenges associated with using electronic voting or counting technologies in an election. These include the management of electronic voting or counting projects; the education of voters on new technologies; the maintenance, storage and update of equipment and software; certification and testing; Election Day implementation; tabulation of results; challenges and recounts; post-election audits; evaluation of the system and Internet voting.

Each electoral environment will be different, and some of the issues outlined in this part of the manual may be more or less relevant in particular country contexts. However, all election management bodies considering the implementation of electronic voting or counting solutions should be aware of all of the implementation issues outlined below, and should ensure they have adequately considered and dealt with them. Likewise, electoral stakeholders such as political parties or civil society groups should be aware of these issues when planning a strategy for oversight of the process.

2.1 MAKING A DECISION ON E-VOTING OR E-COUNTING

••

The first step in implementing electronic voting or counting technologies is the decision-making process concerning the adoption of the technologies. This process has varied considerably in the countries that have used electronic voting or counting technologies. The institution making the decision has also differed; in some countries, parliament has made the decision through the passage of legislation, and in others the election management body has made the decision under its authority over operational matters.

But no matter which institution has decision-making authority, the way in which the decision is reached is vitally important. A decision is more likely to meet the needs of the electoral environment if it is made after consulting openly and widely with electoral stakeholders, based on comprehensive research into available technologies and judged against clearly identified objectives for the implementation of electronic voting or counting technologies. A decision based on these characteristics is also likely to be a far more stable decision that is less likely to face concerted challenges from electoral stakeholders.

Conceptually the decision-making process can be divided into three main phases. The first is the decision in principle, which consists, first and foremost, of assessing whether there is a problem with the current voting or counting process (i.e., a needs assessment), followed by assessing the technical feasibility of addressing that problem with the technology, anticipated benefits and potential risks, financial feasibility and stakeholder reactions to the technology. If the decision in principle indicates that an electronic voting or counting technology might be appropriate, the second stage of the decision-making process should be conducting one or more pilots of the technology. Finally, once pilots have been conducted, a decision can be made regarding the adoption of the technology.[27] Though all three of these stages may not have been followed in each instance where electronic voting or counting has been implemented, they provide a framework for understanding best practices when making such a decision.

An important component of a good decision-making process is the inclusion of a range of stakeholders and interests in dialogue about the possibility of adopting electronic voting or counting solutions. The use of such technologies affects many vital components of the electoral process, and the inclusion of a wide range of stakeholders in the debate helps ensure that all of the necessary perspectives are discussed. While it may be easier to exclude certain skeptical groups from the debate about the possible introduction of electronic voting or counting technologies, especially those who are very critical of such technologies, the perspectives that they bring to the debate may still be very useful and provide valuable insight. Engaging skeptical groups can often be a way to anticipate and address concerns that could later evolve into significant public resistance or that might threaten the integrity or security of the election.

---

27 This conceptual framework is offered as a model of good practice for sound decision making about the adoption of electoral technologies in Goldsmith, B. (2011) Electronic Voting and Counting Technologies: A Guide to Conducting Feasibility Studies.

DECISION IN PRINCIPLE

The decision-in-principle stage of the decision-making process is vitally important, as it helps to establish the parameters for the consideration of electronic voting and counting technologies. This stage involves several essential steps:

- Provision of authority and clear mandate to an institution to consider the use of new technologies;
- An assessment of needs or challenges in the current voting and counting system;
- An assessment of the advantages and disadvantages offered by different technologies in addressing those needs;
- A comprehensive assessment of financial feasibility;
- Consideration of the proportionality of benefits vis-à-vis costs of implementation;
- An assessment of the necessary institutional capacity to implement the new technology;
- A legal framework review; and
- Consideration of support and opposition of stakeholders.

The first step in the decision-in-principle stage is that an institution needs to be provided with the authority to consider the use of voting and counting technologies. In some cases an institution (e.g., the election management body) will have standing authority to investigate and implement trial improvements in the procedure for conducting elections. In other cases this authority will have to be specifically provided.

Regardless, it is important that the mandate for the consideration of these technologies is clearly defined. The institution that will consider the introduction of voting or counting technology needs to be identified; the objectives of the study should be well defined (i.e., whether it involves consideration of voting technology, counting technology, Internet voting, biometric voter identification, etc.); a timeline for the decision-in-principle process should be outlined, and the outputs expected from the process should be defined (e.g., a report, recommendations on technologies, suggestions on vendors, a plan for the conduct of pilots, an indicative budget for the adoption of the technology, etc.).

A comprehensive consideration of electronic voting or counting technologies should reflect on a number of issues. Initially these issues include an assessment of the current system of voting and counting and any existing needs for improvement in the system; an assessment of the advantages and disadvantages offered by the technologies; and a review of IT security issues related to the use of the technologies. The advantages of introducing these technologies should also be proportional to the full costs through the life cycle of its implementation – not only in financial terms but also in terms of staffing resources and other nonfinancial costs triggered by changing the voting or counting system, as outlined in more detail below.

This initial process should lead to the development of a set of requirements for any new technology and a list of anticipated benefits and challenges against which any future use or pilot of the technology can be assessed. Product information will need to be gathered from vendors of electronic voting and counting technologies to allow for a determination of technical feasibility (i.e., whether products are actually available that meet the requirements). If no products are found that meet the requirements, it may be that the requirements identified were too ambitious or that insufficient suppliers were contacted. Even after reconsideration, it may be that no products exist or can be developed that meet the requirements. The conclusion then would have to be that the available technology does not meet the needs identified. This would indicate the end of the decision-making process, with a finding that electronic voting and counting technology was not appropriate for use at that time.

In many cases, however, technology solutions will meet the electoral requirements identified, allowing the next steps in the decision-in-principle process to be conducted. These involve several additional components of assessment: a cost-benefit analysis; an assessment of institutional capacity; an assessment of the vendors' track records for timely delivery of technologies that perform reliably in conditions that exist in the country and under the timelines required by the electoral calendar; and an assessment of the legality of using electronic voting or counting technologies.

Even when electronic voting or counting technologies exist that meet requirements and can offer significant benefits in the conduct of elections, the financial feasibility and sustainability of their use must be assessed. In order to do this, a number of possible products must be selected for analysis, and a full assessment of all of the costs involved in the use of the technology compared to existing electoral procedures will need to be conducted. This assessment will need to take into consideration that, although the initial investment in electronic voting or counting technology might be high, the technology may be in use over several elections; thus, the initial investment costs must be spread over this period, and the additional costs associated with maintenance and software updates must be considered as well. There may also be significant costs incurred in the storage and disposal of equipment.

It may also be the case that the introduction of a new voting or counting technology will represent an additional channel of voting or counting, to be implemented alongside existing voting and counting systems. This is the case in some U.S. electoral jurisdictions, where voters at the polling station are offered the choice between paper ballots or electronic voting machines, and in some countries, such as Estonia, where both Internet voting and paper voting are available. In such cases the introduction of voting or counting technologies may be expected to increase the costs of conducting elections, possibly by a significant amount, but this could be justified through the better realization of other electoral principles, such as greater accessibility for voters.

The use of electronic voting and counting technologies also requires very different skill sets for election management body and polling station staff if the voting or counting technology is being implemented in the polling station. Staff with suitable information technology skills will need to be identified and trained. The election management body will also need to educate voters and other stakeholders on any changes in the voting process, which will be a significant organizational challenge. The election management body will need to manage the change from the existing system to the use of the new voting and counting technologies. Managing such change is a huge project in itself. A realistic assessment of the organizational challenges involved in implementing voting and counting technologies will need to be made, and might impact the final decision on whether to adopt the technology.

Finally, an assessment of the electoral legal framework will need to be conducted. There are two aspects to this legal analysis. First, the existing constitutional and legal framework will need to be assessed to determine if the use of electronic voting and counting technologies complies with relevant constitutional and legal provisions. If the use of the technology is seen as breaching constitutional or legal provisions, then implementation would not be possible unless and until those provisions were amended.

Second, an assessment will need to be conducted as to whether the constitution and legal framework cover the significant changes in the way that elections are conducted due to the use of the new technologies. For example, the law may make reference to paper ballots and physical ballot boxes, which would no longer exist if electronic voting machines were used. Also, new legal provisions might be needed to address issues specific to electronic voting and counting, such as data privacy and proper disposal of obsolete data storage devices. A comprehensive review of existing provisions and new provisions will need to be conducted, with recommended legislative amendments identified.

An important aspect of this decision-in-principle process is the inclusion of key stakeholder representatives. These stakeholders, especially political parties, civil society, and the media, will need to understand why voting or counting technology is being considered, the potential advantages and disadvantages, and the implications that the technologies have for the way that voting and counting are conducted. Once this understanding is achieved, the support or opposition of these stakeholders will be an important consideration.

The decision in principle will need to balance the various issues considered above – technical feasibility, benefits to be achieved, financial feasibility, proportionality of benefits vis-à-vis costs of implementation, institutional capacity to implement the new technology, legal implications, and support or opposition of stakeholders. Each electoral environment may find a different balance among these factors. For example richer countries or countries that can leverage donor funding may be more willing to invest significant resources for fewer anticipated benefits than less wealthy countries without donor funding.

A decision in principle that favors adoption of electronic technologies does not commit a country to adopting voting or counting technologies; it merely recommends progressing to the next stage of the feasibility assessment and overall decision-making process: the pilot project.

FIGURE 6 – THE RATIONALE FOR E-VOTING IN BRAZIL

Electronic voting in Brazil was introduced to reduce fraud in the results-tabulation process and increase voter accessibility to the ballot. Such problems had consistently compromised the integrity of elections, and electronic voting was seen as a method of combating previous shortcomings attributed to the Brazilian paper-ballot system.

The adoption of electronic voting in Brazil was initiated by the Superior Electoral Tribunal (Tribunal Superior Eleitoral or TSE), the judicial body charged with implementing Brazil's electoral laws. While outside actors had some input, the move to electronic voting was largely an autonomous process carried out by the TSE; and consequently, actors within the judicial institution made most major decisions.

The primary reason for adopting electronic voting machines was to combat endemic fraud in the paper ballot tabulation process. Due to the complex electoral environment created by Brazil's electoral rules, where voters would regularly have to choose among thousands of legislative candidates, the tabulation of votes was a complex and lengthy affair. Vote tabulation was also a huge logistical challenge, involving hundreds of thousands of vote counters who were often government employees from the state-owned banks or the postal service. In the 1994 national elections, for example, vote tabulation required about 170,000 people. Because of the scale of the task, vote counting could take weeks, and the post-election period was a time of great uncertainty and tension.

Most importantly, the lengthy tabulation period increased the opportunity for vote counters allied with candidates to manipulate the vote count. While representatives of political parties could observe the vote count, the lengthy vote count period made it difficult for partisan and other civil society actors to fully monitor the process. The most common type of fraud was manipulation of the tabulation sheets, where vote counters who were allied with candidates would subtract votes from some candidates' tallies and add them to their favored candidates' counts.

A secondary motivation for switching to electronic voting was accessibility problems in the paper system. Because of the large number of candidates that ran in legislative elections, the TSE used paper ballots that required voters to write in the names or identifying numbers of their preferred legislative candidates. Because of the difficulty of casting and counting hand-written ballots, the fraction of blank and invalid votes approached 40 percent in legislative elections in 1994. For the approximately 20 percent (according to the 1990 census) of the electorate that was illiterate, writing a five- or six-digit sequence of numbers was not a trivial task. This was compounded by the fact that, in legislative elections, voters vote for multiple offices and would have to fill in a total of 16 to 19 numbers if they were to cast votes for all offices. Furthermore, voters had no way to verify that the numbers they wrote on their ballots actually corresponded to the candidates or parties they intended to vote for.

Electronic voting machines have been able to eliminate some of these significant problems, delivering results much more quickly and eliminating many of the means by which the results were previously manipulated, although they clearly brought new challenges to the conduct of elections.

FIGURE 7 – THE DECISION IN PRINCIPLE IN PAKISTAN

Pakistan's decision-in-principle process provides an example in which the relevant technical, operational, financial and legal issues surrounding electronic voting were taken into consideration.

To assess the potential for using election technologies, the Election Commission of Pakistan (ECP) established a Committee on the Use of Electronic Voting Machines (EVM Committee). Established in November 2009, the EVM

Committee consisted of staff from different departments of the Secretariat for the ECP as well as representatives from the International Foundation for Electoral Systems (IFES) office in Pakistan. The decision to form such a body originated from a presidential request. On the basis of this request, the EVM Committee engaged in a comprehensive feasibility study.

The EVM Committee established four smaller working groups composed of its own members to look at the different aspects of this study. These working groups assessed the strengths and weaknesses of the existing system, the potential benefits offered by new technologies, the likely cost implications of adopting new technologies and the legal implications.

The EVM Committee also arranged for leading electronic voting machine vendors to demonstrate their technologies to the Election Commission of Pakistan. Three vendors made the trip to Pakistan to demonstrate their products. Political parties, civil society and international stakeholders were invited to these demonstrations, and were able to provide their opinions on the possible use of electronic voting machines.

The findings of the working groups, the vendor demonstration and the consultation process were used to complete a final report and recommendations from the EVM Committee. This report detailed the requirements for an electronic voting system to be used in Pakistan, the challenges to meeting these requirements in the Pakistani context, the likely costs and benefits that could be achieved and the legal changes that would be required before an electronic voting system could be implemented.

The EVM Committee found that solutions did exist that could meet the needs of Pakistan. It recommended that the use of electronic voting machines be further explored through the conduct of pilot projects for electronic voting. The committee also recommended that Pakistani technology companies be encouraged to begin developing domestic electronic voting solutions, possibly in partnership with international electronic voting machine suppliers.

Since the report, Pakistan piloted electronic voting machines in by-elections. Voters cast their ballots by paper as normal, and these paper ballots were counted to generate the results; but each voter could also cast a test ballot on one of the electronic voting machines being piloted. A number of different electronic voting machines were piloted in this way.

KEY CONSIDERATIONS: DECISION IN PRINCIPLE

FOR IMPLEMENTING BODIES

- ☑ To what extent have key electoral stakeholders been consulted openly and widely in the decision making process on the adoption of electronic voting or counting technologies?

- ☑ Is the decision making process based on the research into available technologies and judged against clearly identified objectives?

- ☑ Does the implementing body have the necessary authority to consider the use of voting and counting technologies?

- ☑ Is the decision making process based on a needs assessment that identifies whether there are problems with the current voting or counting process?

- ☑ Do products which meet the requirements set out for the chosen technology exist and if such products do exist, has an assessment of their financial feasibility and sustainability of been conducted?

FOR OVERSIGHT ACTORS

- ☑ Have the primary reasons for considering the adoption of new technologies been clearly and publicly explained, including which specific problems technology is meant to address?

- ☑ Has the decision-making process assessed the current system; proportionality of advantages and disadvantages; costs versus benefits; technical feasibility; EMB institutional capacity; and legality of using e-technologies?

☑ Have key stakeholders, including parties, civil society, and the media, and the public been informed of the above assessments?

☑ To what extent have key stakeholders' support, opposition or other input been considered?

PILOT PROJECTS

Pilot projects are an essential assessment tool for evaluating the possible use of new technologies. They should be used to test assumptions about possible benefits and challenges in using new technology, as well as the costs of implementation and the reaction of stakeholders to the technology. The conduct and evaluation of a pilot project on the use of electronic voting or counting technology is a complex task. It needs to be resourced and managed effectively if it is to serve its purpose of providing an adequate assessment of the technology. The pilot process should be transparent and include mechanisms for feedback from stakeholders.

Pilot projects require all aspects of election administration to be adapted to the new technology, but implemented on a smaller scale. Therefore, all of the issues listed in sections 2.2 and 2.3 are relevant when conducting a pilot project. These issues are not repeated here; instead, this section focuses on issues specific to pilot projects.

- **Implementing Agency** – The institution that is responsible for implementing the pilot project(s) will need to be clearly defined, as will any support that it can expect from other state institutions. The implementing agency will normally be the election management body, but this does not have to be the case, especially if electronic voting or counting technologies are piloted in nonpolitical elections (e.g., student elections). It is recommended that, even if electoral stakeholders are not formally included in the project management body established by the implementing agency, they are included and consulted as much as possible throughout the pilot project process.

- **Resources** – The conduct of a pilot will require that financial resources are made available, not only for procurement of the technologies to be piloted, but also for other new aspects of the electoral process, such as testing and certification of the technologies, the conduct of voter education and IT support staff. Human resources will also be required to implement the project, and it is recommended that dedicated resources be allocated to manage and support the pilot project.

- **Mandate** – The mandate of the pilot project should be clearly identified. This mandate should include the technology or technologies that are to be piloted, the scale and locations of the pilot to be conducted, the kind of pilot to be conducted (i.e., in an actual election, in parallel to an actual election, or for a mock election), the issues to be addressed in the pilot and the evaluative criteria to be utilized in the pilot.

- **Timeline** – A clear timeline should be identified, for the conduct of the pilot as well as for delivery of the outputs from the process. The timeline for the conduct of the pilot project must be realistic given the likely need to procure and test the new electronic voting or counting systems, in addition to the other activities required to implement such projects.

- **Transparency** – The need for transparency cuts across all aspects of the implementation of pilot projects. There may be significant distrust about the potential change in the way that elections are implemented. Stakeholder concerns will best be addressed by including political parties, civil society, the media and voters in the process through consultations and briefings as the process develops.

- **Technology Specification** – The decision-in-principle process should pass on a detailed specification for the procurement of the technology to be used in the pilot project(s). This specification should be based on the requirements of the electoral environment and an assessment of existing products. If this is not provided, then the pilot project management body will need to develop it based on the findings of the decision-in-principle process, and then use this specification for the procurement of the pilot technologies.

- **Legal Framework** – The legislative amendment process necessary to enable the conduct of pilot projects, if any amendments are required, may be different for a pilot than for a more general implementation of electronic voting or counting technology. Enabling legislation may be passed for a temporary period, during which the pilot(s) will take place; likewise, temporary rules or regulations may be passed to implement the pilots at a procedural level.

- **Testing of Assumptions** – The decision-in-principle process will make a large number of assumptions about the operational challenges of implementing electronic voting or counting technologies, the expected benefits and costs, and the way in which voters, election administrators, political parties and observers interact with and experience the new system. The pilot project must, to the extent possible, test and challenge these assumptions so that a final decision can be made based on as many facts – and as few assumptions – as possible.

- **Evaluation** – While the issue of evaluating the use of electronic voting and counting technologies is relevant in general terms for the implementation of these technologies, it should play an especially important role during pilot projects. Extra efforts should be made to evaluate the performance of voting and counting technologies during pilots and also to evaluate the reactions of key stakeholders, including political parties, civil society and voters, to the use of the technology. Conducting audits of the piloted technology's performance will be an especially important aspect of this evaluation. These evaluation mechanisms will play a critical role in the next stage of the decision-making process: the decision on adoption.

- **Outputs** – The body responsible for conducting the pilot project should be directed as to the expected outputs of the process. The output could be as simple as a recommendation on whether to adopt the piloted technology. Alternatively, the pilot project might be expected to result in a comprehensive report on the pilot process, lessons learned, a plan for larger-scale implementation, a revised specification for the voting or counting technology, and so on.

FIGURE 8 – PILOTING ELECTRONIC VOTING IN PERU

In 2010 the Peruvian Congress called on its electoral institutions to explore electronic voting following delayed election results during regional and municipal elections earlier that year. As part of the exploration process, Peru's National Office of Electoral Processes (La Oficina Nacional de Procesos Electorales, ONPE) was charged with conducting a pilot of electronic voting technology. Because the ONPE had no previous experience with electronic voting, the International Republican Institute (IRI), with support from USAID, provided technical assistance to the ONPE in planning, conducting and evaluating the pilot.

The ONPE ran the e-voting pilot in the mountain town of Pacarán, chosen for its small size and rural location. While the location and demographics of Pacarán would challenge the introduction of e-voting machines, issues unique to remote communities had to be tested to ensure the technology would meet the needs of Peru's entire citizenry.

The pilot began with IRI working with the ONPE to conduct a baseline study to determine the most effective voter education and training tools. The results of the study helped to clarify the appropriate voting hardware and software for Pacarán. After determining the technical aspects of the pilot, the ONPE designed a plan for poll worker and voter outreach. The outreach plan provided technical training to poll workers and reached 86 percent of the 1,354 registered voters through a variety of e-voting technical training events, including community fairs, door-to-door outreach and scheduled informative workshops. On Election Day, voters also had the opportunity to practice on e-voting simulators prior to casting their ballots.

After the pilot, ONPE and IRI developed detailed recommendations, results and conclusions from the pilot. The main conclusion was that, although the many technical and logistical obstacles to implementing a national electronic voting system might be overcome, implementing such a system would be very costly. Since the pilot evaluation, the Peruvian Congress has not demonstrated serious interest in allocating any significant level of funding for electronic voting. However, since the first pilot in 2011, ONPE has been asked by Congress to conduct additional small-scale pilots for local elections, most recently during July 2013 municipal elections.

KEY CONSIDERATIONS: PILOT PROJECTS

FOR IMPLEMENTING BODIES

- ☑ Has it been made clear which institution is responsible for implementing the pilot projects?

- ☑ Are sufficient financial and human resources available to implement the pilot project?

- ☑ Does the mandate of the pilot project define the technologies to be piloted, the scale and locations of the pilot, the kind of pilot to be conducted (i.e. in an actual election, or in parallel to an actual election, or for a mock election), and the issues to be addressed and evaluative criteria to be utilized?

- ☑ Is the timeline for the pilot realistic?

- ☑ Has a detailed specification for the procurement of the technology

☑ been made for use in the pilot projects?

☑ Does the legal framework permit piloting of electronic voting and counting technologies, or are legislative amendments needed to enable the conduct of pilot projects?

☑ Does the pilot project test and challenge the assumptions about the operation challenges of implementing electronic voting or counting technologies, the expected benefits or costs, and the way in which voters, election administrators, political parties and observers interact with and experience the new system?

☑ Has an evaluation plan been developed for the pilot projects, and are the outputs of the pilot project clearly defined?

FOR OVERSIGHT ACTORS

☑ Is the process of procuring the pilot technology open and impartial to all vendors?

☑ Does the EMB provide periodic public updates and consultations related to the development and procurement of the pilot technology?

☑ Are voters aware of the existence of and rationale behind the pilot?

☑ Are stakeholders, including observer groups, political actors and voters, permitted and encouraged to observe the pilot process, and are they invited to provide feedback on the piloted technologies during the evaluation process?

DECISION ON ADOPTION

The decision on whether to adopt electronic voting or counting technologies should be a direct result of both the decision-in-principle and pilot project stages of the decision-making process. Regardless of whether the decision is to adopt, not adopt or conduct further pilots of technologies, the preliminary recommendation should be discussed with key stakeholders, and the reasons for the final decision should be well documented and shared with the public. A decision to adopt voting or counting technologies should ideally be based on successful pilots in different locations over time and should take into account lessons from those pilots.

The body authorized to make the decision on adoption, which may be the same body that conducted the earlier stages of the decision-making process, has a number of options available to it.

It may be decided that electronic voting and counting technologies do not meet the needs of the electoral environment, from a technical, cost-benefit, resource or stakeholder perspective, and that, therefore, the technologies should not be adopted. Even if this is the case, it is important that the reasons for the decision not to proceed with the technology are well documented in order to ensure accountability regarding the decision. This would provide the opportunity for the decision to be revisited in the future, if the factors supporting nonadoption change.

Alternatively, a decision might be made to adopt certain voting or counting technologies. This will likely only happen if the pilot is seen as successful and the anticipated benefits are achieved. Such a decision should not be based on a single small-scale pilot project, but ideally on the successful conduct of a series of pilots in different locations or over a period of time. Even where the decision is to adopt voting or counting technologies, it is important to recognize that there may be lessons to be learned from the pilot process and ways in which the voting or counting system could be improved when implemented on a larger scale.

The decision to adopt a voting or counting technology may also be implemented in a staggered manner, with some constituencies or regions adopting the technology first. However, while it may be beneficial to do so in order to manage the change more easily, this will entail different voting opportunities for different sets of voters. Some political actors might see this as problematic, if they view the opportunities presented by the voting or counting technology as being preferential to some voters, possibly along partisan lines.

A third alternative is that the pilot process should continue, with the final decision on adoption being delayed until further pilots can be reviewed. This option might be chosen in a number of scenarios: the pilots have indicated that an alternative technology that was not piloted might be more beneficial; the pilots were inconclusive; the pilots were not designed well enough to test the assumptions about challenges and benefits; or the pilot evaluation resulted in a revision of the specifications for the technology being assessed.

This third alternative highlights the fact that the feasibility process is not necessarily linear and may entail several iterations of pilot projects before a final decision can be made on the adoption of electronic voting or counting technologies.

FIGURE 9 – DECISION MAKING IN THE PHILIPPINES: ADVISORY BODY TO THE ELECTION COMMISSION

During the Philippines' transition to electronic counting in 2010, an advisory council was created to assist the Commission on Elections (COMELEC). While the formation and operation of this council came with several challenges, it provides an example of one type of mechanism that can help promote transparency and inclusiveness of decision-making processes on whether and how to adopt voting and/or counting technologies.

Mandated by the national legislature of the Philippines, the COMELEC Advisory Council (CAC) consisted of nine members from government, academia, the IT community and civil society. It provided recommendations and oversight to the COMELEC during all stages of the transition to e-counting technologies, including the following:

- Recommending the most appropriate, secure and cost-effective technology
- Observing and participating as nonvoting members of the Special Bids and Awards Committee, which was established to conduct the bidding and vendor selection process
- Participating as nonvoting members of the steering committee that implemented the new system

- Planning and testing the technology
- Identifying potential problems or inadequacies with the system
- Designing plans for the bidding process and the use and eventual disposal of the new system
- Conducting an evaluation of the new system after the election

The CAC's ability to provide guidance on key decisions during the 2010 elections was cited by many as an important factor in building trust and confidence during the transition from manual to electronic counting. The CAC also issued a number of recommendations for future elections in the Philippines, addressing issues such as the procurement process, timing, implementation, capacity building, legislation and technical aspects of automated elections.

While the creation of the CAC helped promote inclusiveness and transparency, it also came with challenges. The COMELEC decided to exclude CAC members with IT expertise from two key aspects of the transition process: (1) the design and selection of technology and (2) the procurement process. IT experts' participation was seen by the COMELEC as a potential conflict of interest if they were to become bidders. However, several civil society groups and IT experts criticized the decision to exclude those with IT expertise, noting that the selection of technology was then conducted without expert input from the IT community.

KEY CONSIDERATIONS: DECISION ON ADOPTION

FOR IMPLEMENTING BODIES

☑ Is the decision to adopt counting or voting technologies based on the successful conduct of a series of pilots in different locations or over a period of time?

☑ Have lessons learned from pilots been acknowledged in the decision?

☑ Are the reasons for recommending adoption, additional piloting or non-adoption of technologies well-documented and made public?

☑ Where adoption has been recommended, has detailed guidance been provided as to the kinds of technology that should be used, technical specifications, implementation steps and a timeline for adoption?

FOR OVERSIGHT ACTORS

☑ Are the reasons for recommending adoption, additional piloting or non-adoption of technologies well-documented and made public?

☑ If decision to adopt is made, is it based on successful pilots in different locations and/or over a period of time? Has the decision taken into account lessons from pilots?

☑ Is the preliminary recommendation discussed (i.e., through consultations) with key stakeholders?

2.2 BUILDING THE SYSTEM FOR E-VOTING OR E-COUNTING

STANDARDS FOR IMPLEMENTATION

Once a decision is reached that a country will adopt electronic voting and counting technologies, the nation should define standards for the implementation of the system. Such national standards provide overall principles that can help to guide the development of electronic voting and counting technologies as well as the legal framework that regulates them.

The process of defining national standards for electronic and voting technologies should be as open and transparent as possible, with broad participation by recognized technical institutions and experts. Public consultation should also be part of the process, with opportunities for civil society, political actors and voters to review proposals and offer their views.

When defining national standards, countries may choose to make reference to or incorporate international standards for the use of voting and counting technologies (for example, the Council of Europe [CoE] recommendation on e-voting[28]). International standards for democratic elections defined in public international law apply equally to elections using electronic voting and counting technologies and must be taken into account. However, as explained above, international electoral standards are still evolving in order to cope with the specific challenges of using voting and counting technologies; and there is no consensus yet on their content. Even the CoE recommendation on e-voting, which is the most authoritative of the emerging standards documents, is only a recommendation and only directly applicable to CoE member states.

The CoE recommendation provides a good starting point for establishing general standards specific to electronic voting and counting technologies, both in member states of the Council of Europe, in which the recommendation has legal standing, as well as in nonmember states. Norway, for example, incorporated the CoE recommendations (with several noted exceptions[29]) in its Regulations Relating to Trial Electronic Voting, making the CoE recommendations part of the regulatory framework for the electronic voting trial. The regulations emphasize that voting should be free, direct and secret, and sets basic principles to ensure the integrity, accessibility and security of the system during the trial.

In addition to general principles for the implementation of electronic voting and counting, national standards may also include technical requirements for the systems. For instance, in Belgium, the election law includes the technical features that voting machines must comply with as well as steps for certification of equipment. Similarly, Section 301A of the Help America Vote Act (HAVA) in the United States includes technical requirements for voting machines used in federal elec-

---

[28] Council of Europe. Recommendation of the Committee of Ministers to Member States on Legal, Operational and Technical Standards for E-voting, adopted September 30, 2004.

[29] These exceptions were largely related to the requirement to certify electronic voting solutions, which the Norwegian ministry responsible for managing elections did not wish to include for the pilot process.

tions related to verifiability, audit capacity, accessibility for individuals with disabilities, alternative language accessibility, error rate and a requirement that all states adopt uniform and nondiscriminatory standards that define what constitutes a vote and what will be counted as a vote for each category of voting system.

Although not specific to e-voting or elections, there are a number of other international and national standards with which an electronic voting or counting system may need to comply. Standards on such issues as data processing, data protection, electronic transactions, usability, accessibility, security and project management are all relevant and must be taken into consideration.

It is important at the initial stages of implementation to research what standards may apply to ensure that systems are developed to be compliant. Countries may also wish to develop standards for electronic voting and counting systems by using existing private and public institutions that develop technical standards or by drawing experts from such institutions into an expert committee for this purpose.

FIGURE 10 – GUIDELINES DEVELOPMENT IN THE U.S.

Following problems with punch-card voting systems in the 2000 elections, the United States made a concerted effort to develop election standards, including standards for election equipment, that aimed to ensure a level of integrity in the country's numerous electoral jurisdictions. While this effort has been conducted in a transparent manner and has resulted in a detailed set of guidelines, it also highlights the challenges of gaining consensus on and implementing such guidelines.

The U.S. Election Assistance Commission (EAC) was established by the Help America Vote Act (HAVA) of 2002 to serve as an information clearinghouse regarding election administration; testing and certifying voting systems; and promulgating standard voting system requirements.

HAVA also established the Technical Guidelines Development Committee (TGDC), a 14-member expert board drawn from a combination of technical standards agencies and state election officials and chaired by the director of the National Institute of Standards and Technology. The purpose of the TGDC is to assist the EAC with the development of the Voluntary Voting System Guidelines (VVSG), a series of specifications and requirements that voting systems would have to meet to be certified by the EAC. The TGDC works in a transparent way, opening its meetings and archives to the public and inviting public comment and position papers on its current initiatives.

In 2005, the EAC released the VVSG for a 90-day public comment period prior to adoption of the guidelines and reviewed more than 6,000 comments. Under HAVA, adoption of the VVSG by states is voluntary, but adoption by a state brings the guidelines into force for all of the state's electoral jurisdictions.

In 2007, the TGDC prepared a set of recommendations for a revised version of the VVSG, parts of which were incorporated into a new draft proposal by the EAC. The proposed revised guidelines were released for a 120-day period of public comment in 2009, but have not yet been finally adopted.

KEY CONSIDERATIONS: STANDARDS FOR IMPLEMENTATION

FOR IMPLEMENTING BODIES

☑ How broad is participation by recognized technical institutions in the process for defining national standards for implementation of electronic and voting technologies?

☑ Has an expert committee been established to help define the national standards?

☑ To what extent have international/regional standards been considered in the development of national standards?

☑ Do the national standards consider technical features that must be complied with?

☑ Has consensus been achieved among experts on the defined standards?

☑ Have the experiences of other countries been considered in the development of national standards?

FOR OVERSIGHT ACTORS

☑ How transparent and inclusive is the process of defining national standards for electronic technologies? For example, are technical institutions/experts involved, and are public consultations held with civil society, political actors and voters?

☑ To what extent do the national standards comply with have international and regional principles, and standards, and best practices been considered in the development of national standards?

☑ To what extent have existing national technical requirements been taken into account?

LEGAL AND PROCEDURAL FRAMEWORK

The use of electronic voting and counting technologies should be defined in the legal framework. This process can take a considerable amount of time, particularly since key legal provisions are incorporated at the legislative level (i.e., in constitutions and electoral laws) as well as the regulatory level. Amendments should, at a minimum, address the following: physical and procedural aspects of voting or counting processes; testing and certification; audit mechanisms and conduct; status of audit records versus electronic records; transparency mechanisms; data security and retention; voter identification; and access to source code. The process of developing amendments should involve input from electoral stakeholders, including political parties and civil society.

In order to properly implement electronic voting or counting technologies, the use of these technologies needs to not only be in compliance with the constitutional and legal provisions relating to elections and the general conduct of public affairs, but must also be defined in the legal framework for elections. The legal framework includes the constitution, if there is one, the laws relating to elections, and the secondary legislation (such as regulations, rules and procedures often passed by electoral management bodies).

While constitutions rarely say anything specific about electronic voting or counting technologies, they may include general provisions that are relevant to the use of these technologies. Germany provides a good example of this (see Figure 11 below for more details), with the German Constitutional Court deciding in 2009 that the electronic voting machines used in Germany did not comply with general transparency requirements for the electoral process established in the constitution.

FIGURE 11 – THE CONSTITUTIONALITY OF ELECTRONIC VOTING IN GERMANY

After a largely successful trial period spanning from 1998 to 2005, two citizens challenged the constitutionality of electronic voting before the German Constitutional Court. Though the public generally viewed the voting system in a favorable manner throughout the trial period, the actual legality of the technology was not fully assessed in advance of implementation.

Germany piloted its first electronic voting machines, supplied by the Dutch company NEDAP, in Cologne in 1998. The trial was seen as successful, and one year later Cologne used electronic voting machines for its entire European Parliament elections. Soon other cities followed suit, and by the 2005 general election nearly 2 million German voters were using these NEDAP machines to cast votes. Reaction to the use of these electronic voting machines was generally very positive among voters, who found the machines to be easy to use, and among election administrators, who were able to reduce the number of polling stations and staff in each polling station.

However, after the 2005 election, two voters brought a case before the German Constitutional Court after unsuccessfully raising a complaint with the Committee for the Scrutiny of Elections. The case argued that the use of electronic voting machines was unconstitutional and that it was possible to hack the voting machines, thus the results of the 2005 election could not be trusted.

The German Constitutional Court upheld the first argument, concurring that the use of the NEDAP voting machines was unconstitutional. The Court noted that, under the constitution, elections are required to be public in nature and

> that all essential steps of an election are subject to the possibility of public scrutiny unless other constitutional interests justify an exception ... The use of voting machines which electronically record the voters' votes and electronically ascertain the election result only meets the constitutional requirements if the essential steps of the voting and of the ascertainment of the result can be examined reliably and without any specialist knowledge of the subject ... The very wide-reaching effect of possible errors of

> the voting machines or of deliberate electoral fraud make special precautions necessary in order to safeguard the principle of the public nature of elections.[30]

Making it clear that the court's decision did not rule out the use of voting machines in principle, it stated that:

> The legislature is not prevented from using electronic voting machines in elections if the possibility of a reliable examination of correctness, which is constitutionally prescribed, is safeguarded. A complementary examination by the voter, by the electoral bodies or the general public is possible for example with electronic voting machines in which the votes are recorded in another way beside electronic storage.

This decision by the German Constitutional Court, stressing the need for transparency in the electoral process without specialist technical knowledge, effectively ended Germany's recent use of electronic voting. Although the Court decision does not rule out electronic voting machines entirely, no further moves to adopt machines that meet the transparency requirements have been made.

---

[30] A link to the German Federal Constitutional Court's 2009 ruling can be found in the Resources section of this manual.

In addition to ensuring that suggested technology solutions are in compliance with the constitutional framework of a country, consideration should also be given to whether suggested solutions meet international standards, including emerging standards for the use of electronic voting and counting technologies. Election officials and lawmakers may wish to study other countries' experiences when considering whether to adopt such technologies.

Primary and secondary legislation will inevitably need to be amended in order to accommodate the use of electronic voting and counting technologies. It is important that key legal provisions relating to the use of electronic voting or counting system are included at a legislative level so that the use of these technologies is not entirely legislated at the regulatory level. The necessary amendments to the electoral legal framework will vary depending on the technology being implemented but should cover, at a minimum, the issues listed below:

- **Physical Aspects of the Voting or Counting Process** – The use of electronic voting or counting machines will entail changes to the procedure for the setup and conduct of voting and/or counting. For example, when direct-recording electronic voting machines are used, there is no ballot box to prepare and seal. The common practice of displaying the empty physical ballot box before polling starts does have a comparable procedure for electronic voting or counting machines; a display demonstrating that no ballots have been stored is conducted for observers at the beginning of the process. Some of the procedures relating to the setup and conduct of voting and/or counting may be in the election law(s) or may be in secondary legislation, and both will need to be reviewed and amended to accommodate the setup and use of electronic voting or counting technologies.

- **Procedural Aspects of the Voting and Counting Process** – The timeline for the preparation of the voting or counting systems should be clearly outlined, as should details of how the system is to be operated, who is allowed access to it during elections, how equipment should be stored between elections and how access to equipment in storage should be regulated and reported.

- **Testing and Certification of Technologies** – Electronic voting and counting technologies clearly need to be tested before they are used. While any responsible election management body would ensure that sufficient testing of such technologies takes place before they are used for elections, it may be useful to guarantee that testing takes place and specify the kinds of testing to be conducted by including these requirements in the law or in secondary legislation. Likewise, if there is a process of formal certification of electronic voting and counting technologies, this should be included in the law as well. The law should also clearly identify the institutions with the authority to provide this certification, the timeframe for certification and the standards and requirements against which certification will take place.

- **Audit Mechanisms** – The need for audit mechanisms for electronic voting and counting technologies is an emerging international standard. In order to ensure that this standard is met, the requirement for an audit trail should be included in the law. The nature of the audit mechanisms may also be specified if relevant — for example, any requirement for a voter-verifiable audit trail often used with electronic voting machines.

- **Conduct of Audits** – Audits should be conducted in order to generate trust in the use of electronic voting or counting machines and to ensure that these technologies function correctly. Many different kinds of audits can be conducted, including audits of the results, audits of internal logs, audits of storage and access to devices, and so on. The law should clearly identify which audits are to be implemented, when such audits are to take place and the scale of the audits. In addition to requiring audits, which should be provided irrespective of whether there are any electoral challenges, the law should also identify conditions under which recounts are to take place.

- **Status of Audit Records Versus Electronic Records** – In the event that the conduct of an audit determines a different result than is produced electronically by an electronic voting or counting machine, the law should specify how to deal with the situation.

- **Transparency Mechanisms** – The use of electronic voting and counting machines entails the conduct of existing electoral procedures in different ways, as well as the conduct of new stages in the electoral process (for example, the configuration of electronic voting machines). In the interest of transparency, appropriate procedures will need to be developed to ensure that political actors and observers have access to these different and new processes so that they can provide meaningful oversight of the process. These transparency measures should be clearly defined in the legal framework so that observers and party representatives understand and can utilize their access rights.

- **Data Security and Retention** – It is unlikely that existing laws and procedures adequately cover the issue of electronic data security when using electronic voting or counting machines. The way in which all electoral data is secured and stored will need to be provided for in the legal framework, as will the timeframe and procedures for deletion of the electronic data, and these provisions must be in accordance with existing data protection legislation.

- **Voter Identification** – If identification/authentication is being incorporated into the electronic voting process, then this may require legislation, whether using biometrics or making mandatory a particular form of machine-readable ID. In such cases it is essential that the secrecy of the vote be protected through de-linking the vote and the identity of the voter.

- **Access to Source Code** – It may be prudent to legislate whether source code is open source or not, in addition to legislating the mechanisms for any access by stakeholders.

Many of these issues are covered in greater detail later in this part of the guide, and the intention here is to identify the issues that are relevant for inclusion in order to properly legislate for the use of electronic voting or counting technologies.

It is clear from the preceding discussion that adapting the legal framework for the use of electronic voting or counting technologies will entail considerable amendments to laws and secondary legislation. Electoral stakeholders must be involved in the development of these legislative and regulatory amendments. Initially, political parties and observers should be consulted on the ways in which the legislation needs to be changed, especially from a transparency and oversight perspective. Once legislation is passed, the election management body will need to fully brief political parties, the media and civil society on the changes that have been made.

KEY CONSIDERATIONS:
LEGAL AND PROCEDURAL FRAMEWORK

FOR IMPLEMENTING BODIES

- ☑ Are the electronic voting and counting technologies in compliance with the constitution and/or electoral legislation?

- ☑ Are suggested electronic voting and counting technology solutions in line with international and emerging standards?

- ☑ Is the timeline for preparation of voting and counting systems clearly outlined in the legal framework?

- ☑ Are requirements included for the testing of voting and counting technologies prior to their use in the elections?

- ☑ Is an audit trail legally mandated, and if so, is the nature of the audit mechanism specified and is the type of audit, timeframe and scale of audit clearly identified?

- ☑ Have conditions under which audits and recounts are to take place been identified?

- ☑ Are there specifications for dealing with a situation in which the audit produces a different result than by an electronic voting or counting machine?

- ☑ Does the legal framework include specifications for how electoral data will be stored, and the timeframe and procedures for deletion of electronic data in accordance with existing data protection legislation?

☑ Does the legislation address identification/authentication issues if they are being incorporated into the electronic voting process?

FOR OVERSIGHT ACTORS

☑ Are the electronic voting and counting technologies in compliance with the constitution and/or electoral legislation? Are they in line with international and emerging standards?

☑ Is the appropriate secondary legislation in place to accommodate the implementation of electronic voting and counting and the processes associated with such technologies?

☑ Are transparency mechanisms included and clearly defined in the legal framework, such that oversight actors have sufficient access to the new processes associated with the technologies?

☑ During the electoral legal framework reform process, has the election management and/or legislative committee consulted political parties and civil society on the ways in which the legislation needs to be changed?

☑ After the legal framework has been revised, have parties and civil society been briefed on the reforms enacted pertaining to election technologies?

DESIGN REQUIREMENTS

By defining general requirements on the design of the electronic voting or counting system, electoral authorities provide an indication to potential suppliers of what their overall needs are. System design should ensure transparency, accountability, secrecy, usability, accessibility and security. Design requirements should ideally be informed by testing of equipment on different groups of voters. The design process should involve the input of relevant stakeholders, such as parties and civil society. The design process should also consider and specify any additional components (beyond electronic voting and counting equipment) that must be provided as part of an overall election management system.

The starting point for the development of an electronic voting or counting system is for the election administration body to define a set of general requirements that a system should meet. These general requirements should be in line with any national or international standards (including emerging electronic voting standards), as well as the country's own legal framework.

General requirements should provide broad guidance on the design of the electronic voting or counting system. They should address issues such as secrecy, transparency, accountability, usability/accessibility and security. For instance, such requirements might indicate what kind of audit trail is necessary or whether source code must be open or verifiable.

The process of defining design requirements should be an inclusive one, seeking the input of various stakeholders, including political parties and civil society. Such consultation will help to ensure broad support for the system that is eventually selected, as well as provide specific information on the needs of particular target groups.

By defining general requirements, election authorities give potential suppliers of voting and counting equipment an indication of what their overall needs are. Once these requirements are agreed on, authorities can review different options offered by vendors to determine whether any already developed off-the-shelf products meet the requirements or whether a new system will need to be designed.

Of particular importance are design requirements regarding the usability and accessibility of the electronic voting or counting system. The system should be as user-friendly as possible to maximize the ability of all voters to cast their ballots in an accurate, effective and efficient manner. At the same time, electronic voting and counting systems should be designed to maximize opportunities for the inclusion of voters who may normally struggle to participate in the electoral process, such as voters with visual impairments, hearing impairments or motor difficulties, as well as those from minority language groups. New technologies can increase the ease of access for such groups, and election authorities should make requirements for such accessibility explicit in their initial design requirements.

The UN Convention on the Rights of Persons with Disabilities sets the overall norm for ensuring that persons with disabilities have equal access to the same services as the rest of the population. Article 29 of the convention explicitly requires state parties to ensure that persons with disabilities can participate in political and public life on an equal basis with others; this includes the right and opportunity to vote. It further requires that appropriate procedures, facilities and materials be provided that are accessible for persons with disabilities and that protect their right to cast secret ballots. The Council of Europe Recommendation on Legal, Operational and Technical Standards for E-voting also addresses accessibility, suggesting that e-voting systems should maximize opportunities for people with disabilities.

A number of standards relating to usability and accessibility are not tied specifically to voting, but instead seek to make technology as accessible as possible, and are therefore directly relevant to the design of electronic voting and counting equipment. For instance, the International Standards Organization (ISO) has developed standards on the interaction between humans and machines that do not specifically relate to electronic voting and counting, but that can be usefully adopted to maximize the accessibility of such systems. Similarly, the Web Accessibility Initiative (WAI) has developed operational guidelines to ensure that persons with disabilities have the best possible access to content on the web. WAI guidelines are particularly relevant for Internet voting.

Election authorities can incorporate standards related to usability and accessibility into their design requirements to ensure that voting and counting systems are developed in a manner that maximizes usability for all voters as well as the access afforded to particular groups of voters. For instance, in Norway, election authorities referenced specific accessibility and usability requirements as part of their tender for electronic voting solutions. This reflected the emphasis Norway put on making elections as inclusive as possible.

The usability and accessibility of a particular voting or counting system can best be assessed through the testing of equipment on different groups of voters throughout the design phase. Such testing should be as inclusive as possible, involving voters from different demographics as well as those who might normally struggle to participate. Election authorities should liaise closely with NGOs that represent particular groups such as persons with disabilities, minority language communities and illiterate or low-literacy voters to understand their needs in the voting process and to maintain an ongoing dialogue about the development and testing of the equipment.

Testing of electronic voting and counting options with voters also provides an opportunity to enhance the transparency of the development process and boost public confidence in the system. Involving political actors and citizen observer groups in the development testing process should also help to promote transparency and confidence in the resulting system.

If election authorities determine that off-the-shelf solutions are not available that meet the general requirements, it is likely that customized equipment will need to be developed. In such cases, technical experts will need to develop the specific technical requirements for the equipment. It is important that throughout the development process, details of the work of such experts is made available to the public. Such experts should be independent from state authorities and political contestants, and should disclose any affiliations with interested parties so as to avoid any perceived or real conflicts of interest where particular vendors could be seen to receive preferential treatment.

Additional factors for practical use and storage of the equipment should also be considered in the design phase, such as: whether there are particular environmental conditions in which the equipment will be required to function (e.g., high temperatures, humidity or dust); whether the power supply is uncertain in some parts of the country; how equipment should be transported and whether this is an issue for the design; and the environmental requirements that should exist for storing the equipment between elections.

For Bhutan's 2008 parliamentary elections, election authorities decided to use the lightweight (5 kilogram) battery-powered electronic voting machine used in India, as the machines needed to be transported by officials to distant villages, sometimes on foot.[31] Consideration of such factors early in the design phase is absolutely crucial for the successful implementation of electronic voting and counting equipment.

It should also be noted that it is not only the design of voting or counting machines themselves that needs to be considered and specified. An electronic voting or counting system may be part of an overall election management sys-

---

31 Election Commission of Bhutan, "Electronic Voting Machines," www.election-bhutan.org.bt.

tem. This election management system may be used to manage the administrative aspects of the election related to the machines (for example the pre-election configuration) and also to integrate candidate registration and verification with ballot production, issue of election notices, production of polling cards, count tabulation and results publication. If any or all of these components are required to be provided as part of an overall election management system, then they will need to be specified in advance.

FIGURE 12 – DESIGN AND PROCUREMENT OF E-VOTING MACHINES IN BRAZIL

The design and procurement processes carried out in Brazil demonstrate the importance of transparency and inclusiveness in building trust not only in the design and procurement of technology, but also in the eventual technology itself.

In 1994, Brazil's Tribunal Superior Eleitoral (TSE) established a committee to assess the feasibility of transitioning to electronic voting. While the committee was largely made up of legal professionals, it reached out to a wide range of stakeholders through the consideration and design stages of its work. Stakeholders within government were consulted, but so were outside experts at a range of computer companies. Existing commercial electronic voting packages were also assessed, and a visit was conducted to the U.S. state of Virginia to see the electronic voting machines in use there.

The committee's conclusion from this consultation and research process was that no existing electronic voting systems met the specific requirements of Brazil's elections; therefore, a custom solution would have to be developed. In its 1995 report, the committee elaborated a set of initial requirements that would need to be met by the new electronic voting system.

The recommendations of this report led to the establishment of a "technical" committee tasked with further defining the requirements of the new system and outlining the procurement process and the evaluation of bids. In order to develop the request for tender, the technical committee first published a request for comments and suggestions. Dozens of reports from companies, government entities and universities were received in response to this request; and with the information received, the technical committee wrote detailed tender documents. The procurement process included a requirement that all bids include a working model of the proposed voting machine that could pass 96 separate tests before being considered. Five companies submitted bids initially, but only three of these provided working models that passed all 96 tests. Procurement rules for government purchases were followed, and all criteria for judging bids by companies were made public.

This open and consultative design and procurement process did much to generate trust in the process and the eventual use of electronic voting machines in Brazil.

KEY CONSIDERATIONS: DESIGN REQUIREMENTS

FOR IMPLEMENTING BODIES

- ☑ Do the general requirements set out for an electronic voting and/or counting system address issues of secrecy, transparency, accountability, usability/accessibility and security?

- ☑ Is there a process to ensure consultation and solicit feedback on the general requirements for an electronic voting or counting system?

- ☑ Do existing products meet the requirements or will a new system need to be designed?

- ☑ Does the system maximize the ability for all voters to cast their ballots in an accurate, effective and efficient manner?

- ☑ Does the system meet existing standards on usability and accessibility?

- ☑ Are external factors such as the environmental conditions in which the equipment will be required to function and the reliability of the power supply throughout the country been considered for the design requirements?

- ☑ How will equipment be transported and stored and do these considerations impact the design of the equipment?

FOR OVERSIGHT ACTORS

- ☑ Is the process of defining design requirements inclusive by, for example, seeking the input of various stakeholders, including political parties and civil society?

- ☑ Are there specific requirements to ensure that the systems are developed in a manner that maximizes the usability for all voters and the access afforded to groups of voters who may normally struggle to participate in the electoral process, such as voters with visual impairments, hearing impairments or motor difficulties, as well as illiterates or those from minority language groups?

- ☑ What tests and/or research, if any, have been conducted to assess the usability and accessibility of equipment? Was it conducted among voters from diverse demographics and among those who may normally struggle to participate?

- ☑ Is the work of developing technical requirements made available to the public?

- ☑ Are the experts responsible for developing design requirements mandated, and are they required to disclose any affiliations with interested parties (i.e., potential vendors)?

PROCUREMENT, PRODUCTION AND DELIVERY

The procurement and production processes are vitally important to building trust in the process. The procurement specification should cover everything that is required from the technology provider. It is especially important that the procurement of such technologies is conducted in an impartial manner through a transparent, competitive bidding process. Conducting such a process takes a significant amount of time and involves several different steps, as detailed below. The evaluation of bids should provide sufficient written documentation so that observers can learn whether the decisions were made strictly on the basis of the evaluation criteria laid out in the procurement documents. Contractual documents should be made available to stakeholders to the extent the law allows. Observers should use these contractual documents as tools to monitor the extent to which vendors meet their obligations. Because there is a need for frequent communication between supplier and election management body to ensure that the technology solution delivered meets the exact needs of the users, sufficient time for this interaction should be factored into the production and delivery timeline.

Once the decision to conduct a pilot or to implement electronic voting or counting technologies more generally has been made, a critical first step is procuring the equipment needed to implement the technology. A comprehensive specification is essential for this procurement process. Ideally a specification will have been developed during the decision-in-principle process and refined during the pilot, if there was one. Regardless, it is crucially important to ensure that a specification is developed that covers everything that is required from the technology provider.

A comprehensive specification should include the following issues:

- **Type of Technology** – The specification should indicate whether the election management body is interested in electronic voting, electronic counting, remote voting or a combination of these.

- **Scale** – The quantity of any equipment or services required may influence the ability of the supplier to deliver these items on time and therefore should be clearly specified, especially if custom-made equipment and software need to be developed. The anticipated number of voters using a system will also impact the suitability of systems and will be highly relevant for solutions such as remote voting systems.

- **Timeframe** – The timeframe for delivery will also have a significant influence on suppliers' ability to deliver and, potentially, on the cost of equipment and services as well.

- **Voter Authentication** – Any requirements for voting machines to also authenticate the identity of voters should be clearly identified, as should the mechanisms that will be used to conduct this authentication, such as biometric fingerprint identification.

- **Audit Mechanisms** – Any requirements for audit mechanisms should be clearly outlined.

- **Results Transmission Mechanisms** – The means by which results are to be transmitted or transferred from individual voting or counting machines to the central vote tabulation system should be defined.

- **Power and Environmental Conditions** – Any requirements for machines to operate for periods of time without mains power or to function in extreme temperatures, humidity or dusty conditions should be identified.

- **Electoral Systems** – The electoral systems that the electronic voting or counting equipment are to be used for should be identified. It may also be prudent to ensure that the equipment is able to cope with other electoral systems that are not currently used but might be adopted in the future. The specification should also indicate if each voter will need to cast multiple ballots and whether different electoral systems will apply to different ballots.

- **Accessibility Requirements** – Any requirement for the equipment to deal with multiple languages and voters with disabilities should be detailed, including the need for visual, audible and tactile interfaces, as applicable.

- **Security Requirements** – Security requirements for the electronic voting or counting machines, as well as any security standards that they should comply with, should be detailed.

- **Access to Source Code** – It is seen as increasingly important that electronic voting and counting solution source code be open to external inspection, if not fully open source, and any such requirements should be included in the specification.

- **Additional Services** – Other required services, such as project management, configuration, training and support during implementation of the electronic voting or counting technology, should be identified.

- **Consumables** – The specification should indicate whether it is acceptable for consumables, including paper, ink, cutters, batteries, memory storage units and devices, to be proprietary or whether they must be generic. If only supplier consumables can be used, will the supplier guarantee availability throughout the lifespan of the device, which might be as long as 15 years?

- **Additional Software Systems** – There may also be a requirement to procure a results transmission, receipt and tabulation system or a more general election management system that would include the electronic voting or counting system.

Comprehensive specifications will form the basis for the procurement of electronic voting or counting equipment.

While not part of the specification of requirements for electronic voting or counting technologies, the request for proposals issued with the specification may also seek information on a range of other issues relevant to the suitability of the proposals made by suppliers. These include:

- The institution that will own the intellectual property rights for the procured electronic voting or counting solution (for example, the EMB or the supplier)

- Responsibility for the repair of faulty or damaged equipment (whether it lies with the EMB or the vendor) and whether the EMB is authorized to make any repairs

- Mechanisms for configuration of electronic voting or counting machines prior to each election

- The vendor's responsibilities regarding transferring skills and knowledge to the EMB for training its staff and staff operation of the technologies

- Consequences for the integrity of stored or in-process data transactions in the instance of a sudden loss of power to equipment

- Maximum capacity of electronic voting or counting machines in terms of the number of electoral races and candidates that can be accommodated

- Means of verifying that loaded software is the approved version

- Mechanisms to demonstrate that the electronic version of the ballot box is empty at the beginning of voting and/or counting

- Capacity of the electronic voting system to display photographs or symbols for ballot entities

- Mechanisms for review and confirmation of voter choices on the electronic voting solution

- Specifications and reliability of any printing device attached to the voting machine

- Mechanisms for ensuring the protection of data and secrecy of voters' choices

- Mechanism for generation of results at the end of voting or counting, and the ways in which these results are transferred or transmitted for tabulation

- Details of the election management system used with the electronic voting or counting technology, including whether the supplier is responsible for providing the tabulation system (software and hardware)

- Responsibilities and capacities for troubleshooting and other servicing before and during Election Day processes

- Life expectancy of electronic voting or counting equipment

- Maintenance and storage requirements for equipment between elections

Given that the use of electronic voting and counting technologies presents particular challenges to the transparency of and trust in the electoral process, it is especially important that the procurement of such technologies is conducted in an impartial manner, ideally using an open and transparent competitive bidding process. The conduct of an open and impartial procurement process takes time and may involve many different steps and accommodations, including:

- Consultations with technical experts during the preparation of specifications

- Establishment of eligibility requirements for bidders

- Submission of expressions of interest by suppliers

- Evaluation and prequalification of suppliers based on the expressions of interest

- Publication of the final request for proposals (RFP)

- Conduct of a vendor conference to answer questions concerning the RFP

- Time allocation for drafting and submission of proposals

- Evaluation of proposals

- Submission and responses to clarifying questions on proposals

- Publication of the selection decision

- Time for contracting the selected supplier

As can be seen from this long list, the procurement process can be lengthy, and election management bodies need to plan accordingly.

Often a committee is established to review proposals received by suppliers; the committee then evaluates the bids according to the criteria established and decides on which proposal best meets the needs of the election management body. The criteria that will be used for evaluation should be defined before the procurement process and, ideally, communicated in the RFP. Evaluation criteria might include compliance with technical specifications, experience in delivering similar solutions, quality and experience of the project management team offered by the vendor, access provided to source code and cost of the proposed solution.

The work of this evaluation committee should be transparent, and the committee should provide sufficient written documentation so that observers can learn whether the decisions were made strictly on the basis of the evaluation criteria laid out in the procurement documents. Opening the evaluation process to observers would further help to promote transparency.

Even after selection of a vendor, there should be sufficient time allocated for reaching agreement on a contract. Many vendors have their own contract templates, as do many procuring entities. Discrepancies often arise as to the specific details, such as where the equipment will be delivered (to the airport or to the warehouses of the EMB, for example), the schedule of payments, the schedule of deliveries, factory acceptance test plan, the court system that will have final jurisdiction in case of legal dispute, any exemption from taxes or the party responsible for any taxes, and whether the equipment can be used for other purposes besides the conduct of elections.

The contract should include a timeframe for the delivery of equipment and services. The election management body will need to carefully monitor the progress of the supplier in meeting its contractual obligations and must have in place contingencies for the possibility that the supplier does not deliver on time. The election management body may consider including penalties in the contract for late delivery of equipment and services to protect itself against costs associated with late delivery and provide incentives for the supplier to meet its delivery obligations.

To the extent possible under existing administrative statutes or legal mandates, contractual documents should be made available to stakeholders. In this way, observers can evaluate the contractual terms and assess, for example, whether the timeline is realistic and what the obligations of vendors are if the timeline or other terms are not met. Observers can then also monitor the extent to which vendors comply with their obligations during the process.

It should also be noted that considerable communication will likely be required between the supplier and the election management body as electronic voting or counting equipment is developed, in order to clarify and add detail to the specifications used in the procurement process. This will especially be the case where a custom-made solution, rather than an off-the-shelf solution, is delivered. This interaction between supplier and election management body is essential in ensuring that the technology solution delivered meets the exact needs of the users, and adequate time for this interaction should be included in the timeline for production and delivery.

KEY CONSIDERATIONS: PROCUREMENT, PRODUCTION AND DELIVERY

FOR IMPLEMENTING BODIES

- ☑ Do the procurement documents for e-voting or e-counting hardware include technical specifications that detail key issues required of vendors including types of technology, security and authentication mechanisms, environmental conditions, accessibility requirements, software and source code requirements?

- ☑ Does the Request for Proposals outline expectations regarding intellectual property rights agreements; division of responsibilities between vendor and EMB; specifics of electoral system that equipment has to address; specifics for security of voting or counting equipment; hardware and software requirements for results production and dissemination systems; and maintenance and storage requirements.

- ☑ Is the evaluation criteria detailed in the Request for Proposals?

- ☑ Does the procurement process put in place mechanisms to ensure that all steps of the process are transparent and engage electoral stakeholders at appropriate steps in the process?

- ☑ Is sufficient time allocated for the procurement process to meet transparency and inclusiveness goals?

☑ Is there sufficient time allocated for the EMB to come to terms on a contract with the selected vendor?

☑ Does the contract vehicle contain specific benchmarks for timely delivery of equipment and services from the selected vendor, as well as clearly defined penalties for failure to meet benchmarks?

☑ Are contractual agreements made publicly available?

FOR OVERSIGHT ACTORS

☑ Do the procurement documents cover everything that is required from the technology provider (see above)?

☑ Is the overall procurement process conducted in an impartial and transparent manner?

☑ Is the bidding process open to all vendors and competitive?

☑ Are the criteria for evaluation defined before the procurement process and communicated in the bidding document?

☑ Is the evaluation process transparent, and does it provide sufficient written documentation that allows observers to determine whether decisions were made strictly on the basis of the evaluation criteria?

☑ Does the selected vendor have any links to and/or conflicts of interest with relevant public officials, political leaders, candidates and/or parties?

☑ Are contractual documents made available to the public, so that observers can monitor the extent to which vendors comply with their obligations during the process?

☑ Does the contractual arrangement ensure that the EMB will remain in control of the relationship with the vendor and that the vendor is accountable to the EMB? Similarly, is the role of the vendor vis-à-vis the EMB clearly defined?

☑ Is the contractual timeline realistic? What are the obligations of vendors if the timeline or other terms are not met?

SECURITY MECHANISMS

The security of electronic voting and counting systems is essential to ensuring public confidence and overall electoral integrity. At the same time, these technologies present a host of security challenges, including physical security of equipment, openness to review of the source code, secrecy of voting data, encryption of data stored on machines and transmitted to tabulation centers and verification of the legitimacy of the sources of data transmitted to tabulation centers. Because numerous security flaws have been detected in voting and counting machines in many countries, public debate on and scrutiny of the security of such technologies has increased. EMBs too often assume that systems are secure, while other electoral stakeholders often have greater distrust in technologies. Thus, EMBs need to take security concerns extremely seriously.

System security is a crucial feature of electronic voting and counting technologies. These technologies are inherently less transparent than the use of paper ballots, where all steps of the voting and counting process are observable. If an electronic voting or counting system is to be trusted by electoral stakeholders, it is important that the security challenges presented by the use of the technologies are understood and addressed.

Many aspects of this issue of system and data security need to be considered.

One key concern is the openness to review of the source code for the electronic voting or counting machine, as well as any other software related to the machines. Whether the source code for electronic voting and counting applications should be open source (i.e., published for anyone to inspect) is a significant issue in the debate about the transparency and security of these technologies.

Traditionally the source code for these machines and supporting applications has been seen as proprietary in nature, exclusively owned by the supplier and not provided for any independent review. Proprietary source code carries two inherent risks for the EMB: that it may be locked into a long-term agreement with the solution provider; and/or that future supplemental procurement of new machines may not be compatible with the ballot or results format of the existing systems. The need for transparency in the electoral process has led to increasing demands from election management bodies for this source code to be open to inspection by external stakeholders, and increasingly, suppliers are meeting these demands.

This issue is relevant for security, in that the source code for voting and counting applications is often very long and complex. Errors and omissions, whether accidental or otherwise, may exist in the software and not be found, despite internal review. Allowing external stakeholders to inspect the code should dissuade the inclusion of deliberately malicious code by suppliers or rogue programmers. It is also expected that the more people that can check the source code, the more likely it is that errors in the code can be identified and corrected. Given the complexity of source code, political party observers and nonpartisan election observer groups will likely need to engage IT security experts to review the code and other aspects of the security mechanisms.

Maintaining secrecy of the voting data, including ensuring that votes are not linked to voters' identification information, is a particular security challenge for electronic voting and counting machines, especially with remote voting, where identification details need to be entered into the same device on which the vote is cast (for example, a personal computer). However, this is increasingly an issue with electronic voting machines used in supervised environments, as voting machines are now being developed to identify each voter through a personal ID number or through biometrics.

FIGURE 13 - THE IMPORTANT USES OF CRYPTOGRAPHY IN ELECTRONIC VOTING AND COUNTING

Cryptography offers a number of benefits to electronic voting and counting solutions. It may be used to perform tasks such as encrypting votes and digital ballot boxes, ensuring votes and software are unmodified, verifying the identity of a voter before he or she casts a ballot, and assisting in auditing and tallying the results of an election. Traditionally, cryptography (from the Greek for "hidden writing") was used to conceal information between two people using a secret key known only to them. Over time, it expanded into the art and science of using mathematics (in the form of algorithms) to hide information, protect privacy, ensure files are not altered and prove the identity of a message's sender. Considering the paramount importance of ballot secrecy and fraud detection, cryptography has proved a useful tool for countries employing election technologies.

ENCRYPTION AND DECRYPTION

Encryption and decryption are among the most common uses of cryptography. Encryption is the process of obscuring information, and decryption reverses this process. Keys are the secret piece of information necessary to encrypt and decrypt data. Encrypted data is unintelligible; and without the correct decryption key, it cannot be recreated in its original form. An example of a very simple encryption key is to increment each letter in a block of text by one letter (i.e., "a" becomes "b," "b" becomes "c," etc.), so "Election Day" would become "Fmfdujpo Ebz". Decryption of the text requires that each letter be decremented by one.

Ensuring that a key remains secret is paramount to ensuring encrypted information remains hidden. With the advent of computer-based cryptography, keys are now represented as large, nearly random strings of letters and numbers such as 2b7e151628aed2a6abf7158809cf4f3c (this number would typically be much larger). Different methods of encryption and decryption have different properties; some function more quickly, are more difficult to break, can be transmitted more rapidly or work better on slower computer processors.

For electoral purposes, encryption is often used to obscure the contents of a voter's ballot selections and the contents of a digital ballot box. The voter's encrypted ballot selections may be stored on a voting machine or sent over an insecure channel like the Internet or the telephone network. When casting an electronic vote, the value of the vote will be encrypted using an encryption key produced by the EMB and available at all electronic voting locations. However, only the EMB will have the key that is needed to decrypt encrypted data.

HASH FUNCTIONS

Another cryptographic function is the hash (often called cryptographic hashes). Hashes are mathematical functions or equations that "read in" a piece of information (e.g., a file) and output a set of numbers and letters that are unique to the input. Just as with encryption, there are different hashing algorithms with unique characteristics. Using the SHA-256 hashing algorithm, the word "election" hashes to: c7a19845b9e9de079260094d79525957. But when using the same algorithm and inputting the word "elections" (notice there is only a one-letter difference), the output is completely different: b9dd4e28c0fe5673909bb6c0615f5f22. This is the point of hashes – detecting changes. A file of any size can be passed through the hashing algorithm, even large and complex computer programs. Hashes can identify a one-character modification to a vote stored on a computer, the software running on a voting machine, or even an entire operating system.

There are many applications of this concept to voting. In the U.S., a public repository known as the National Software Reference Library (NSRL) stores the hashes of voting system source code and the compiled versions of software that are used for voting and counting systems. Some EMBs verify all software before installing it on voting machines by "hashing" the software and checking the result against the hash values in the NSRL. This process helps to identify malicious modifications to the software, but many election officials also state this process helps identify when incorrect versions are about to be installed or when software is corrupted.

DIGITAL SIGNATURES

Digital signatures are mathematical functions that work in a similar manner to cryptographic hashes and also help identify who sent a message or file. Digital signatures are not analogous to physical handwritten signatures as they provide much stronger proof of who "signed" a message. A digital signature is different for every message, making it much more difficult to forge another person's signature. In elections, digital signatures are used to "sign" the contents of a digital ballot box or a voter's ballot selections, thus helping ensure the ballot box or vote was not altered. If tampering occurred and the digital signature was forged, the attacker would need to know another person's, or the EMB's, secret key.

MIX-NETS

The order in which data is stored on electronic voting or counting systems can be used to link the identity of the voter to the value of the vote, if the order in which voters cast their ballots is also observed. Cryptographic schemes have been developed to protect the secrecy of stored votes. A mix-net takes encrypted, stored data and then re-encrypts it and mixes the order in which it is stored. Only then are the data decrypted and the values of the votes revealed. As the order of the original vote data has been changed and the encrypted value of the stored vote data has also been changed (it was re-encrypted as it passed through the mix-net), there is no way that decrypted vote values can be linked back to either the original data received or the identity of voters.

HOMOMORPHIC CRYPTOGRAPHY

Another solution used to protect the secrecy of stored votes is homomorphic cryptography, which allows the votes in the electronic ballot box to be tabulated while still encrypted. As individual votes are never decrypted, there is no possibility of linking voters to the way that they voted. Votes may even be posted to a public bulletin board for independent tabulation by anyone to verify the outcome of the election.

The physical security of electronic voting or counting machines and the data held on the machines also needs to be protected. Access to voting or counting machines must be controlled, and any access that takes place should be recorded, reported on if it is outside of standard operating procedures and, ideally, conducted by two-person teams. Data ports on electronic voting or counting machines may be essential so that software and configuration data can be loaded onto the machines, but the data ports need to be protected so they cannot be used to manipulate the functioning of the machines or to insert different vote data. It is also important that mechanisms are in place to verify that the software loaded onto any electronic voting or counting machine is the same version that was tested and approved by the election management body and external stakeholders.

Data held on electronic voting or counting machines needs to be encrypted to ensure that, even if the data is accessed by unauthorized persons, this data cannot be read, used or manipulated. Procedures must also be in place to ensure the security of decryption keys and to establish when and how the decryption of data takes place.

The encryption of voting data needs to be maintained when it is transmitted or transported from individual electronic voting or counting machines to the tabulation system for generation of results. There also must be a way to ensure that data uploaded to the results tabulation system has come from a legitimate source. This can be achieved by digitally signing data and only allowing data with an authorized digital signature to be uploaded.

In the public debate about electronic voting and counting systems, their security has become an increasingly important issue, with systems subject to considerable scrutiny. Electronic voting and counting machines and results systems have not fared well under this additional scrutiny. Despite the denial of suppliers (and often of election administrators as well), numerous security flaws have been detected in voting and counting machines. In the Netherlands campaigners argued that it was easy to reprogram voting machines to, for example, play chess or to manipulate the election results. When the suppliers of the machines challenged this, the campaigners reprogrammed one of the voting machines to do exactly that, playing chess against a reprogrammed voting machine (see Figure 14 below for more details).[32]

In India, the election commission claimed that, because the instructions for their voting machine were burned into the circuit board, it was not possible to reprogram their machines. Rop Gonggrijp, a Dutch hacker who was involved in exposing the vulnerability of the Dutch voting machines, along with a number

---

[32] Gonggrijp, R. and Hengeveld, W-J (2006) "Nedap/Groenendaal ES3B Voting Computer: A Security Analysis."

of other researchers, took on the challenge of showing whether the Indian voting machines were secure. They demonstrated that, with little effort, the Indian voting machines could be manipulated to change the results, avoiding this circuitry coding, and that this manipulation could even be activated remotely by mobile phone.[33]

In the U.S., the debate on electronic voting machine security has been particularly intense, with many studies demonstrating how existing voting and counting machines could be hacked in order to manipulate election results. In 2004 the source code for a commonly used electronic voting machine in the U.S. was published online. A group of four computer scientists set about analyzing the source code and discovered several problems, including the incorrect use of cryptography, vulnerabilities to network threats and poor software development processes. This analysis concluded that the voting machine system was vulnerable to both inside and external security threats and failed to meet even minimal security standards.[34]

Concerns about the physical security of the Irish voting machine were also identified by that country's Commission on Electronic Voting. In its first report in 2004 on the electronic voting system chosen in Ireland, after an initial small pilot of the voting machines in 2002, the commission found security defects in both the hardware/software interface and the physical voting machine itself.[35] The system did not use (then) current security mechanisms, such as cryptography, and was vulnerable to attack by an insider with short-term access to the machine, with the result that recorded votes could be significantly affected. The commission raised serious concerns about the integrity of any elections held

---

33 Prasad, H. K., Haldermann, J. A., Gonggrijp, R. Wolchok, S., Wustrow, E., Kankipati, A., Sakhamuri, S. K. and Yagati, V. (2010) "Security Analysis of India's Electronic Voting Machines."
34 Kohno, T., Stubblefield, A., Rubin, A. and Wallach, D. (2004) "Analysis of an Electronic Voting System," IEEE Symposium on Security and Privacy. (Washington, DC: IEEE Computer Society Press) avirubin.com/vote.pdf.
35 Commission on Electronic Voting (2004) "First Report of the Commission on Electronic Voting on the Security, Accuracy and Testing of Chosen Electronic Voting System," Appendix 2B.

using the machines and determined that they should not be used again before further efforts were made to resolve these issues.

The experiences of these countries has led to a tendency to put any electronic voting or counting system under intense scrutiny. All too often election management bodies seem to operate under the assumption that electronic voting and counting systems are secure until proven otherwise. At the same time, electoral stakeholders tend to start from a position of much greater distrust in such technologies. In this context, election management bodies need to take security concerns very seriously and must be seen to address both real and perceived security threats.

FIGURE 14 – THE NGO CAMPAIGN ON THE SECURITY OF E-VOTING MACHINES IN THE NETHERLANDS

The Netherlands' experience provides an example of the challenges that can arise when EMBs, political parties, civil society and other stakeholders do not pay adequate attention to the integrity and security of electronic voting and counting technologies.

In the summer of 2006, a number of computer experts in the Netherlands launched a group called "We Do Not Trust Voting Computers" ("Wij vertrouwen stemcomputers niet") to publicize their concerns about the security of electronic voting machines and their lack of auditability mechanisms. The use of electronic voting machines was already widespread in the Netherlands, although Amsterdam introduced them for the first time during municipal elections in spring 2006.

The campaign set up a website (http://wijvertrouwenstemcomputersniet.nl) and sought to further investigate the use of electronic voting computers through freedom of information requests. The requested documents revealed a number of security flaws in the voting machines, as well as the extent to which the election process had been outsourced to technology suppliers. The campaign posted the documents on its website, generating controversy with the technology suppliers who claimed the documents included confidential information. The controversy brought increased media attention to the campaign.

The campaign received widespread national exposure in early October 2006 when its experts appeared in an investigative television news program demonstrating the security flaws of the voting machines. The program showed the experts replacing the memory chip in a voting machine in less than five minutes, allowing them to manipulate the results of a mock election; later they reprogrammed the machine to play chess. The report also raised serious questions about the physical security of the machines while in storage and during transport, the testing of machines and the adequacy of the regulatory framework. The campaign released a security analysis at the same time detailing the vulnerabilities identified by the experts, including the possible detection of radio emissions outside polling stations that could compromise the secrecy of the vote.

Following government testing of the machines and an independent review of the election process (see Figure 26, "Re-evaluation of the Use of Electronic Voting Machines in the Netherlands" below), the Dutch Parliament withdrew the enabling legislation for electronic voting in October 2007, returning the country to nationwide paper balloting for the first time in over 40 years.

KEY CONSIDERATIONS: SECURITY MECHANISMS

FOR IMPLEMENTING BODIES

- ☑ Have the advantages and disadvantages of open source code versus proprietary code been fully considered in the design process?
- ☑ Is a mechanism in place to control access to voting or counting machines? Does the control mechanism include recording and reporting of access to the machines that is outside of standard operating procedures?
- ☑ Is the data held on electronic voting or counting machines protected through encryption?

☑ Are procedures in place to ensure the security of decryption keys and to establish when and how the decryption of data takes place?

☑ Is the encryption of voting data maintained when it is transmitted or transported from individual electronic voting or counting machines to the tabulation system for generation of results?

FOR OVERSIGHT ACTORS

☑ Does the system only allow access for authorized users, and is that access provided in a secure manner?

☑ Is the physical security of machines, including data ports, protected from would-be attempts to manipulate the machines? Are party agents and election observers able to monitor any intervention that affects the system while voting and counting being conducted?

☑ Is the secrecy of the vote maintained, such that votes are not linked to voter identification information?

☑ Are there mechanisms, such as hashes, to ensure the software loaded onto machines can be verified as the EMB-tested and approved version?

☑ Is voting data encrypted to ensure it can be securely transmitted or transported from individual machines to the tabulation system? Is there a mechanism, such as a digital signature, to ensure that data transmitted to the tabulation system is from a legitimate source?

RECRUITMENT AND TRAINING OF PERSONNEL

One of the most difficult challenges for EMBs in transitioning to electronic voting and counting technologies is building the capacity at all levels to administer elections with new technologies. This usually involves not only training existing staff, but also creating new structures and hiring new staff with the skills necessary to oversee the technological transition. The long-term goal for EMBs should be to build their capacity to self-administer all aspects of future elections, but initially it is likely that private vendors or technicians would need to be contracted to fulfill specific technological functions. In such cases, vendors' roles should be clearly defined, and the overall responsibility for administering the elections should remain with the EMB. The terms of the relationship with the vendor, as well as trainings and materials for election officials at all levels, should be open to observers so that they can assess the level of preparedness of the EMB.

Introducing electronic voting and counting systems will present the EMB with significant challenges in administering elections with the selected technology. Depending on the complexity of the technologies adopted and the existing technical competencies of the EMB staff, it is likely that new skill sets will be needed to administer the electronic systems. It is important that EMBs develop the capacity to administer as many aspects of the electronic voting and counting system as possible so that they maintain control over the integrity of the election itself. However, building the necessary capacity in various areas may be a gradual process.

Once the decision to adopt electronic voting and counting systems has been made, the EMB will need to designate who at the central level will be responsible for regulating, managing and operating these systems. While most EMBs have an IT department, assigning it responsibility for overseeing electronic voting and counting would likely overstretch the department's capacity, having a potentially detrimental effect on the project. Instead, an EMB will likely need to create new structures to conduct these tasks.

An analysis of the staffing requirements associated with the project will need to be conducted as early as possible so that decisions can be made regarding whether the necessary competencies can be filled by training current staff or whether new personnel must be identified and recruited. The same issue will be replicated at the regional, local and polling station levels, in regard to both permanent staff and temporary election staff. Observers should be afforded access to such staffing plans, as these plans are critical to the successful implementation of new technologies.

It may be difficult for EMBs to recruit personnel with the necessary qualifications and experience to operate and update the new systems. EMBs may instead have to rely either on technicians provided by the equipment supplier or on the contracted services of private firms to fulfill specific technological functions, such as software programming and management of security features. Should such personnel be employed, their level of access to systems should be strictly defined and recorded, and their role should be transparent to observers.

Care should be taken to ensure that overall management of the systems remains within the EMB's authority, as it is responsible for the administration of elections and accountable to the public for their integrity. While private firms or other state actors may conduct important parts of the election process, they should not have overall responsibility for the administration of elections. Over time EMBs should prioritize building their capacity to administer all aspects of electronic voting and counting systems with their own staff resources.

Given the complex nature of electronic voting and counting systems, extended training of permanent and short-term personnel is likely to be necessary. Even at the polling station level, election officials must be knowledgeable enough about the equipment they are required to operate in order to conduct basic troubleshooting if there is a problem on Election Day, or to correctly identify a problem so that the necessary technicians can be contacted. Polling officials must also understand the equipment well enough to explain the process to voters, which will help to increase public confidence in the systems. Similarly, training needs at the regional and central levels will also be significant, as officials must be able not only to operate the equipment, but also to solve problems and, in addition, must be able to explain the process to voters and other stakeholders.

Training for personnel at all levels, therefore, must be comprehensive and effective. Especially when voting and counting systems are used for the first time, it might be necessary for the equipment supplier to play a role in providing training. To the degree possible, the EMB should work with the supplier to develop the in-house capacity to conduct such training. For instance, the equipment supplier can conduct "training of trainers" courses for the in-house EMB trainers to gain the knowledge required to conduct the trainings themselves.

Training events and training materials should be open to scrutiny by observers and stakeholders. Observers should assess the effectiveness of the trainings and materials, and make any recommendations regarding improvements that may be necessary. Through such efforts, observers will also build their own understanding of the procedures and operation of the electronic voting and counting systems, as well as any possible weaknesses they should be aware of on Election Day.

KEY CONSIDERATIONS: RECRUITMENT AND TRAINING OF PERSONNEL

FOR IMPLEMENTING BODIES

☑ Has an analysis of the staffing needs associated with the project been conducted at both national as well as the regional, local, and polling station levels for staffing needs?

☑ Are levels of access to systems appropriately defined for external technicians that may be hired to assist in the process?

☑ Is training for personnel at all levels based on cooperation with the equipment supplier in order to develop in-house capacity to conduct trainings?

☑ Does the process include a training of trainers to build internal capacity?

FOR OVERSIGHT ACTORS

☑ Is the EMB staffing plan adequate for successfully implementing electronic voting and counting technologies, and are staffing plans made available to oversight actors?

☑ If outside technicians or consultants are involved, are their roles clearly defined and transparent?

☑ Do election officials, including at the polling station level, have sufficient understanding of the technologies, allowing them to clearly explain the voting and counting process to voters?

- ☑ Does the EMB have a long-term goal and plan to self-administer all aspects of electronic voting and counting in future elections?

- ☑ Do oversight actors, including parties and observer groups, have access to EMB trainings and training materials, allowing them to assess the adequacy of training, provide recommendations and build their own understanding of the technologies?

2.3 IMPLEMENTING ELECTRONIC VOTING OR ELECTRONIC COUNTING IN AN ELECTION

PROJECT AND RISK MANAGEMENT

The successful implementation of electronic voting or counting in an election should have as a first step a comprehensive project management plan. The management plan should detail the steps necessary for effective implementation, the schedule for these steps, as well as the personnel responsible for carrying them out, and should identify risks associated with the implementation and how these risks can be addressed. The management plan is a key resource for managers to gauge progress on the implementation of electronic voting or counting technologies and to respond to delays or obstacles. Observers should use the management plan to provide oversight of the implementation process and make recommendations in cases where deadlines are not being met according to schedule or where risks are not being effectively addressed.

Elections are a complex logistical exercise. The introduction of electronic voting and counting systems makes them even more complex. As has been discussed previously in this manual, the successful implementation of electronic voting and counting technologies depends on a broad number of variables working together properly. For this to happen, the project needs – first and foremost – effective planning and management.

Although this manual attempts to present the implementation of electronic voting and counting in as straightforward a manner as possible, discussing it as a coherent process, implementation is much more likely to involve a diverse range of processes conducted by official and unofficial actors, dispersed across institutions and over a lengthy period of time. The EMB must establish mechanisms for overall project management and coordination, including the establishment of a project management group. Such a group can include members from a diverse range of relevant institutions to ensure the smooth coordination and timely progress of the project. It is important that a broad set of skills be represented among members (e.g., project management, field operations, training, logistics, voter education, legal and IT) so that all aspects of various issues are considered.

Two important questions for the election authorities and other relevant institutions are whether to devote dedicated staff to the project and whether project staff should have additional responsibilities. While it may be preferable to have staff dedicated to the project, this might not be possible – particularly if there is a long time period between the project's conception and its actual implementation. In a situation where there are few or no dedicated project staff, the role and importance of a project management group is further increased.

From the outset, it is important that the EMB and other relevant institutions (or the project management group) conduct a planning process that lays out step-by-step how the project will be implemented, who (or which institution) has responsibility for each aspect and how long it is expected to take. The project management group should draft a detailed plan and timeline that set out each stage of the project as well as the deadlines to be met. This plan and timeline should be publicly available and reviewed by EMBs on a regular basis to ensure that targets are being met.

As has been stressed elsewhere in this document, the amount of time necessary to implement electronic voting and counting systems should not be underestimated, and the schedule should include adequate time for public consultation, drafting of the necessary legal framework, feasibility studies, pilot testing, design of appropriate technology, security testing, expert review, personnel recruitment and training and voter education. The timeline should also include some flexibility in case some of the activities take longer than anticipated.

In Norway, for example, the Parliament decided in 2008 to pilot Internet voting during the September 2011 local elections. This timeframe provided several years for development of the system and pre-testing, with the 2011 pilot taking place in only 10 out of 429 municipalities. Despite this extended timeframe, the project team still had to work very hard to get the Internet voting system ready in time for the pilot.

FIGURE 15 – UK ELECTORAL COMMISSION REPORT CRITIQUES THE 2007 ELECTRONIC VOTING PILOTS

The UK Electoral Commission conducted comprehensive assessments of all of the voting pilots that it conducted between 2002 and 2007. After the 2007 pilots, it identified several project management issues that had not been properly addressed:

"It is important to realise that these remote e-voting pilots are complex IT projects and therefore require effective planning, testing and quality management. The lack of these elements in the 2007 pilots resulted in significantly higher implementation risks than necessary. The relative success of the delivery of the pilots, notwithstanding some issues at individual pilots, was due to the efforts of individual local authorities and their suppliers, combined with good luck."

The report also went on to emphasize the need to allow adequate time for testing prior to polling so that identified issues can be properly resolved and retesting can take place.

The project management group should meet on a regular basis to review the project's progress. Periodic progress reports can refer back to the original plan and timeline in order to assess progress made to date; these reports should also be publicly available. The project management group can further promote transparency by allowing political actors and independent observers to attend some of its meetings and by regularly briefing them on project progress.

It may be advisable to establish a broader consultation group in addition to the formal project management group. This group could be kept informed of project progress and consulted periodically and at key stages during the project implementation process. This consultation group should have a wide range of interests and organizations represented, such as members from academia, civil society and professional communities. The inclusion of those who advocate against the use of electronic voting or counting in this consultation group will also be important, as those critical of the use of such technologies often raise important issues and perspectives that may need to be addressed to some extent.

A critical aspect of project management is developing a risk assessment tool that realistically identifies possible sources of risk, considers any mitigating factors and provides appropriate responses. This will involve a full assessment of potential security risks, as these are among the most critical for an electronic voting and counting system and should be carefully considered; but other types of risk related to logistical or even legal issues should be considered as well.

Although each project will have its own risks, a risk plan should address:

- Late or failed delivery of equipment and services
- Failure of security mechanisms (e.g., breach of electronic voting machine security)
- Missing, malfunctioning or late delivery of equipment, software or supplies (e.g., thermal paper, backup batteries, and other consumables)
- Communications failure (e.g., nonfunctioning Internet connection)
- Power failure
- Problems with staff recruitment
- Legal challenges to the use of the technology
- Public (mis)perception and resistance
- Attempts to discredit the system by those with competing commercial or political interests

A risk management plan should be developed early in the project and should be made publicly available so as to increase public confidence in the election authorities' ability to face the challenges of implementing electronic voting or counting.

Election observers should review the project management documents on an ongoing basis and highlight any gaps that they identify in a timely manner so that recommendations can be made to improve the project. Using the project documents, observers can also provide oversight to ensure that deadlines are being met and the project remains on track in terms of its timeline. Observers should also review the risk management plan to determine whether risks have been realistically anticipated and countermeasures devised. Observers are in a key position to provide this assessment of project progress to citizens on an ongoing basis through periodic statements. Such reporting can enhance public confidence in the election administration and also highlight any areas of concern in a timely manner so that action can be taken.

FIGURE 16 – ELECTRONIC VOTING PROJECT MANAGEMENT IN THE NETHERLANDS

Despite using electronic voting for many years in the Netherlands, the Ministry of Interior, which is in charge of the overall framework for elections, did not have the technical capacity to properly manage and regulate the electronic voting process. This allowed vendors too much control over the implementation of electronic voting technologies and the setting of standards for these technologies. Consequently, vendors and the ministry failed to update voting technology in line with modern security requirements, posing severe security risks to the electronic voting process.

In the late 1960s, the government of the Netherlands commissioned the Dutch Organization for Applied Scientific

Research (Toegepast Natuurwetenschappelijk Onderzoek, TNO) and the Dutch Apparatus Factory (Nederlandse Apparatenfabriek NV, NEDAP) to design and build a voting machine. At this time, the Ministry of the Interior was responsible for developing the overall legal framework for elections, including ensuring proper standards and regulation of voting machines. During the initial design process, the ministry chose not to set any legal requirements for TNO and NEDAP. The decision to award TNO and NEDAP creative control over the voting machines set a precedent that gave Dutch suppliers control over the ministry on electronic voting project management and regulation.

Voting machines became more widespread in Dutch elections during the late 1980s and 90s, yet the ministry's regulation of these technologies remained limited. Vendor influence over electronic voting continued in part because of the ministry's lack of knowledge of electronic voting technologies. The ministry was unable to determine clear requirements regarding functionality, integrity and security of voting machines. One paragraph of the Electoral Code (Article J33, paragraph 2) did specify some requirements for voting machines (such as secrecy of the vote and a clear candidate list; however, legislation was largely process oriented and did not delve into standards or technical requirements.

The ministry also relied heavily on vendor knowledge when revising standards on electronic voting, which created a conflict of interest. TNO, for example, was included in a ministry working group in 1990 and tasked with drafting technical regulations for voting machines. Their suggestions did not require any security features or a voter-verified paper audit trail (VVPAT), nor did it address the possibility of manipulation. Consistent with TNO's recommendations, no such regulations were ever issued by the ministry.

In the absence of a strong regulatory framework, vendors did not update technology in line with modern security requirements, making the voting machines vulnerable to internal and external security threats. The ministry also overlooked several warning signs with the voting machines, including problems that were discovered with similar machines in Ireland as well as concerns raised by the Electoral Council. For example, the Electoral Council advised the ministry on several occasions to introduce a certification procedure for the tabulation software. The ministry did not enact regulations in response to these concerns.

KEY CONSIDERATIONS: PROJECT AND RISK MANAGEMENT

FOR IMPLEMENTING BODIES

☑ Has a project management body been established?

☑ Are measures in place to ensure that project staff time can be sufficiently devoted to the project in the presence of other responsibilities?

☑ Has a detailed plan and timeline that sets out each stage of the project as well as the deadlines to be met been drafted? Is there some flexibility built into the plan in case some activities take longer than anticipated?

☑ Has a full management plan been developed?

☑ Will the plan be reviewed on a regular basis by the project management body to ensure that targets are being met?

☑ Is a broader consultation group with a wide range of interests and organizations represented also involved in the process of implementing the project?

FOR OVERSIGHT ACTORS

☑ Is the project management body inclusive and diverse so as to involve a broad set of skills in implementing electronic voting and counting?

☑ Has the project management body made its detailed plan and timeline available to the public so that stakeholders can hold management bodies accountable to targets and deadlines?

☑ Does the project management body produce periodic progress reports for the public, and/or are stakeholders invited to attend certain meetings to be briefed on progress?

☑ Has the EMB conducted a full security risk assessment, taking into account technical, logistical and legal issues that could arise?

☑ Has the risk management plan been made public so that stakeholders may provide input?

VOTER EDUCATION AND INFORMATION

Voter education and information are critical elements in building voters' confidence in newly introduced technologies. EMBs should be strategic and proactive in providing information on how to vote, how the overall system works, why the new technology has been adopted and methods to ensure the system's integrity. Voter education strategies should consider the target audiences and use different types of outreach methods based on how different segments of voters commonly access information. Particular consideration should be given to targeting groups, such as voters with disabilities, and rural and elderly voters, that may be less comfortable with technology. It is also important to provide opportunities for voters to try out the new voting equipment in person. Election observers have a responsibility to assess the adequacy and effectiveness of voter education efforts and make recommendations on how any identified gaps can be filled.

Experience has demonstrated that due consideration of voters' level of awareness about and confidence in the new technologies is key to the success of any electronic voting or counting system. It is not enough for voters to know how to vote using this new technology; they must also have confidence in the integrity of the technology that is being used. Providing voters with the information necessary to cast their votes using a new system efficiently and with confidence requires a comprehensive approach to voter education and public outreach. Such efforts should therefore start as early as possible and continue until results are certified.

The main responsibility for informing and educating voters rests with the EMB. As part of its overall strategy for introducing electronic voting and counting, the EMB should have an accompanying plan for educating and informing voters including the allocation of sufficient resources to meet these requirements. A public outreach strategy should include detailed information about how to vote, as well as how the overall system works. The strategy should consider the target audiences and use different types of media (TV, radio, press, Internet) based on the country context and, in particular, the mediums through which different segments of voters most commonly consume information. Voters should also have an understanding of the reasons why the new technology is being adopted, how it will be implemented and what mechanisms have been included to ensure its integrity. EMBs should be proactive in providing such information, in order to demonstrate transparency and build public trust in the system.

The EMB's public outreach plan should also include strategies for how to react to stakeholder comments or media stories about the voting and counting technology that might not be accurate or that might cast doubt over the technology in some way. Particularly in the age of 24-hour news and viral social media, media officers have to be ready to provide any necessary clarifications at short notice. By responding quickly to critical stories about the voting or counting system, the EMB may be able to avoid a story gaining momentum disproportionate to its accuracy or relevance. It will be useful for EMBs to prepare a comprehensive booklet containing frequently asked questions (FAQ) and talking points regarding e-voting or counting, for use by election commissioners, senior managers and public relations personnel, which includes responses to common and often-repeated criticisms of electronic voting machines. Responses to questions from journalists or stakeholders should always aim to inform and educate, rather than to dismiss concerns.

In addition to a media campaign, the EMB should identify as many opportunities as possible for voters to try out the new voting equipment in person. Information transmitted by media cannot replace the experience of trying the equipment in real life. As mentioned above, usability tests as well as pre-pilot and mock elections are good initial opportunities for voters to try out and become comfortable with the equipment, as well as to receive assistance on how to use it. Election officials should be creative and take advantage of all possible opportunities to share information on the electronic systems throughout the pre-election period. Voters are likely to be curious about the new technology and interested in trying it for themselves. In Geneva, authorities installed test machines using the new Internet voting interface in the waiting room of the passport service office so that citizens could test the voting system while they waited.

Since increased accessibility of elections is a frequently cited goal of electronic voting and counting projects, particular consideration should be given to reaching out to target groups with special voter education messages and campaigns. Voters with disabilities and elderly voters should be informed about any new functionality that may facilitate their ability to vote unassisted, and should be provided with relevant information about any further steps they need to take prior to voting. Elderly voters may be particularly hesitant to use new technology, and special efforts should be made so that they feel comfortable with the equipment. Voters from minority language groups should receive voter information in their own languages to inform them about new opportunities to use ballot interfaces in alternative languages. Specific TV and radio campaigns should also provide information for illiterate and low-literacy voters, to explain how they will be able to vote using the new system (e.g., by displaying candidate photos or party symbols on the ballot) and to encourage their participation, given that they may be unfamiliar or uncomfortable with electronic technologies.

The adoption of new election technologies may offer opportunities for election officials to reach out to young voters and encourage their participation. In addition to voter education campaigns in the traditional media, voter education efforts aimed at young voters should take full advantage of social media.

While the primary responsibility for voter education rests with the EMB, civil society groups may also be usefully engaged in educating voters about electronic voting and counting systems. To play this role, civil society groups must have access to accurate and timely information from the EMB about how the new system will work and what voter education messages should be disseminated. Voter education messages should be carefully formulated to transmit the most necessary information in a user-friendly format.

Voter information should also be available at polling stations – including leaflets or posters that explain to voters how to cast a ballot using the new equipment. Polling officials should be well prepared to answer any questions about the voting machines – such as how to use the machines, how the vote is counted and transmitted and how the security and secrecy of the vote are protected. Providing this kind of information will help to increase voter confidence and trust in electronic voting and counting.

As representatives of citizens, domestic election observer groups have a particular responsibility to ensure that the public is adequately informed about elections. Election observers should assess the provision of voter education by election officials throughout the election process and should determine whether adequate information has been provided. Such information can be collected by long-term observers, and data may also be available in public opinion surveys. If any gaps in knowledge or among particular target groups or regions are identified, election observer groups should make recommendations to election officials about how such gaps can be filled so that voters have the information they need to vote and have confidence that their votes will be accurately reflected in the election result.

FIGURE 17 – MEDIA ENGAGEMENT IN THE PHILIPPINES

When the Philippines began to implement its new optical-scan ballot-counting system, the Commission on Elections's (COMELEC) Project Management Office embarked on a widespread public acceptance program with three objectives: first, to educate the electorate on how the automated electoral system worked; second, to promote acceptance of the system as a guarantee of speedy and credible results; and third, to manage expectations. Dissemination of messages for the campaign through private TV networks was critical for its success, as was ongoing engagement with the media on Election Day. While the COMELEC's policy of open and transparent engagement with the media was challenging at times, the Commission believed that it was a considerable asset to engage and inform the media in such an open manner.

The three major TV networks considered it part of their corporate social responsibility to spread information about the new ballot-counting machines, and as a result, developed and aired information clips in the run-up to the election at no cost to the government. The core content of these information clips was approved by COMELEC to ensure accuracy and consistency. One network released a music video that featured a well-known dance troupe singing a catchy tune about the automated election system. This tune became so pervasive that it was one of the most recognizable tunes in the country at the time. Even children knew the lyrics to the song, and voters waiting in line on Election Day were observed singing it together.

On Election Day COMELEC deployed over 40,000 technical staff to monitor how the new technology was working. All issues were reported to a situation room in the capital. COMELEC adopted a policy of transparency about these incidents. A press center was placed in the situation room, and COMELEC kept the press fully informed about any reported problems, even those that did not reflect well on COMELEC. The result of this was that the media were well informed throughout Election Day about issues that had arisen as well as COMELEC's response to these issues, and the coverage that this provided meant that COMELEC was easily able to get airtime to explain what was being done about reported problems.[36]

---

[36] Taken from a presentation by Gregorio Larrazabal, former COMELEC commissioner.

KEY CONSIDERATIONS: VOTER EDUCATION AND INFORMATION

FOR IMPLEMENTING BODIES

- ☑ Has a comprehensive plan for educating and informing voters about the new technologies been developed and have sufficient resources been allocated to conduct voter education and information activities?

- ☑ Does the public outreach strategy include detailed information about how to vote as well as how the overall system works?

- ☑ Have strategies been developed for how to react to stakeholder comments or media stories about the voting and counting technology?

- ☑ Is a set of Frequently Asked Questions (FAQ) available for reference to election commissioners, senior managers and public relations personnel that include responses to common and often-repeated criticisms of electronic voting machines?

- ☑ Are opportunities available for the public to engage with the new voting equipment in person in the pre-election period?

- ☑ Are targeted efforts in place to address voter education for specific populations such as the elderly, minority ethnic/language groups, and youth?

- ☑ Is voter information available at polling stations?

- ☑ Are polling officials sufficiently prepared to answer any questions about the voting machines?

FOR OVERSIGHT ACTORS

☑ Has the EMB developed a comprehensive plan for voter education, including sufficient time and resource allocation?

☑ Does the EMB strategy for voter education identify target audiences and incorporate a variety of media sources and other mediums through which those target audiences commonly consume information?

☑ Has the EMB provided opportunities for citizens to engage with the new voting equipment in person?

☑ Has the EMB made extra efforts to engage target groups, such as the elderly and disabled, via specialized voter education messages and campaigns? Have voters from minority language groups received voter information in their language?

☑ Have civil society groups actively engaged in voter education efforts themselves, and have they received the necessary technical information on the new technologies from the EMB to produce effective voter education materials?

☑ Have civil society assessed the adequacy and effectiveness of EMB public outreach efforts? Has any public opinion polling been conducted to gauge the readiness of voters?

SOFTWARE AND HARDWARE MAINTENANCE, STORAGE AND UPDATE

Vital functions such as secure storage of electronic voting and counting equipment, maintenance, upgrades, and reconfiguration need to be performed in the period between elections. Care should be taken to ensure that these processes are planned for and that appropriate procedures are put in place to undertake these functions securely and with as much transparency as possible. EMBs should also focus on identifying staffing and training needs to address maintenance and storage as much as possible without the support of vendors.

Equipment used for electronic voting or counting will remain unused between elections, possibly for long periods of time. In the case of electronic voting or counting machines, these machines will need to be placed in storage between elections. EMBs may choose to store this equipment centrally or in regional storage facilities, depending on the logistics involved in moving the equipment and the availability of suitable storage locations.

The EMB will need to be aware of any environmental conditions that are required when storing the electronic voting or counting equipment, as the equipment may be sensitive to extremes of temperature and humidity or may require dust-free environments. Finding suitable storage locations may be especially challenging in very hot countries, where extreme heat may degrade the reliability of the equipment.

Even where a relatively small amount of equipment is used, such as for Internet voting systems, it will be important that this equipment is placed in a secure location between elections so that the perception and reality that the equipment could be tampered with can be countered. The storage location(s) should be guarded and should have appropriate and clearly identified access control systems. All access to the storage location should be logged, with the reasons for the access clearly identified in the log. It is good practice for party representatives and observers to be invited to supervise any routine access to stored electronic voting or counting equipment; this may also take place in the storage locations due to the space requirements of maintaining or configuring a large number of machines.

Electronic voting and counting machines need to be maintained and checked, especially when left for long periods of time between elections. Machines may also need to be upgraded through their life cycle, which may be fifteen to twenty years. Electronic voting and counting machines will need to be configured before elections so that they are programmed for the types of elections being conducted and the political entities on the ballots. Observers and party representatives should be provided access to these configuration processes.

The conduct of this checking, maintenance, upgrade and configuration may be covered by the supply contract for the electronic voting or counting equipment, or it may be the responsibility of the EMB. In order to avoid dependence on suppliers, it is preferable that the election management body handle these functions. The development of the capacity within the EMB to conduct these tasks may require significant staff training. Thus, it may decide to build this independent capacity over the course of several elections, with reduced dependence on the supplier as time progresses.

KEY CONSIDERATIONS: SOFTWARE/HARDWARE MAINTENANCE, STORAGE AND UPDATE

FOR IMPLEMENTING BODIES

☑ Is the EMB aware of the environmental conditions that should be addressed when storing the electronic voting or counting equipment?

☑ Are suitable storage locations available, and are these storage locations guarded and do they have appropriate and clearly identified access control systems?

☑ Is a maintenance schedule for the equipment established and implemented?

☑ Is all access to the storage location logged and explained?

☑ Are the electronic voting and counting machines configured before the elections so that they are programmed for the type of elections being conducted and the political entities on the ballots?

FOR OVERSIGHT ACTORS

☑ Has the electronic equipment been stored in a secure location between elections in a manner that prevents unauthorized tampering?

☑ Are party representatives and observers allowed to monitor routine access to stored electronic equipment?

☑ Do observers and party observers have access to monitor the process of configuring and upgrading machines before elections?

☑ Are the checking, maintenance, upgrade and configuration of equipment conducted by the EMB or the vendor? If by the vendor, does the EMB have the capacity to properly oversee these processes?

TESTING, SOURCE CODE REVIEW AND CERTIFICATION

EMBs must ensure that there is appropriate and systematic testing of electronic voting and counting systems in the period before an election so that problems can be highlighted and addressed in a timely fashion before Election Day. EMBs should also provide access to independent experts to review the source code in order to engender transparency and build confidence in the electronic systems. EMBs may also require independent bodies to certify the electronic voting and counting systems prior to their use. Both testing and certification are time-consuming processes, and EMBs should ensure sufficient time before Election Day for these steps in the process to take place. Observers and parties should ensure they have the expertise and capacity to comprehensively inspect the source code and assess the testing and certification processes.

Testing and Source Code Review

Ensuring that electronic voting or counting systems function correctly and generate accurate results based on the votes cast is critically important. Not only must election management bodies ensure this, but they also must convince key electoral stakeholders that this is the case so that they will trust and accept the results. Unlike other electronic transactions, one cannot check afterward that his or her vote was recorded correctly.[37] For example, with electronic banking, people can check their statements to see if any incorrect transactions were made and can have mistakes corrected. The need for a secret vote denies the possibility for this level of transparency.

As a result, the EMB needs to make additional efforts to test the electronic voting or counting system before it is used to ensure that it works correctly. Figure 5 in the Overview section shows the different kinds of tests that the Council of Europe recommends for electronic voting and counting systems; these include acceptance testing, performance testing, stress testing, security testing, usability testing and source code review.

All of these tests will be conducted by, or on behalf of, the EMB. The more these tests can be conducted by the EMB, the better, as long as it has the competency to do so. If any aspect of testing is outsourced, EMB personnel must remain engaged and provide oversight of the testing process. From a transparency and confidence-building perspective, it is also useful to have an external, independent body conduct some level of testing. In the US, local EMBs carry out testing before each election. In Maryland, this testing consists of preparing and configuring the machines, casting hundreds of votes on each voting machine, and producing and checking results on the voting machine as well as through the central tabulation system, before clearing the voting machines of voting data, sealing them and securing them so they are ready for use in the election.

While different EMBs will take varying approaches to the testing regime that is used, it is vital that the EMB does some level of testing and that testing is done

---

[37] It should be noted that there are electronic voting and counting schemes designed to provide this level of verifiability for voters (such as Scantegrity, Prêt à Voter and Punchscan voting systems). However, these systems can be seen as quite complex for voters and have challenges in terms of scalability when it comes to larger elections. The crux of the challenge for such end-to-end verifiable voting schemes is to provide verifiability without violating the secrecy of the vote. This is a particular challenge in countries where employers or others could demand that a voter use such mechanisms after the election to prove she or he voted as instructed or where vote-buying schemes could easily be adapted to take advantage of such mechanisms.

before each election. Testing before each election is necessary to check the election-specific configuration and also to deal with any technology changes, which is especially important for Internet voting where new browsers as well as updated versions of existing browsers may need to be accommodated.

Full system testing also needs to take place sufficiently in advance of elections to enable the remedy of any problems encountered. It is also prudent to do a final check of equipment closer to Election Day. In the 2010 Philippine election, during which electronic counting machines were being used for the first time, the machines were scheduled for final testing and sealing one day before the election. The COMELEC IT Department decided to test some machines earlier and discovered less than a week before the election that a bug in the configuration of the scanning software would cause the machines to register votes incorrectly. The decision to do early testing and sealing detected the problem in time, so that new compact flash cards could be distributed nationwide, rescuing the election from disaster.

Access to the source code for electronic voting and counting applications may also be made available so that independent experts can check that no errors exist in the source code (see the previous discussion of open source code in the "Security Mechanisms" section). Additional scrutiny of the source code may help to identify the existence of any errors, oversights or malicious code, but will also importantly help to build confidence in the electronic voting or counting systems by increasing transparency.

Fully open source code is not necessary to provide these confidence-building mechanisms, but it is the more preferable option. Should open source code not be used, experts representing key electoral stakeholders (political actors and civil society) should be allowed sufficient access to review the source code and should not be restricted in reporting their analysis of its content by the use of any nondisclosure agreements. The EMB may also decide to engage an external body to conduct an independent review of the source code as a confidence-building measure.

All of the reports on the testing of electronic voting or counting systems should be made available for review by political actors and observers. Again, this transparency will help to build confidence in the system.

It is important to recognize that conducting these different kinds of tests takes a significant amount of time and resources. Electronic voting and counting systems are complex; and especially when new systems are developed, they will often contain errors that need to be corrected. Each time an error is identified and corrected, it may be necessary to conduct the full test process again, as even a small change may lead to unforeseen consequences. Therefore, sufficient time and resources must be allocated for this testing to take place, as well as for any corrections and retesting to be implemented.

FIGURE 18 – SOURCE CODE REVIEW MECHANISMS IN BRAZIL

Brazil's electoral commission (Tribunal Superior Eleitoral, TSE) is credited for making the source code to its electronic voting system available for review by electoral stakeholders. In addition to providing access to the source code, the TSE invites computer scientists and interested parties to find system vulnerabilities. Despite these efforts, electoral stakeholders believe that the TSE can take further steps to ensure greater transparency in this process. Among the steps suggested are providing more time for experts to analyze the system and source code, and placing fewer restrictions on public comments resulting from the expert analysis.

The Tribunal Superior Eleitoral (TSE) takes steps to provide transparency for electoral stakeholders by offering access to the source code for the electronic voting system as well as opening the system for hacking competitions. However, the TSE has come under some criticism in recent years because of the manner in which these initiatives have been implemented, which has led to calls for greater transparency with regard to technical aspects of the electronic voting system.

Brazilian electoral law stipulates that the source code should be made available for review by political parties and the Brazilian bar association (Ordem dos Advogados do Brasil, OAM). Electoral stakeholders in Brazil believe that the TSE failed to meet this requirement for the 1996, 1998, and 2000 elections. The TSE did start to make the source code available for review after the 2000 elections, but the manner in which the source code is provided has also come under some criticism. Computer scientists criticize the fact that auditors must sign a nondisclosure agreement and, consequently, any problems found during the audit are not made public. Auditors also point out that only a few days are given for auditing and the examination of the code occurs in very controlled conditions on the TSE's computers, which are insufficient to comprehensively examine the code. In some cases, the code was modified after it had been given to the parties for review.

To its credit, the TSE has gone beyond its legally mandated requirements to make the source code available for review to independent computer scientists. These computer scientists have generally found the system to be robust, but have made several recommendations to improve the system, including instituting a voter-verified paper audit trail (VVPAT) to enhance the auditability of the system. The TSE has thus far resisted instituting VVPAT in the electronic voting system. Since 2009, the TSE has also organized hacking competitions, inviting computer scientists and other interested parties to find external vulnerabilities in the electronic voting system, but there have been complaints that the TSE does not allow enough time (three days are provided) to thoroughly test the system and that those participating in the competitions do not have enough time to analyze the code.

Certification

In addition to comprehensive testing of electronic voting and counting technologies prior to use, it is good practice to have these systems certified prior to use.[38] The purpose of certification is similar to testing in that it determines whether the electronic voting or counting technology operates effectively. The difference is that an authority independent of the EMB, political parties,

---

38 The Council of Europe (2004) recommendation on e-voting requires that, before any e-voting system is introduced, it be certified by an independent body to verify that it is working correctly and meets all necessary security measures (Recommendations 25 and 111).

the government and suppliers conducts certification. The certification process should be carried out in an open and transparent manner and is intended to build confidence in the operation of the electronic technology.

This certification process will provide independent assurance that the electronic voting or counting solutions meet a certain set of standards. If any changes are subsequently made to the hardware or software, the certification process will need to be completed again, although it may be possible to conduct an abbreviated recertification if changes are minimal and can be categorically identified. Time is again an issue, and the process of certification may take between six and 12 months, depending on how many issues are found that require fixing and how complex the system is. While certification can be a strong mechanism for ensuring the integrity of the electronic voting or counting system and in building trust in the system, it does limit the flexibility of the EMB in making last-minute improvements to the system, as any such improvements would require recertification.

A number of institutions, such as university information technology departments or technology institutes, could play a role as certifying bodies. It is important that the process of certification is well defined. In some countries the certifying institutions themselves have to be preauthorized and must meet a series of standards for the work they will conduct certifying electronic voting and counting technologies. Clear guidance will need to be developed for certifying institutions on the certification requirements (which should be publicly available), the records they should make of their findings, the consequences of a product failing to comply in some way, the mechanisms for a vendor to resubmit after failing certification and the openness of the certification process and certification reports.

FIGURE 19 – E-VOTING CERTIFICATION PROCEDURES IN THE UNITED STATES

In 2005 the U.S. Election Assistance Commission (EAC) established Voluntary Voting System Guidelines (VVSG) to accredit the functional capabilities, accessibility and security requirements of electronic voting and counting systems. These requirements have to be met for systems to gain EAC certification, and the EAC has accredited several testing labs to conduct the certification process. Individual states, however, may decide whether or not to use VVSG for the electronic voting and counting systems employed in their elections.

Electronic voting systems, both direct-recording electronic and optical-scan ballot counting, are used extensively throughout the U.S. Under the Help America Vote Act (HAVA) of 2002, the Election Assistance Commission (EAC) was established and empowered with adopting voluntary voting system guidelines, accrediting voting system test laboratories and certifying electronic voting and counting systems. In 2005 the EAC adopted the Voluntary Voting System Guidelines (VVSG), thereby establishing standards relating to the functional capabilities, accessibility and security requirements of electronic voting and counting systems. These are the standards that the EAC's certification process applies to systems. The VVSG contains approximately 1,200 requirements that systems are required to comply with in order to obtain certification by the EAC.

The EAC does not test electronic voting and counting systems itself, but provides accreditation to a number of testing labs which conduct the certification process. Suppliers of electronic voting and counting systems must apply to one of the approved testing laboratories in order to obtain accreditation for their system. Certification requirements under the VVSG are quite rigorous, and systems may initially fail to meet the requirements. In such cases the system must be modified and resubmitted through the certification process. Typically it will take between six and 18 months to obtain certification for a system, although there is no guarantee that a system will ever be certified.

It is important to note that this EAC certification process is voluntary in the U.S., with each state deciding if it will make certification by the EAC a requirement for the voting and counting systems used in the state's elections. Each state may also apply state-level certification requirements. This state-level certification process will typically be used to ensure that electronic voting and counting systems comply with state-specific electoral legislation. It may also be used to complement the EAC certification process or as an alternative to certification by the EAC.

KEY CONSIDERATIONS: TESTING, SOURCE CODE REVIEW AND CERTIFICATION

FOR IMPLEMENTING BODIES

☑ Are necessary levels of testing of the electronic voting and counting systems going to take place, including, as recommended, acceptance testing, performance testing, stress testing, security testing, usability testing and source code review?

☑ Are any external independent actors involved in the review process?

☑ Is there a plan in place to conduct full system testing sufficiently in advance of the elections?

☑ Is access to the source code also made available to independent experts and stakeholders to check for errors or malicious code?

☑ Will a certification process be conducted by an authority independent of the EMB to provide independent assurance that the electronic voting or counting solutions meet a certain set of standards?

☑ Have sufficient time and resources been allocated for the testing and certification process to address any issues that are identified during these processes?

FOR OVERSIGHT ACTORS

☑ Which tests are conducted?

☑ Does the EMB conduct the tests or does the vendor? If the vendor, does the EMB remain engaged and provide oversight of the process?

☑ Are tests conducted sufficiently in advance of elections so that any problems encountered can be addressed?

☑ Is the source code for the electronic technologies open source? If not fully open source, do observers and party representatives have sufficient access to inspect the source code, including not being restricted in reporting their analysis of its content by the use of any non-disclosure agreements? For their part, election observers and parties should ensure they have the capacity and/or expertise to comprehensively inspect the source code.

☑ Are all test reports available for review by political actors and observers?

☑ Is an independent certification process conducted, and, if so, are the processes and results publicly available?

ELECTION DAY (SETUP, TESTING, SECURITY, TROUBLESHOOTING)

Election officials should ensure that sufficient resources are in place at every polling station to receive and properly operate electronic voting equipment on Election Day. These resources should include sufficient personnel (including technicians) and processes to address any issues that may arise with the proper operation of the electronic equipment on Election Day. Observers should assess whether all procedures are appropriately followed in the setup, operation and closing of electronic voting equipment at the polling station, whether the technologies are usable and accessible for all voters and whether sufficient measures are taken to ensure election security.

Electronic voting and counting equipment should be delivered to polling stations just prior to Election Day and issued to a designated person (usually the head of the polling station committee) using appropriate handover procedures and documentation. As electronic voting and counting equipment is considered to be sensitive balloting material, all access to the equipment must be controlled and recorded, and proper security precautions must be in place to secure the machines until voting starts. Party representatives and accredited observers should be permitted to witness the delivery and setup of voting and counting equipment.

On Election Day, polling officials follow procedures to initialize the voting and/or counting machines. Typically there is a demonstration in front of any party representatives and/or observers present to show that there are "zero votes" recorded in the machine during the initialization process prior to the start of voting. Test elections are also sometimes conducted for party representatives and observers to show that ballot choices are accurately recorded.

A sufficient number of technicians should be available to provide assistance, either on the premises, on call or via telephone hotlines should officials have any problems with the setup, initialization or functioning of voting and counting equipment. Specific procedures and contingency plans must also be in place for the possibility that a voting or counting machine does not work and cannot be fixed. These could include the rapid replacement of nonfunctioning or malfunctioning machines from a store of spare machines kept under the same security protocols, postponement of elections in that polling location or the use of alternative means of voting, such as paper balloting.

During the voting period, party representatives and observers should assess whether polling officials are adhering to proper procedures for processing voters, providing assistance when necessary and respecting all security safeguards. It is particularly important for observers to consider whether the secrecy of the vote is being respected – both through the arrangement of the polling station and the way that assistance is offered to voters. Observers should also pay particular attention to any technical problems that arise with the equipment during the voting and how such problems are resolved. The introduction of technology into the voting process is likely to increase the possibility of technical problems, but they should be dealt with efficiently and according to procedures, in a manner that does not interrupt the voting process if possible.

Security safeguards during voting should include procedures for controlling access to electronic voting and counting equipment. It should be clear who is allowed access to machines in any given situation (for instance if repairs are needed), and any access should be properly documented in the polling station protocol. Safeguards such as authentication codes and tamper-proof seals on any external ports should also be used.

While electronic voting and counting equipment should have been already submitted to several rounds of usability testing during its development and in any pilots, Election Day is the real test for how well voters interact with the technology. Observers should pay close attention to the accessibility of electronic voting and counting machines, including the experiences of special groups of voters such as those with disabilities, and elderly, illiterate or minority-language voters.

At the close of voting, officials should carry out closing procedures for the electronic voting and counting equipment. Polling officials should carry out the relevant command to close voting on each voting (or counting) machine. Depending on the type of equipment, individual machines may produce a tally sheet of results for that machine. Should each machine produce its own tally, these figures should be aggregated into a polling station results protocol.

The printouts for each voting or counting machine should be posted outside the polling station, together with the overall results protocol for the polling station. Party representatives and observers should be given copies of results printouts or should be permitted to copy the figures. As in traditional voting, results protocols should be signed by members of the polling station commission. Electronic voting and counting machines may also produce an activity log, detailing all actions taken on the machine during Election Day. These should also be available for observers.

FIGURE 20 – ELECTION DAY PLANNING IN THE PHILIPPINES

In the Philippines, the nationwide shift to electronic counting machines led to several logistical challenges during the 2010 national election. Due in part to budgetary constraints, the Commission on Elections (COMELEC) was unable to procure enough precinct count optical scan (PCOS) machines to accommodate as many polling locations as under the manual election system. On Election Day the reduction in polling locations led to long lines, shortages of poll workers and poorly managed technical support for PCOS machines. There were also challenges in providing Election Day support for the electronic counting machines and in transmitting the results at the close of polling.

The transition to nationwide use of electronic counting machines during the 2010 Philippines elections presented a number of logistical challenges for election officials in preparation for Election Day. Due in part to budgetary constraints, the Commission on Elections (COMELEC) was only able to lease enough precinct count optical scan (PCOS) machines to accommodate approximately 80,000 precincts. As a result, precincts had to be clustered, significantly reducing the number of precincts, down from approximately 250,000 in 2007. Instead of 200 voters per precinct, there were up to 1,000 voters per precinct. On Election Day, voters across the country had to wait for hours in line. Although precincts were clustered, the number of polling station workers per precinct was not increased accordingly, which compounded the already lengthy wait times. International and domestic observers noted that this may have led to disenfranchisement of voters who could not wait or decided against waiting in long lines.

The use of PCOS machines also required significant preparations for providing real-time technical support on Election Day. A number of issues arose on Election Day, including missing or drained batteries, paper jams and precincts running out of thermal paper. Some incidents resulted in PCOS machines not being used at all on Election Day. Although the vendor, Smartmatic, claimed to have recruited and trained over 48,000 technical assistance providers to be deployed on Election Day, many election officials complained that most PCOS technicians did not have the proper skills to assist them with mechanical problems that occurred during Election Day processes.

Data transmission and results tabulation also presented enormous challenges on Election Day. Although the transmission was in general fast and efficient, there were reports of transmission failures, delays or the inability of the consolidation centers to receive data. Problems emerged, in part, due to the fact that the reporting hierarchy required for electronically transmitting election results was the same as that used in manual elections. This system stipulated that data be reported from precinct to municipality to province to central server. According to several post-election assessments, this reporting hierarchy should have been adjusted to allow for direct transmission to a central server, which would have been much more timely and cost-effective.

FIGURE 21 – NONPARTISAN CITIZEN OVERSIGHT OF ELECTIONS IN THE PHILIPPINES

The experience of citizen observer groups during the 2010 Philippine elections points to a number of challenges oversight groups face as they transition from observing paper-based elections to observing elections that utilize electronic voting and counting technologies. In the 2010 national election, these groups observed several aspects of the electoral process, especially during the pre-election stage and on Election Day. However, they faced significant internal and external challenges in effectively observing the mechanics of the new process. The foremost lesson learned was that better coordination and cooperation among civil society actors could have helped pair IT expertise with election-monitoring experience and methodologies to more effectively observe the new election system.

Just as the transition from manual to electronic technologies in the Philippines triggered significant adaptations among EMBs, it also necessitated major changes in the organizational structures and methodologies of civil society actors. By 2010, some groups had accumulated decades of experience monitoring manual elections, such as the country's first observation group, the National Citizens' Movements for Free Elections (NAMFREL), but they had to quickly attempt to acquire and apply IT knowledge to their efforts. Other groups, including the Center for People Empowerment in Governance (CenPEG), brought their IT expertise to the new electoral environment, but they lacked election observation experience. In addition to the challenge of acquiring IT knowledge, several groups faced challenges observing the election due to a lack of accreditation by the COMELEC, which only provided official accreditation status to one group, the Parish Pastoral Council for Responsible Voting (PPCRV). While many organizations still monitored without accreditation, this greatly restricted observer groups' access to a number of critical parts of the electoral process.

Despite these internal and external challenges, civil society groups were proactive in promoting transparency and accountability from the early phases, including during legal reforms, system design, and procurement, through Election Day processes and the post-election period.

In the years leading up to the 2010 elections, as the Philippines adapted its legislative framework and standards to accommodate electronic technologies, civil society organizations such as NAMFREL provided input on reforms. In the pre-election period, IT-focused groups such as CenPEG, through its "Project 30-30", advocated for measures to improve the integrity of the new automated system. For example, CenPEG attempted to review the source code used for the new automated system. The COMELEC, however, regulated access to the source code and did not agree to have the source code taken out of its headquarters, citing intellectual property rights and security concerns. CenPEG subsequently filed a legal complaint against the COMELEC. The Supreme Court eventually issued a ruling after the elections directing the COMELEC to provide source code access to CenPEG. After years of court battles and negotiations between the COMELEC and Dominion Voting Systems, which owns the source code, the COMELEC offered the source code for public review on May 9, 2013, just four days before the May 13 general elections. Watchdog groups and some political parties commented that the source code release had come too late for a meaningful review.

To monitor the transmission and tabulation processes, several election observation groups had planned to collect the results at the precinct level and compare them to the precinct-level results published on the COMELEC's website. However, the comparison of results for a sizeable portion of precincts was not possible, in part because observers were not able to collect election results in many locations. In a number of cases, poll workers refused to provide PPCRV's accredited observers with a copy of the election results. Unaccredited observers from NAMFREL; Bantay Eleksyon, a coalition of 47 organizations formed by the Consortium on Electoral Reforms; and other groups had an even more difficult time entering polling stations and obtaining copies of election results. Another major obstacle was that, on election night, the COMELEC stopped posting precinct-level results to its website after approximately 90 percent of the results had been posted. Then the COMELEC took the data down. Before it was taken down, a group of IT experts created a mirror image of the site and, upon later analysis, found a number of anomalies and missing data. COMELEC has never explained why the full precinct-level results were not released publicly, nor why the website had a number of data errors. This raised serious concerns among some political contestants and citizen observation groups.

Following the 2010 elections, civil society groups reported a number of lessons learned from their observation efforts. In particular, they emphasized the need for better coordination between traditional election observers and IT experts so that they could take advantage of each other's comparative strengths, knowledge and networks. Citizen observation groups, particularly those which lacked IT capacity prior to

2009, did not sufficiently refine their monitoring methodologies and tools to take into account the new technologies of the 2010 elections. In many cases, they did not have the specific expertise to anticipate where problems or vulnerabilities could occur, or to develop the tools and observer training necessary to collect evidence of these problems. Similarly, IT experts and groups with higher IT capacity did not have the experience or organizational structures of the more experienced observation groups, which limited their ability to effectively observe processes during the days immediately surrounding Election Day.

KEY CONSIDERATIONS: ELECTION DAY (SET-UP, TESTING, SECURITY, TROUBLESHOOTING)

FOR IMPLEMENTING BODIES

- [✓] Are a sufficient number of technicians available to provide assistance, either on the premises, on call or via telephone hotlines should officials have any problems with the set-up, initialization and function of voting and counting equipment?

- [✓] Are specific procedures and contingency plans in place for the possibility that a voting or counting machine does not work and cannot be fixed?

- [✓] Is it clear who has access to machines in any given situation, and is there a process for properly documenting any access in the polling station protocol?

☑ Will safeguards such as authentication codes and tamper proof seals be used on any external ports?

☑ Are closing procedures to be carried out by polling officials clearly defined with the relevant command to close voting or counting on each machine?

☑ If individual tally sheets are produced, will the results be aggregated into a polling station results protocol?

FOR OVERSIGHT ACTORS

☑ How have observer groups and political parties had to change their election day strategies to effectively monitor new technologies on election day? Do they have the necessary technical expertise?

☑ Are machines secure during and after the transfer from storage to the polling location until voting starts? Are observers permitted to observe the delivery of equipment?

☑ Is there a demonstration to show that no votes have been recorded in the machine prior to the start of voting?

☑ Do polling officials follow procedures for set-up, processing of voters and closing the polling station, and do observers have access to all of these processes?

☑ Is secrecy of the vote ensured, both through the polling station arrangement and the way that assistance is offered to voters?

☑ If problems with equipment arise, are polling officials or authorized technicians capable of resolving them efficiently, according to procedures, and without interrupting the voting process?

☑ Is access to the equipment and sensitive materials sufficiently secure, controlled and recorded?

☑ How accessible and usable are electronic machines for voters? In particular, what are the experiences of special groups, such as disabled, elderly, illiterate or minority language voters?

☑ Are printouts for each voting or counting machine posted outside the polling station, together with the overall results protocol for the polling station? Are party representatives and observers given copies of results printouts or at least permitted to copy the figures?

☑ Are electronic voting and counting machines activity logs available for observers?

☑ How has the implementation of new technologies affected the conduct of voting? Have any new problems been introduced that were unforeseen, and if so, how did the EMB respond?

TABULATION

Electronic voting and counting technologies allow for quicker tabulation and transmission of results when compared to paper-based systems, but election authorities must ensure that these processes are undertaken with as much transparency as possible and with a strict focus on the security of results data. Results can be transmitted either through secure communication channels or by encrypted data. And as these security measures are taken to safeguard the data, election authorities must ensure that observers and oversight groups are able to observe the data being uploaded. Results data from the polling station to central level should be made publicly available online.

Once votes from electronic voting or counting machines have been aggregated at the polling station level and recorded in a polling station protocol, they must be delivered in a secure and efficient manner either to the next level of the election administration or to the central election authorities for tabulation, depending on the election legislation.

Results transmission is likely to be simultaneously conducted through more than one channel. Often unofficial results are transmitted first, and then official results follow. Results may be transmitted electronically through the Internet (using a modem or satellite device) or by mobile phone. Security measures should be in place to prevent any interference with the electronic transmission process. For instance, data may be encrypted, and secure communication channels may be used, along with digital signatures to verify the integrity of the data that is received. At the same time, hardware devices such as memory cards or memory sticks may also be transported to the next-level election commission, with encrypted and signed data. Paper results protocols may be sent through an additional channel.

At the next stage in the tabulation process, for instance at a district-level tabulation center, election officials will feed results from polling stations into the system. If results have been submitted electronically or using electronic hardware, then results may be automatically uploaded without the need for any data input, saving time and avoiding errors.

The tabulation process at all levels should be fully transparent for party representatives and observers. Observers should be able to witness the data being uploaded or entered into the tabulation computers. If observers have collected results protocols from polling stations, they should be able to verify that these figures have been properly recorded at each higher level of the tabulation process. The full tabulation from the central level down to the polling station should be publicly available on the Internet in an easily verifiable format.

Depending on the technology adopted, the tabulation process when using electronic voting and counting systems has the potential to be extremely quick – even instantaneous. In such cases, consideration must be given to how results will be presented. One criticism of the Ireland pilot of electronic voting was that the tabulation and announcement of results happened too suddenly, before the losing candidates could prepare for defeat. Traditionally in Ireland the tabulation process takes one or even several days,[39] and is conducted in front of party representatives, who are able to make an early calculation of the results. There have been similar objections to rapid reporting of results in the United States, where multiple time zones create the possibility that the outcome of a presidential election may be known even before the polls close on the West Coast.

FIGURE 22 – OBSERVATION IN LONDON CRITIQUES ELECTRONIC COUNTING

In the 2008 London mayoral and assembly elections, electronic ballot scanners were used in three centralized counting centers. However, after observing the process, the British NGO Open Rights Group cited a lack of transparency in several areas that did not allow for observers to confirm that the results were an accurate reflection of voters' intentions. In its report, Open Rights Group made a number of recommendations for the use of electronic counting systems in future elections.

In 2008, the British digital rights NGO Open Rights Group deployed 27 observers to follow voting and counting during the London mayoral and London Assembly elections. The group focused in particular

---

[39] The length of vote counting in Ireland is due to the country's use of the STV (single transferable vote) proportional representation electoral system.

on assessing the counting process, as the vote count was conducted using electronic ballot scanners at three centralized counting centers. The final report released by Open Rights Group concluded that "there is insufficient evidence available to allow independent observers to state reliably whether the results are an accurate reflection of voters' intentions."

In particular the group criticized inadequate transparency of the process, including the inability of observers to witness the recording of valid votes and the lack of a random manual audit on a sample of ballot scanning machines to assess the overall accuracy of the counting process. The group also criticized the lack of observer access to the control desk of the equipment supplier, despite the fact that its computers were connected to the counting server.

In its report, Open Rights Group offered five key recommendations to authorities for improving the system in the future. The group also provided recommendations for the future consideration of using e-counting technologies more broadly, which included conducting a thorough cost-benefit analysis of the use of e-counting machines; allowing sufficient time for formal consultations with key stakeholders before deciding whether to use e-counting technologies in the future; and building in sufficient time for procurement and implementation of any new technologies.[40]

---

[40] The full report can be found here: www.openrightsgroup.org/wp-content/uploads/orglondonelectionsreport.pdf.

KEY CONSIDERATIONS: TABULATION

FOR IMPLEMENTING BODIES

- ☑ Is results transmission simultaneously conducted through more than one channel?

- ☑ Is the path of results transmission clearly defined?

- ☑ Is the tabulation process designed to be transparent for party representatives and observers, and is the tabulation publicly available in a verifiable format?

FOR OVERSIGHT ACTORS

- ☑ Are sufficient security measures in place to prevent interference with the electronic transmission process?

- ☑ Are polling station level results published on the Internet in an easily-verifiable format?

- ☑ Is the tabulation process at all levels fully transparent for party representatives and observers? For example, can observers witness the data being uploaded or entered into the tabulation computers?

- ☑ How has the announcement of results changed with the implementation of new technologies (i.e., are results announced more quickly?), and how does this affect the post-election political dynamic and overall public confidence?

CHALLENGES AND RECOUNTS

Electoral authorities generally follow the same procedures for challenges and recounts for an election with electronic voting or counting as they do for paper-based elections. However, in the case of electronic voting, some form of audit trail must exist so that the results can be verified and electoral authorities should consider this requirement during the planning stages for electronic voting systems. In the case of electronic counting systems, clear guidelines and rules should be established regarding the counting of ballots that are not read by scanners.

A key part of ensuring the integrity of the results is the ability of political competitors to lodge challenges to the results and receive effective redress. This is first of all a question of the legal framework. It must clearly define who can lodge a challenge against the results, which body the challenge should be lodged with, what circumstances an investigation will be conducted in and what situation a recount of the results will occur in. As the counting and tabulation processes are likely to be much faster using electronic voting and counting equipment, the deadlines for responding to challenges will need to reflect this.

Generally complaints and appeals procedures should remain the same as in traditional elections. However, the additional question of whether the equipment functioned properly may account for a greater number of challenges, and mechanisms must be in place to demonstrate that the count reflects the votes as cast through the conduct of recounts.

In order to determine whether votes have been accurately counted by a voting or counting machine, some kind of voter-verified audit trail – either paper or electronic – must exist that can serve as the basis for a recount. Without this audit trail, it is not possible to conduct a recount. While some voting machines do not produce a voter-verified audit trail, having such a trail is increasingly viewed as an emerging standard in the field. Simply recalculating the votes using the same machine is not sufficient to independently verify the accuracy of the results. In the case of electronic counting machines, the ballots that have been counted serve as the audit trail and can be manually recounted.

When electronic counting machines are used, blank ballots or ballots that cannot be read by scanners (e.g., damaged ballots or ballots with unclear or stray marks) must be set aside for adjudication, typically in the presence of candidate representatives and observers. In such cases officials must manually determine whether a vote is valid and, if so, for which candidate or party it has been marked. If candidate representatives disagree with the determination, the disputed ballots may be reviewed with a more senior-level election official who will determine if and how to count the ballot.

Manual recounts may be also called in the case of a very narrow margin of victory. Some election laws may require a manual recount should the results fall within a prescribed margin of victory. Clear and unambiguous legal guidelines must be in place for what steps should be taken if the results do not match or are not within a certain margin of error, especially whether the paper or electronic results should take precedence. Observers should closely follow the process of challenges and recounts, and audit reports should be publicly available.

FIGURE 23 – CHALLENGES AND RECOUNTS: POLITICAL PARTIES AND THE COMPLAINTS PROCESS IN THE PHILIPPINES

The electoral complaints and protests filed by political parties after the 2010 Philippines elections point to several issues that are important for political contestants in countries with electronic voting and counting systems: the need for specialized technical expertise, effective training of party observers to collect appropriate documentary evidence, and IT capacity in courts making decisions on electoral complaints.

In 2010, political parties in the Philippines observed the country's first nationwide use of electronic technology for elections. The introduction of e-counting technology was expected to reduce fraud and errors during counting and tabulation (canvassing). Thus, it was hoped that the number of electoral complaints and protests filed by parties and candidates would decrease. However, due to several factors, electoral protests increased in 2010. The House of Representatives Electoral Tribunal received a record number of cases (65) in 2010. The COMELEC also received more cases filed by losing candidates in 2010 (98) than in the 2007 elections (73).[41]

---

41 Libertas. Issues and Challenges to Dispute Resolution under the PSCOS AES.

Some of the protests were related to the electronic technology used in the elections, including complaints about: erroneous counting of votes or misreading of ballots by the optical-scan machines; errors in the initialization of optical-scan machines; errors in transmission and consolidation of results; erroneous rejection of ballots; nonimplementation of security measures; and manipulation of optical-scan machines and/or compact flash cards. Ultimately, many cases were dismissed due to insufficient evidence or on procedural grounds.

Reflecting upon their experiences with monitoring and filing complaints, the major political parties cited a number of lessons learned. A lack of IT training and tools for observing the new technologies made it difficult for party agents to collect the necessary evidence to support their candidates' claims. Parties also pointed to the importance of making sure the courts have the IT capacity to effectively rule on technology-related cases. They also noted that the cost of filing complaints has increased, since parties have to hire more specialized legal and IT expertise, significantly adapt party pollwatcher trainings and tools, and educate themselves in more detail about the new technologies.

KEY CONSIDERATIONS: CHALLENGES AND RECOUNTS

FOR IMPLEMENTING BODIES

- ☑ Does the legal framework clearly define who can lodge a challenge against the results, to which body the challenge should be lodged, in what circumstances an investigation will be conducted and in what situation a recount of the results will occur?

- ☑ Do deadlines for responding to challenges reflect the fact that counting and tabulation processes are likely to be much faster using electronic voting and counting equipment?

- ☑ Does a voter verified audit trail exist as the basis for a recount?

- ☑ Is there a process in place for adjudicating blank ballots or ballots that cannot be read by scanners?

- ☑ Are clear legal guidelines in place for what steps should be taken if the original and recounted results do not match or are not within a certain margin of error?

FOR OVERSIGHT ACTORS

- ☑ Does the legal framework clearly define who can lodge challenges against results, to which body the challenge should be lodged, in what circumstances and investigation will be conducted, and in what situation a recount of the results will occur?

- ☑ Is there a voter verified paper audit trail in place that can serve as the basis for a recount?

- ☑ If relevant, is there a clear process for adjudicating ballots that cannot be read by scanners, and are stakeholders allowed and encouraged to oversee this process?

- ☑ Do the legal guidelines clearly establish what must take place in instances where recounted and original results do not match sufficiently?

- ☑ Are audit reports made publicly available?

- ☑ Does the court or adjudicating body have sufficient IT capacity to effectively rule on election technology-related cases?

POST-ELECTION AUDITS

Trust in electronic voting and counting systems can be strengthened through mandatory auditing of these systems as soon as possible after an election to verify that the system was able to accurately capture results from the election. The legal framework for elections should specify the process through which a post-election audit should be implemented as well as the consequences of any difference found between electronic and paper records. The audit should take place as soon as possible after an election and should be open for observation by oversight groups.

Comprehensive testing and source code reviews, as well as possible certification mechanisms, will do much to ensure that electronic voting and counting systems deliver accurate results. However, to ensure trust in these systems, it is crucial that they be auditable and audited after use so that the results can be verified as accurate, ideally by an independent organization.

The way in which this auditability is provided varies depending on the type of electronic voting or counting system in question (e.g., it is different for electronic voting systems, electronic counting systems and especially for remote electronic voting systems). The most common way in which auditability is achieved for electronic voting machines[42] is through the use of a voter-verified paper audit trail, which can be manually counted as a check against the electronic result generated by the electronic voting machine.

Regardless, an audit mechanism is a way both of checking that the technologies worked properly and of verifying the results, by comparing the electronic and auditable versions of the results. In addition to checking the operation of the

---

42 Auditability is mainly a challenge for electronic voting systems, as electronic counting systems normally use a paper ballot completed by the voter, which naturally provides a paper audit mechanism.

system, this also helps build confidence in the system, more so if the audit is done under the full observation of stakeholders in the process.

In order to build and maintain confidence, conducting audits of the results generated by electronic voting or counting systems should be mandatory.[43] The (paper) audit trail should be manually counted and the results compared to the electronic results generated. Because it is unlikely that such an audit will be possible in every location, audits should be conducted in a randomly selected sample of locations that are only informed of the impending audit after the close of polling or counting. In contentious elections it may be appropriate to allow candidates to select a predetermined number of polling stations for manual audit in addition to the randomly selected samples. This allows the candidate to focus on areas where fraud may be suspected.

The legal framework should make clear how this audit process takes places, the number of locations, the ways in which the locations are selected and informed, when the audit takes place, the people who may be present during the audit, how the results of the audit are reported, and the consequences of any difference between electronic and paper records.

The audit process should be conducted as soon as possible after the election. An audit right after the close of voting and counting avoids the possibility or perception of tampering or manipulation before the audit takes place. If an immediate audit is not possible, then the sample to be audited should be sealed in a tamper evident way until the audit can take place. The audit should be fully observable by election observers as well as the media and political party and candidate agents.

---

[43] This is supported by the Council of Europe (2010) in its E-voting Handbook in which it recommends that a paper audit trail should be combined with a mandatory count of paper votes in a small but statistically meaningful number of randomly selected polling stations, p. 12.

The results of the audit process will need to be interpreted differently depending on the kind of technology being used. With electronic voting technologies there should be no differences at all between the result generated from the audit trail and the electronically generated result. If a difference is found, then it will be prudent to conduct a recount of the audit trail to make sure that the manual process has not generated a mistake. Should a difference between the manual count of the audit trail and electronic count of votes still persist, even if only by one vote, this will be seen as an indication of some flaw in the operation of the electronic voting machine or the audit trail. Even a small deviation would be a critical concern. Without an understanding of why a difference is possible, it also cannot be known if this flaw could lead to much larger deviations between the electronic result and audit trail in other locations that are not being audited or in future elections.

With electronic counting technologies, the interpretation of differences between the manual recount of the audit trail and electronically generated results is more difficult. Different voters mark paper ballots in different ways, and sometimes these voter marks are interpreted differently by electoral officials. The advantage of electronic voting technologies is that they interpret ballot marking in a consistent manner, according to the instructions provided to them. A difference in vote totals through a manual count of the ballots may be due to the counting machine reading voter marks in a different way than the election official. It may be the election official has made a mistake, or it could be a simple difference in the ability of individuals to discern small differences in shading that may clearly indicate the intent of a voter, but which the machine is incapable of detecting. In extreme cases, it could be that the difference represents an error in the ballot-counting rules provided to the counting machine. This requires an amendment to the counting machine software. Depending on the severity of any error in the ballot-counting rules provided to the counting machine, this may have implications, even serious implications, for the results generated by counting machines across the election.

FIGURE 24 – E-VOTING AUDITS IN VENEZUELA

Electronic voting is a heavily audited process in Venezuela. Upon casting a vote electronically, a voter can verify that his or her vote was cast as intended through a paper receipt, which the voter then places into the ballot box. After the close of polling in randomly selected polling stations, officials conduct an audit to ensure that the count from the paper ballots matches the electronic records.

Venezuela is one of only four countries that uses electronic voting machines for its entire electorate (India, Brazil and Bhutan are the others). The voting machines used in Venezuela are touch-screen direct-recording electronic voting machines (DREs) that produce a paper receipt for the ballot once the ballot choices have been made. In the 2012 presidential election, voters were also authenticated using a biometric authentication device. After casting their ballots, voters are able to check that the paper receipt matched the selections they had made on the electronic voting machine. The voter then placed this paper receipt into a ballot box in the polling station.

While the voting machine itself tallies the votes and produces the results for the polling station, the paper record in the ballot box enables verification that this electronic record is accurate. This verification method is used extensively in Venezuela, with over 50 percent of randomly selected polling stations counting the paper records to ensure that they match the electronic results. This "hot audit" is conducted immediately after the close of polling and in the presence of observers and party representatives. No significant anomalies between the paper and electronic records have ever been found.

Prior to this, a number of other audits and oversight mechanisms are implemented. The source code for the electronic voting machines is audited before each election. Technical teams assembled by government institutions, independent institutions and political parties review the source code line by line in a "clean room," where code can be viewed in its entirety but not modified or taken away. As part of this audit process, the source code is compiled and hash functions of the final versions are registered. These hash functions can then be used to verify that the audited version of the software is being used on Election Day.

KEY CONSIDERATIONS: POST-ELECTION AUDITS

FOR IMPLEMENTING BODIES

☑ Does the legal framework make clear how the audit process takes place, the number of locations, the ways in which the locations are selected and informed, when the audit takes place, the people who may be present during the audit, how the results of the audit are reported, and the consequences of any difference between electronic and paper records?

☑ Is a randomly selected sample of locations chosen for audits, and only informed after the close of polling or counting?

☑ Will audits take place as soon as possible after the election?

FOR OVERSIGHT ACTORS

☑ Is there a way to compare the electronic and auditable versions of the results to confirm whether the technologies worked properly and to verify the results, such as through the use of a voter verified paper audit trail?

☑ Is a random manual audit conducted, during which the audit trail is manually counted and the results compared to the electronic results generated in a random selection of polling stations? Is it conducted as soon as possible after the election, and is it fully observable by election observers, the media and political party and candidate agents? Are the results made publicly available?

☑ If a difference is found during the audit, is there a robust process to determine the cause of the difference and to address the cause(s) to the extent possible?

EVALUATION OF SYSTEM

Comprehensive evaluations of electronic voting and counting systems after an election can be critical for the long-term viability of these systems. The evaluation should take place not too long after an election and should involve a variety of data sources and electoral stakeholders so that a well-rounded assessment of the electronic voting and counting systems can be conducted. The EMB should have a mechanism for tracking and implementing evaluation recommendations in advance of the next electoral cycle.

A comprehensive evaluation of an electronic voting or counting system is critical to its success, particularly in the longer term. Only through an honest evaluation can the positive and negative lessons learned from the use of electronic voting or counting be captured to improve the process in the future.

An evaluation may be carried out by the project management committee or by another oversight body, or it may be contracted out to independent consultants. The evaluation should focus on the original objectives of the project and the extent to which those objectives have been achieved with the adoption of the electronic voting or counting system. Issues such as efficiency, usability, accessibility, accuracy, security and cost, among others, should be considered.

An evaluation may include several components, carried out by different bodies. Post-election surveys and focus groups can be a useful way to collect valuable information about voters' experiences using the technology, if the jurisdiction has the resources to commission such an exercise. Partnering with a university may be a useful way to conduct such activities. The number of complaints received about the electronic voting or counting system and the nature of these complaints should also be evaluated.

Evaluators should seek to involve a broad range of stakeholders in the assessment of electronic voting and counting systems. Interviews should be conducted with voters as well as with election officials at various levels, candidate and party representatives, election observers and journalists to learn about their experiences with the electronic voting and counting and whether they have recommendations to offer for the future implementation of the system.

Evaluation reports should be made available to the public and can serve as the basis for post-election roundtable discussions about the project among stakeholders, with an eye to offering recommendations for future improvement. Facilitating broad post-election dialogue about the electronic voting and counting systems can help to promote transparency and public confidence in the process as a whole, and offer valuable lessons as well.

Once the evaluation process is complete, it is important that the findings are used to improve the process in the future. A mechanism should be designed to ensure that recommendations and lessons learned are considered and implemented promptly, in time for the next election cycle.

FIGURE 25 – EVALUATION OF E-VOTING IN NORWAY

Following the 2011 trials of Internet voting in 10 of Norway's 429 municipalities, authorities contracted two research centers and IFES to carry out a thorough evaluation of the system. The evaluation used both qualitative and quantitative research methods, including questionnaire surveys in the trial municipalities, in-depth interviews with selected groups, focus groups for young people and observation studies of user-friendliness for voters with disabilities.

The evaluation sought to assess the project in the following seven areas:
- Availability and accessibility
- Trust and credibility
- Secrecy of voting (e.g., family voting, undue influence)
- Efficient counting of votes/fast electoral results
- Participation and turnout
- International experience with e-voting
- Compliance with international standards

The evaluation reports are available on the website of the Ministry of Local Government and Regional Development at: www.regjeringen.no/en/dep/krd/prosjekter/e-vote-2011-project/evaluations-of-the-e-voting-trials/evaluation-of-the-e-voting-trials-in-201.html?id=684642

FIGURE 26 – RE-EVALUATION OF THE USE OF ELECTRONIC VOTING IN THE NETHERLANDS

The Netherlands in 2006 decided to re-evaluate the use of electronic voting technologies after the system in use came under criticism for security and other reasons. To facilitate this process, the nation's parliament created commissions to investigate how past decisions on the approval of voting machines had been made and to review the organization of the election process. The findings of both commissions strongly criticized the government's management of voter technologies, and subsequently the government abandoned electronic voting, returning to paper-based voting.

Following decades of using electronic technologies in elections in the Netherlands, such technologies came under heavy criticism in 2006. In response to the publicizing of concerns about the lack of security and auditability mechanisms in the country's electronic voting machines by a group of computer experts called "We Do Not Trust Voting Computers" (described in more detail in Figure 14 above), the parliament requested that the government establish two independent commissions to consider the past and future of electronic voting.

The Voting Machines Decision-making Commission was tasked with reviewing how decisions on the approval of voting machines had been made in the past and what lessons could be learned. In its April 2007 report "Voting Machines: An Orphaned File," the commission was critical of the government's past role in electronic voting, concluding that (1) voting machines did not receive enough attention; (2) the Ministry of Interior lacked technical knowledge, resulting in officials becoming overly dependent on external actors, including technology vendors; and (3) the government did not react to signs that should have raised concern. The report also concluded that certification and testing of the voting machines was based on outdated standards and that reports from these tests should have been made public. The report noted that the legal framework did not adequately address the specifics of electronic voting, particularly the security requirements.

A second commission, the Election Process Advisory Commission, was set up to evaluate the organization of the election process and to make recommendations for future elections. In its September 2007 report "Voting with Confidence," the commission noted that requirements for election-related equipment had not been adequately established and that the security and management of the equipment were not properly regulated. It also noted that the electronic voting machines in use were not sufficiently transparent and verifiable. The commission concluded that all municipalities should have the same method of voting and that voting by paper ballot would be the most appropriate method.

> The government acted quickly in the wake of the release of the commissions' reports. Within a year of release of the Election Process Advisory Commission's report, the government had decided that voting and counting in the Netherlands would fully return to paper-based, manual processes.

KEY CONSIDERATIONS: EVALUATION OF SYSTEM

FOR IMPLEMENTING BODIES

- ☑ Is a comprehensive post-election system of evaluation in place, and are the responsibilities for this evaluation clearly defined (for example, between project management committee, another oversight body, or independent consultants)?

- ☑ Are resources available to commission post-election surveys and focus groups to collect information about voters' experiences using the technology?

- ☑ Does the evaluation focus on the original objectives of the project, and to what extent they have been achieved with the adoption of the electronic voting or counting system?

- ☑ Are issues such as efficiency, usability, accessibility, accuracy, security, and cost among others considered in the evaluation?

- ☑ Are the number of complaints received about the electronic voting or counting system and the nature of these complaints also evaluated?

- ☑ Will interviews be conducted with voters, election officials at various levels, candidate and party representatives, election observers and journalists?

- ☑ Will post election evaluation reports serve as the basis for post-election roundtable discussions among stakeholders about the project?

- ☑ How will the findings from the evaluation be used to improve the process in the future, in time for the next election cycle?

FOR OVERSIGHT ACTORS

- ☑ Does the evaluation of the electronic technologies involve a broad range of stakeholders, including election officials, party representatives, observers, and voters?

- ☑ Are evaluation reports made available to the public?

- ☑ Have election officials facilitated any post-election dialogues or other mechanisms to provide stakeholders an opportunity to offer recommendations for future improvements?

- ☑ Is there an EMB mechanism in place for tracking the implementation of stakeholder and evaluator recommendations ahead of the next election cycle?

- ☑ Have oversight actors evaluated their own efforts to monitor the new technologies and have they shared their findings with the EMB and the public?

- ☑ Are oversight actors preparing to assess and adapt their own methodologies in relation to future electronic voting and counting implementation plans?

INTERNET VOTING

While Internet voting has been utilized for national-level elections in only a few countries, it is a voting mechanism that is increasingly being explored as a means to allow access to the election process for voters who may otherwise find it difficult to go to their polling location on Election Day. Internet voting, however, presents a number of technological challenges focused on security, privacy, and secrecy issues, as well as challenges for stakeholder involvement in and observation of the process. All of these must be comprehensively addressed for election authorities to consider moving forward with Internet voting.

The first use of Internet voting for a binding political election took place in the US in 2000, with more countries subsequently beginning to conduct trials of and/or use Internet voting. A total of 14 countries have now used remote Internet voting for binding political elections or referenda. Within the group of Internet voting system users, four core countries have been using Internet voting over the course of several elections/referenda: Canada, Estonia, France and Switzerland. Estonia is the only country to offer Internet voting to the entire electorate. The remaining ten countries have either just adopted it, are currently piloting Internet voting, have piloted it and not pursued its further use, or have discontinued its use.

Examples of Internet voting in other countries around the world vary widely in scope and functionality. The early cases of Internet voting were less technically advanced than those being developed more recently. Many of the changes seen in Internet voting systems have been aimed at improving the quality of elections delivered by these systems and meeting emerging standards for electronic voting.

It is fair to say that Internet voting is not a commonly used means of voting. Of the 14 countries that have so far used it in any form, only ten currently have expressed any intention of using it in the future. However, Internet voting is a relatively new voting technology and has been developing significantly over the previous ten years. Internet voting seems to fit, for many countries, a niche corner of the electoral process. It is largely targeted at those who cannot attend their polling station in person on Election Day. In fact many more countries have expressed or shown an interest in the use of Internet voting, especially when they have large numbers of expatriate voters. However, the implementation of Internet voting, according to emerging standards, is a very technical exercise. It can also pose some difficult political questions if the aim is to facilitate the inclusion of large numbers of expatriate citizens in the political process.

The technicalities of implementing Internet voting systems are largely a result of attempts to reconcile the use of Internet voting with emerging and existing standards to which elections and electronic elections should adhere. These standards include the need for secure online voter authentication, protection of the secrecy of the vote, appropriate transparency mechanisms, testing and certification regimes. The need for secure online voter authentication mechanisms may be one of the biggest hurdles in implementing Internet voting. It presents a challenge for many established democracies, which often do not have ID card systems with secure online authentication mechanisms.

FIGURE 27 – INTERNET VOTING IN ESTONIA

Estonia has implemented Internet voting in national elections since 2005 and the percentage of voters voting via Internet has trended up in each successive election. Estonia has taken several measures to ensure the secrecy of the vote, primarily through allowing multiple votes to be cast over the Internet by a voter (only the last one is counted) and also prioritizing any paper ballot cast by a voter over Internet votes cast.

Estonia became the first country to offer Internet voting to the entire electorate for nationwide, binding elections. Internet voting has now been provided in local (2005, 2009), parliamentary (2007, 2011), presidential (2011) and European (2009) elections. The first three elections were carried out without major criticisms and with a growing percentage of Internet voters. The 2011 parliamentary elections saw a significant increase in the usage of Internet voting (over 24 percent of all votes were cast using the Internet).

Internet voting is only available before Election Day during an early voting period that normally lasts for one week. Voters may cast their Internet ballots multiple times during this period, and only the last Internet ballot cast is considered valid for the official tally. Various paper ballot options are also available. Voters can cast early paper ballots. Estonians living abroad may cast their ballots by post or vote at an embassy. Voting from ships is also offered.

The names of those voting by Internet are removed from the electoral register used on Election day in the polling station. Any paper ballot cast in the early voting period will be counted, canceling any Internet ballot cast by the voter. The strategy of allowing multiple votes and the primacy of the paper ballot is intended to protect the secrecy of the vote by allowing any voter who may have been coerced or intimidated to vote a certain way the opportunity to vote again in secrecy and overwrite their previous, tainted vote.

Internet voters identify themselves with a smart national ID card or a "mobile ID" (a new authentication channel using mobile phones with specific SIM cards that was introduced in 2011). Once authenticated, the voter casts the ballot through a platform that sends the vote to a central database. The vote is digitally signed (inner "envelope") and inserted in another virtual and signed "envelope" (outer one) that contains the identification of the voter and the session log.

In reviewing the use of Internet voting since 2000, a number of important themes emerge:

Trust in Internet Voting – As already discussed, trust in the electoral process is essential for successful democracy. However, trust is a complex concept, which requires that individuals make rational decisions based on the facts to accept the integrity of Internet voting. The problem is that Internet voting is so complex that few voters have the technical expertise necessary to make the informed decision to place their trust in it. In order to compensate for the inherent complexity of Internet voting, extra measures need to be taken to ensure that voters have a sound basis on which to give their trust to Internet voting systems. Technical institutions and experts can play an important role in this process, with voters trusting the procedural role played by independent institutions and experts in ensuring the overall integrity of the system, rather than their own limited understanding of how Internet voting works and the verification mechanisms used.

A number of mechanisms can be used to enable the development and maintenance of trust in Internet voting systems. One of the fundamental ways to enable trust is to ensure that information about the Internet voting system is made publicly available. The system must also be trustworthy, and measures to ensure the integrity of the system are important. A vital aspect of integrity is ensured through testing, certification and audit mechanisms. These mechanisms will need to demonstrate that the security concerns presented by Internet voting have been adequately dealt with, and will need to recognize that there are some aspects of security that are outside of the control of the Internet voting system – such as the devices (i.e., the computers) that voters use to cast their ballots.

Due to the inherent lack of transparency with Internet voting, it is important to separate the responsibilities for different stages of the Internet voting process. Such a separation of duties will make it more difficult to manipulate the system. Allowing the repeated casting of Internet votes, with only the last vote being counted, also helps generate trust amongst voters. Making the Internet voting system verifiable, so that the results can be independently verified against the votes cast, is an increasingly important trust mechanism, although this needs to be done in a way that does not violate the secrecy of the ballot. Finally, Internet voting systems should be subjected to various evaluation mechanisms.

The Secrecy and Freedom of the Vote – Ensuring the secrecy of the ballot is a significant concern in every voting situation. In the case of Internet voting from unsupervised environments, this principle may easily become the main challenge. Given that an Internet voting system cannot ensure that voters are casting their ballots alone, the validity of Internet voting must be demonstrated on other grounds. One relevant argument is the similarity of Internet voting with postal voting, a method of voting considered to meet standards of secrecy by the Venice Commission. The chance to repeat and cancel an Internet vote is a common argument for the acceptance of Internet voting, as it means that a vote buyer or coercer will not know for sure which ballot will be counted for a voter. Finally, Estonia has argued that the principle of secrecy entails an obligation to provide the opportunity for a secret vote, but that voters are free to choose less secret voting options if they desire.

Accessibility of Internet Voting – Improving accessibility to the voting process is often cited as a reason for introducing Internet voting. The accessibility of voting systems, closely linked to usability, is an international standard for elections, and is relevant not only for voters with disabilities and linguistic minorities, but also for the average voter. Internet voting can have a significant impact on the accessibility of the voting process. It is important that voters, especially those who may have special accessibility issues, are involved in the development of any Internet voting system. The way in which voters are identified and authenticated can have a significant impact on the usability of the system, but a balance needs to be found between accessibility and integrity.

The voting process itself, and vote-verification mechanisms, can also be difficult to design in ways that are accessible to all. Voters will often demand that Internet voting be made available through the end of normal voting, but the duration of voting will need to be determined while considering other factors, such as any requirements for Internet voters to be able to cast a paper ballot. The proliferation of computer operating systems and web browsers presents

Internet voting system developers with increasing challenges in making their systems functional on all or most of these operating systems and browsers.

A counterargument can be made related to the "digital divide" in terms of the accessibility of Internet voting. Different groups in society have different levels of access to the Internet. Therefore, the provision of Internet voting in societies where there is very unequal access to the Internet will have a different impact on accessibility for various communities. Of course, these communities may have very different voting preferences, which could have implications for the results of the election.

Even in well-developed democracies, more affluent voters may be able to vote from the comfort of their own homes, while others may have to take time off work to wait in line to vote. The possible unequal impact on accessibility created by the provision of Internet voting would be far more severe if Internet voting were the only means of casting a ballot. However, as can be seen even where traditional voting mechanisms are also in place, Internet voting can create accessibility concerns, although the accessibility of these other voting mechanisms could be improved in order to compensate.

Electoral Stakeholders and Their Roles – The introduction of Internet voting significantly changes the role that stakeholders play in the electoral process. Not only do new stakeholders, such as voting technology suppliers, assume prominence in the Internet voting process, but existing stakeholders must adapt their roles in order to fulfill their existing functions. While electronic voting in general requires changes in the roles of these stakeholders, the introduction of Internet voting, in particular, changes the roles in a much more fundamental manner as the act of voting is taken outside of the polling station.

This new network of stakeholder roles and relationships may be difficult to manage well, and some of the various stakeholder demands may be contradictory (for example, they may take different positions on the disclosure of information on the Internet voting system). Central to this new network of stakeholder relationships is public administration, especially the role of the EMB. Public administration and the EMB will establish the legal and regulatory framework for the implementation of Internet voting; and this framework will define the roles and rights of the various stakeholders in the Internet voting process. The EMB will also need to manage the implementation of the Internet voting technology, ensure control is maintained over the supplier and facilitate the open involvement of all relevant stakeholders during implementation. An open information policy will be essential to the EMB's interactions with stakeholders to develop trusted relations while implementing Internet voting.

Internet voting presents obvious challenges for party poll watchers and observers. While the role of observers in the pre-election period will be similar to their role with other forms of electronic voting as discussed above (e.g., legal framework, design requirements, testing and certification, security, etc.), observers will be unable to make a systematic assessment of the voting and counting process. Observer groups and political parties must therefore design observation strategies with this in mind and must be candid with the public about any limitations of their assessments. At the same time, Internet voting introduces several new elements and points of inquiry for election observers. These include evaluating the security of voting servers, assessing the EMB's monitoring of voting server security and threat response plans, and the functioning of Internet Service Providers (ISPs).[44] As with other forms of electronic voting, IT expertise will be critical to such efforts. Observers may also use survey techniques to gauge voters' experience with Internet voting, including their level of trust in the system.

---

44 Pran, V. and Merloe, P. (2007) NDI Handbook: Monitoring Electronic Technologies in Electoral Processes, pp. 85–88.

EMBs need to be sensitive and responsive to opposition and concern about the introduction and use of Internet voting systems. There will likely always be some opposition to such systems; however, to ignore opposition and concern is very risky. Even small groups opposing voting technology can have a significant impact by raising concerns that resonate with the public. EMBs that fail to respond to concerns about Internet voting may lose control of any public debate in a way that could be fatal for implementation. Proactive engagement with opponents of Internet voting by the EMB and attempts to mitigate these concerns will serve to diffuse potentially damaging public debates on Internet voting. It will also help ensure that Internet voting does not become a, or the, divisive issue in a country's political discourse.

KEY CONSIDERATIONS: INTERNET VOTING

FOR IMPLEMENTING BODIES

- ☑ What measures have been taken to build trust among stakeholders and especially voters in the development of the internet voting system?

- ☑ What technical solutions have been put in place to respect the secrecy of the vote?

- ☑ As an important goal of electronic voting technology, what efforts were made to ensure and enhance accessibility across all voter groups?

- ☑ How have traditional and new stakeholders been included throughout the design and implementation process of internet voting?

- ☑ Is there proactive engagement with those opposed to internet voting in order to address their concerns?

FOR OVERSIGHT ACTORS

☑ What limitations do observers and parties face in assessing the integrity of internet voting? Are there alternative strategies they can adopt to monitor the process?

☑ What measures have been taken to ensure voters have a solid basis to trust internet voting systems? What level of trust do voters have in the system as a result?

☑ Do all stakeholders support the adoption of internet voting, and if not, how have concerns been addressed by the authorities?

☑ How does internet voting affect accessibility for different communities, who may have highly unequal internet access? If inequities are created, are there alternative (i.e., traditional) means by which voters disadvantaged by internet voting can cast their ballots? Has the accessibility of traditional voting methods been improved to compensate for the improved accessibility for internet voters?

☑ To address the reduced transparency associated with internet voting, are responsibilities separated among those administering elections for different stages of the internet voting process?

☑ To what extent is the secrecy of the vote protected? For example, do voters have the opportunity to repeat and cancel their votes? Is the online voter authentication secure? Are the voting servers secure? How has this security been demonstrated to the public?

CONCLUDING REMARKS

This Manual has introduced the challenges and opportunities relating to the use of electronic voting and counting technologies in the electoral process. General principles and issues, which need to be considered at every stage of the process of consideration and implementation of these technologies, have been covered. A step-by-step guide to the different stages of consideration and implementation of the technologies has been provided to assist EMBs as they move through the process or seek to understand it better, as well as to help other stakeholders, including civil society and electoral contestants, understand how to engage in and monitor these processes. Finally, several detailed case studies have been provided to show how different countries have addressed these general principles and issues as they have implemented electronic voting and counting technologies.

A few concluding remarks are worth making to reemphasize key points for any EMB considering the use of electronic voting or counting technologies, for international donors and technical assistance providers involved in working with EMBs on such decisions, and for oversight actors, including civil society groups, the media and electoral contestants. In particular, EMBs considering these technologies must use well-considered approaches to the decision to adopt or not adopt electronic voting and counting technologies, institute pilot projects as a key component of the decision-making process, ensure that enough time has been allocated for the implementation of electronic voting and counting technologies, and secure appropriate financial and human resources to meet the technological and logistical challenges inherent in the implementation of these technologies.

The decision making process is critical to introducing electronic voting and counting technologies. The potential advantages of such technologies also come with many challenges that EMBs need to effectively consider and address to ensure that the integrity of the electoral process is not undermined. It is important that the decision is taken carefully and with due consideration, that electoral stakeholders understand the rationale being used for moving toward these technologies, and have opportunities for their viewpoints to be taken into account.

Additionally, electoral contestants and stakeholders can view changes in the mechanics of the electoral process with deep suspicion, as they may suspect that a change benefits one competitor over another. The EMB, or other institution tasked with taking the decision on whether to use electronic voting or counting technologies, should be very clear on the issues that the introduction of the technology is meant to address and the objectives that it seeks to achieve. Clarity and consultation with electoral stakeholders on these issues will help the stakeholders understand the motivations for using the technology, and accept the technology if it is adopted for well-founded reasons.

Pilot projects are an essential component of the decision-making process. It is very important that pilots are not implemented only after the decision to adopt a technology has been made, but rather before that decision is made. The pilot project plays a vital role in testing the assumptions about the advantages the technology offers, determining whether the risks and challenges can be adequately managed, and properly evaluating the costs associated with using the technology. Pilots need to be properly assessed after being completed, and this process takes time if it is to be conducted properly – requiring surveys, consultations and internal review.

While there may be political pressure to adopt and implement new technologies quickly, these pressures should be resisted. The implementation of electronic voting and counting technologies can be a costly endeavour, although the costs need to be considered over the course of the many elections for which the equipment will be used. If a decision is taken to adopt such technology without due consideration and is subsequently reversed because of hasty decision-making, then financial and human resource investments may be lost, potentially wasting a large amount of state funds, and public confidence in the electoral process could be reduced.

While it is difficult to generalize what an appropriate timeframe is for deciding on and implementing electronic voting and counting technologies, this Manual has emphasized that a great deal of caution should be taken to ensure sufficient time is allotted for such a transition. The time required for making a decision will depend on the amount of resources applied to the feasibility process and the opportunities that exist for pilot testing the technology in a real electoral environment, for example through by-elections. Still, it is imperative that electoral authorities take appropriate time within the existing context to consider all aspects of the decision and leave ample time for consultation with key electoral stakeholders at all stages of the decision-making process.

Once the process moves on to implementing electronic voting or counting technologies there are a number of other critical pitfalls to take into account. Just as with the decision making process, realistic timeframes for implementation are vital, especially when legislation needs to be amended to permit and properly regulate the use of these technologies. In many countries this alone can take months or years through the parliamentary process. Similarly, there should be ample time allotted for testing and certification, voter education, election official training, and other key elements of the implementation cycle. EMBs must be properly resourced to manage technology projects. Examples from countries implementing electronic voting or counting technologies have shown that often the EMB is not prepared for the complexities of implementing elections using these technologies. Not only have they not had the technical expertise in-house to properly manage or oversee the implementation of the technology, but sometimes they have lacked the project management skills and resources.

This can lead to the project being poorly managed, risking the quality of the elections, and/or vendors of the technology playing too central a role in the implementation of the technology without proper oversight by the EMB. Vendors have very different priorities than EMBs, and when vendors are empowered in this way, these conflicting priorities can have dangerous implications for the conduct of the elections and the perception of the elections by stakeholders.

Just as EMBs must ensure they have the capacity and resources to manage elections involving electronic technologies, civil society groups, political parties and the media also have a responsibility to the public to build their expertise and capacity to provide informed and constructive input during all aspects of the decision making, design and implementation phases, as well as to effectively monitor these processes. Since not all voters can fully understand all aspects of these technologies, they rely heavily on oversight actors to promote transparency and to assess the integrity of elections that involve electronic technologies.

While each implementation of election technology may be different, with a different product and a different electoral environment, there is much that EMBs can learn from others who have implemented similar technologies. Successful implementation approaches and pitfalls experienced can be shared between EMBs so that good practices can be developed and shared between EMBs in this still emerging field of elections. Likewise, civil society groups can also learn from others that have observed transitions to electronic voting and counting technologies.

It is hoped that this Manual will help EMBs, international donors and technical assistance providers, civil society groups, media and electoral contestants to properly take into account these common pitfalls in implementing, supporting and monitoring electronic voting and counting projects in order to strengthen the integrity of electoral processes around the world.

ANNEXES

CASE STUDY REPORT ON BRAZIL ELECTRONIC VOTING, 1996 TO PRESENT

IFES and NDI conducted a case study of Brazil to examine the country's experience and lessons learned from the use of electronic counting technologies in its elections since 1996. Brazil began the process of transitioning to electronic voting after the 1994 general election, and the Brazilian experience since then has been characterized by a rapid transition to universal electronic voting by the 2000 election for approximately 100 million voters. One of the chief characteristics of the Brazilian move toward electronic voting has been the large role played by the *Tribunal Superior Eleitoral* (TSE) – the institution responsible for managing elections, advocating for and implementing electronic voting – and the relatively little role played by civil society and oversight groups, until recently. One of the implications of this development for electronic voting in Brazil is the balance between implementation and oversight, and how this balance has been challenged in recent years through greater calls for transparency and oversight by civil society actors.

DECISION MAKING PROCESS ON ELECTRONIC VOTING

Brazil began shifting toward electronic voting in 1994. The impetus for the initial move to e-voting was largely led and managed by the TSE. The TSE has jurisdiction over all aspects of elections in Brazil and regulates the functioning of political parties. Over its history, the TSE has developed a reputation for trustworthiness, competence and autonomy in the management of the electoral process. In addition to its election management role, the TSE is also responsible for revising the electoral law every two years and submitting it to the legislature for approval, as required by Brazilian law. Because of its good reputation, the electoral law submitted by the TSE is rarely debated; and this gave the TSE significant leeway to purse electronic voting as a solution to challenges faced by the electoral process. While outside actors had some input, the move to electronic voting was largely an autonomous process carried out by the TSE, and consequently, actors within the judicial institution made most of the major decisions.

There were two primary reasons why the TSE adopted electronic voting machines (EVM). The first was to combat endemic fraud in the paper ballot tabulation process. The second was to address issues related to electoral accessibility and spoiled ballots in the paper voting system. Due to Brazil's complex electoral rules, voters regularly have to choose from thousands of legislative candidates. This makes results tabulation a logistical challenge because the paper voting system involves hundreds of thousands of vote counters who were often government employees from State-owned banks or the postal service. Because of the scale of the task, vote counting could take weeks and this post-election period was a time of great uncertainty and tension.

Most importantly, the lengthy tabulation period increased opportunity for vote counters allied with candidates to manipulate the vote count because the lengthy vote count was difficult for partisan and other civil society actors to fully monitor. The most common type of fraud was manipulation of the tabulation sheets known as "maps" where vote counters who were allied with candidates would subtract votes from one candidate's tally and add them to the favored candidate's count.[45] This type of electoral fraud became a national issue after the 1994 presidential and legislative elections when a scheme to manipulate the election results involving electoral judges was uncovered in Rio de Janeiro. The local branch of the TSE was forced to annul the results for the legislative elections and hold a new one, leading to questions about the pervasiveness of fraud in elections.

A secondary motivation for switching to electronic voting was due to accessibility problems in the paper-based system. This system was a hugely complicated, as it required voters to write in the name or identifying number of their preferred legislative candidate. Two factors, the large number of candidates in legislative races, as well as the level of illiteracy in the country (approximately 20 percent, according to the 1990 census) resulted in almost 40 percent of votes being blank or invalid in 1994 legislative elections. These factors were compounded by the fact that, in legislative elections, voters voted for multiple offices and would fill in several names or numbers to cast votes for all offices. TSE officials argued that the high number of blank votes cast could be attributed to illiterate voters, who did not want to take a long time writing in a name, revealing they could not write.

The disenfranchising effect of complex ballots also made fraud easier, as described by Federal Deputy Tourinho Dantas:

> If an illiterate voter doesn't know how to read or write, how can he vote? They humiliate themselves at the moment in which they vote. When he goes to the ballot booth and he doesn't know what to do, he casts a blank vote. This vote, in the majority of places, is filled out by those perpetrating fraud. It is by this means that fraudulent votes are cast in so many places.[46]

---

45 In Portuguese slang, this practice was known as "mapism" ("mapismo").
46 Dantas, Tourinho. Diário do Congresso Nacional, October 27, 1994, p. 13,331

The initial decision to switch to electronic voting was made by President of the TSE, Minister Sepúlveda Pertence, in 1994. He cited the Rio de Janeiro scandal as a factor:

> After the experience we have lived through, not in the poorest regions, but rather in one of the most important cities in the country [Rio de Janeiro], we cannot retreat from the imperative of automation, or if that is not possible, the "mechanization" of the vote.

The impetus to change voting technologies came almost wholly from within the TSE, and was based in part on previous positive experiences with the use of technology in voter registration and results tabulation. When the decision was made between 1994 and 1995, there were no other major societal actors such as political parties, civil society organizations or other government bodies advocating for the abandonment of paper ballots.

In Brazil, a pilot was not carried out to test electronic voting. Instead, a gradual introduction of universal electronic voting was achieved over the course of three elections: in the 1996 elections, 30 percent of voters (33 million) directly voted through the electronic voting machines; in 1998, an additional 30 percent (35 million voters) voted through e-voting machines; and in the 2000 elections, the entire nation voted through electronic voting (100 million voters).

BUILDING THE SYSTEM FOR ELECTRONIC VOTING AND COUNTING

After Minister Carlos Velloso took over as President of the TSE at the end of 1994, he created a feasibility committee composed mostly of notable judges, lawyers and other jurists to investigate the feasibility of transitioning to electronic voting, as well as to determine the basic parameters of any new system. The committee was charged with planning a system with the following characteristics:

- Computers used for both voting and counting
- Could be used across a representative sample of municipalities throughout Brazil in the 1996 municipal elections
- Performed automatic and rapid tabulation of the votes
- Significantly reduced or eliminated fraud
- Implemented with the approval of citizens, political parties and candidates

While a judge formally led the committee, the real leader was Dr. Paulo César Bhering Camarão, a friend of Minister Velloso with expertise on the technical aspects of electronic voting. On technical aspects, the committee consulted with the military, government ministries and experts in universities. To study the legal feasibility of the new system, the committee also consulted the Bar Association (OAB), public prosecutor's office and other lawyers. Simultaneous to the formation of the feasibility committee, Minister Velloso worked to convince judges and technical staff within the TSE to accept the transition to electronic voting. In an interview, Minister Velloso indicated he had the support of President Fernando Henrique Cardoso and Minister of Planning and Budget José Serra. In the initial stages of planning, Congress and political parties had very little role, although they were kept informed. There was not much outreach to the media in the decision making stage, as Minister Velloso only held a press conference to inform the media about the TSE's efforts. There was also little civil society engagement in the decision making stage.

LEGAL FRAMEWORK

The TSE's feasibility committee crafted language to be included in legislation governing the 1996 municipal elections. Overall, the committee sought to create a system that would necessitate as few changes to existing law as possible. The legislature, with little debate, incorporated the legislative language into Articles 18, 19 and 20 of Law 9.100, which passed on September 29,

1995. The law authorized the TSE to use electronic voting, but did not specify in great detail how the system would work. The law required that voters choose a candidate by inputting their preferred candidate's number, and that each mayoral candidate's photo be displayed on the screen. The law also mandated that 120 days before the election, the TSE would allow political parties or companies hired by them to audit the code used in the machines. Finally, Law 9.100 mandated that a paper trail be created. A physical copy of the vote would be printed so the vote count produced by the machine could be checked using the hard copy. However, the law did not require that voters be able to verify the printed version of their vote with their selection on the machine.

Requirements for a voter verified paper audit trail (VVPAT) have undergone several reversals since the initial law governing electronic voting was passed. During this time, the TSE has been opposed to a requirement for VVPAT, but the Brazilian Congress has attempted to introduce this requirement several times. In 2002, Congress passed electoral law 10.408, which mandated that the TSE begin transitioning to a system with a voter verified paper audit trail (VVPAT) and that this be piloted in the 2002 national elections. The TSE argued that the pilot results suggested the VVPAT system increased error rates and re-introduced some of the problems associated with the paper system. Civil society advocates of VVPAT argue that the TSE failed to adequately train poll workers and educate voters about VVPAT, thus stacking the deck against it use.

In 2003, at the behest of the TSE, Congress passed law 1.503, which removed the requirement to adopt VVPAT, instead mandating that each machine record individual votes in a random order. This record would be given the parties so they could tabulate individual votes and check the official vote count. Of course, this digital registry of individual votes does not provide the same level of verifiability as the VVPAT, as voters have no means of verifying their vote.

In 2009, the status quo changed once again. Representatives of the Working Democratic Party (*Partido Democrático Trabalhista* or PDT) successfully included language in Law 12.034/09 passed that year, which once again mandated VVPAT by the 2014 elections. Further, the new law required that voting machines not be connected to the machines that verified voters' identity. The TSE challenged the law in the Supreme Court, which suspended the law on the grounds that if the voter identification machine and the voting machine were not connected, then it would be possible for a voter to vote multiple times. The Supreme Court also expressed concern that if the printer jammed, then polling station workers might see the vote while fixing the printer, compromising the secrecy of the ballot. While it is possible the suspension could be lifted on appeal, civil society activists in favor of VVPAT are not optimistic.

IMPLEMENTING OF ELECTRONIC VOTING AND COUNTING SINCE 1996

While the national TSE determines policy for the overall electoral process, state-level regional electoral courts (*Tribunal Regional Eleitoral* – TRE) implement the policy. Both the TSE and state TREs have high levels of project management capacity accumulated through decades of running Brazil's elections. Election operations are implemented by highly-qualified permanent staff and temporary workers (1.9 million for the 1996 elections). The vast majority of temporary workers in 1996 were poll workers and vote counters in municipalities that retained the paper ballot. In municipalities using electronic voting, the number of required workers was considerably smaller.

The TSE coordinated with the armed forces, the postal service and local governments to distribute voting machines and other materials. For technical assistance with the voting machines, the TSE contracted with a variety of companies. Firms hired in 1996, included HP, Oracle, Embratel, ABASE, MÓDULO and FUBRAS for services, including the creation and maintenance of databases;

preparation of EVMs; training of technicians; provision and support for use of flash cards; and security.

There were relatively few problems with electronic voting on Election Day in 1996. In the first round of the election, 74,127 electronic voting machines were used by about a third of the electorate and relatively few machines (3.65%) had some type of problem. According to the TSE, 1.76 percent of the machines had problems due to improper use, .92 percent had hardware malfunctions, .88 percent had software malfunctions and .09 percent had unidentified problems. The TSE noted the attached printers malfunctioned at unacceptably high rates, which contributed to the TSE's decision to abandon a printed paper trail in future elections. As a result of the printer problems, printed ballots were not used to verify any of the machine vote counts in 1996.

In subsequent years, the error rate has dropped even further. According to the TSE, The failure rate of EVMs is very low (about 0.007%), but if problems do occur, the machines are replaced. If replacement is not possible, then paper ballots are used. The only major logistical problems in subsequent elections occurred in 2008, where a flaw in the code caused widespread problems with a specific brand of memory flash card. In states where EVMs were using this brand of memory card, many voting machines had to be replaced on Election Day. In some cities, specifically Belém, Goiânia and Recife, roughly 30 percent of EVMs had to be replaced.

DESIGN REQUIREMENTS

In the initial design stage, the TSE feasibility commission determined the basic parameters of the new system. While the commission mostly consulted with stakeholders within the government, they also reached out to outside experts at several computer companies, including IBM, Hewlett Packard, ABC-Bull, CPM, Unisys, Microsoft, Digital and Soza International. Dr. Camarão also examined existing commercial systems and observed elections in the state of Virginia in the U.S., which employed electronic voting. The committee concluded that existing systems developed in other countries were insufficiently tailored to the requirements of the Brazilian elections, and consequently decided to seek a custom solution.

The initial requirements of the TSE committee for the electronic voting machine were as follows:

- Easy installation process
- Easy to operate, both by voter and poll worker
- Low cost and ability to be adapted to other uses
- Own source of energy so that external power sources would not be required
- Robustness to different weather conditions
- Machine should be controlled by poll workers to prevent multiple voting
- Machine should have attached printer to enable paper trail
- Printer ballot should be collected automatically without any action by the voter
- Voting machine should not be connected to a network for security reasons
- Equipment should allow for future upgrades
- Screen should allow voter to verify their vote and be capable of presenting instructions
- Screen should display each candidate's photo
- Allow for ability of the voter to use an alphanumeric keyboard to select candidates; this requirement was later abandoned in favor of a purely numeric keyboard. The TSE thought that since knowledge of how to use telephone keypads was widespread, a numeric keypad would not pose any difficulties for the illiterate and semi-literate.

With regard to the procurement process, the initial requirements were as follows:

- Equipment needed to be provided with enough time to conduct a full battery of tests under diverse conditions.
- The company providing the machines had to have the technical and logistical capacity to fully meet the needs of the TSE.
- The contract would cover hardware provision, as well as technical support, logistical support and aid in distribution.

THE PROCUREMENT PROCESS

After the TSE feasibility committee issued its final report in August 1995, a new technical committee was convened to more thoroughly investigate and specify the requirements for the new system. They also elaborated the request for tender to be issued by the TSE. The request would specify how the machine would be developed; how many machines would be required and their geographic distribution; training requirements; technical support requirements; documentation requirements; and plans for testing the submitted models. Importantly, the committee was also charged with specifying how different bids would be evaluated.

To develop the request for tender, the technical committee first published a request for comments and suggestions on their requirements for the electronic voting machine in the government register. They received over a dozen reports from a variety of private companies, government entities and universities. With this information, the TSE technical committee wrote a complete request for tender with three annexes that specified the required products and services; the technical requirements of the voting machine; and how any bid would be judged. Procurement rules for government purchases were followed and all criteria for judging bids by companies were public.

Companies that submitted a bid had to provide a working model that could pass 96 technical tests. Only those companies that passed all the tests would be considered for the bid. Five companies submitted a bid, but only three companies—IBM, Unisys and Procomp—submitted models that passed the 96 tests. Of these three companies, Unisys submitted the lowest bid of R$ 69,762,178.60 (about $63 million USD) and was selected to implement the new system.

Since the 1996 elections, the TSE has continued to use outside contractors to maintain and manufacture the electronic voting machines. In the last several elections, Diebold-Procomp won bids to manufacture the voting machines. In 2009, Diebold-Procomp delivered 194,000 machines for use in the 2010 elections.

CERTIFICATION, SOURCE CODE REVIEW AND TESTING

In the elections held from 1996–2004, the code used in the electronic voting machines was developed by private sector firms. In the initial 1996 elections, Unisys contracted a company called Microbase to develop the software. Microbase used a proprietary operating system called "VirtuOs," whose code base was not generally available for auditing. In models developed for the 2002 and 2004 elections, Microbase used Windows CE as the operating system. In 2006, the TSE transferred software development to their internal team, and in 2008 adopted an operating system based on GNU/Linux.

The TSE reserves final authority over the source code, so no outside authority certified the code used in 1996 or in subsequent elections. The electoral law mandates the TSE make the final source code available to political parties and, after 2003, the Bar Association (Ordem dos Advogados do Brasil or OAB), 120 days before the election. Activists and academics say that that the TSE failed to comply with this requirement for the 1996, 1998 and 2000 elections. After 2000, in the wake of heightened scrutiny of the system, the TSE began to allow outside actors to review the source code, but interviews with activists and congressional staffers indicate that only two parties – PDT and the Worker's Party (Partido dos Trabalhadores or PT) – regularly participated in the audits. PDT typically has computer scientists affiliated with the party examine the code, while PT hires an outside company. The OAB expended considerable effort and money prior to the 2004 elections to audit the code by hiring an outside company and examining the software in various states, but has only conducted minimal auditing since 2004 due to costs and lack of internal capacity. There has been criticism of this auditing process by civil society groups and computer scientists. Computer scientists criticize the fact that auditors must sign a non-disclosure agreement and, consequently, any problems found during the audit are not made public. Auditors also point out that only a few days are given for auditing, and the examination of code occurs in very controlled conditions on the TSE's computers, which is insufficient to comprehensively examine the code.

Academics and the OAB have also reported that there have been cases where the code has been modified after it was given to the parties, meaning parties did not audit the final version of the code. The TSE has argued the code needed to be modified for technical reasons, but has not fully explained the changes.

The first comprehensive, independent and nonpartisan audit of the full electronic voting system code and equipment was conducted several years after the adoption of electronic voting in 2001 and 2002 by eight computer scientists at the State University of Campinas (*Universidade Estadual de Campinas* or UNICAMP). The UNICAMP team concluded the system was "robust, secure, and trustworthy," and they made eight recommendations for improving the system. These recommendations focused on improving how the code is maintained and developed from election to election, as well as details of the cryptographic signing mechanism. According to the TSE, all recommendations made by the UNICAMP report were incorporated into the system after its publication. Since then, the TSE has sponsored a few additional independent audits of the code, generally by university researchers. For example, a 2002 report by Jeroen van de Graaf and Ricardo Felipe, computer scientists at the Federal University of Minas Gerais and the Federal University of Santa Catarina, respectively, found the electronic voting system was an improvement over the paper ballot system. The authors, however, also criticized the time made available for political parties to audit the code. The researchers emphasized the limited utility of the cryptographic authentication safeguards, as there is no way for observers to know if it is functioning properly. Van der Graaf and Felipe argued for the use of a voter verified paper trail as a means of enhancing the audit ability of the system.

Beginning in 2009, the TSE organized public tests of the system, during which they invite computer scientists and interested parties ("hackers") to attempt to find external vulnerabilities in the electronic voting system. The first test in 2009 did not provide access to the voting machine code, while the 2012 test did. Participants in the 2012 test were given only three days to design, execute and evaluate attacks to the system. Further, access to the source code was limited, as only four computers with the source code were provided. Given the number of participants, this left limited time for each team to actually examine code. Basic tools to search and evaluate the code such as "grep" were also unavailable. The security tests focused solely on the voting machines, not other aspects of the system.

One of the teams that participated in the 2012 test succeeded in compromising the anonymity of the vote. After each election and for each machine, parties are provided with a list of individual votes cast (without identifying information of the voter) in a randomized order. The team of computer scientists from the University of Brasilia, led by Professor Diego Aranha, discovered a flaw in how individual votes were stored that would allow parties to recover the precise order in which votes were cast. According to the TSE, the vulnerability identified by Professor Aranha has now been fixed.

The TSE also allows for a form of auditing that they call the "parallel vote." The day before the election, two electronic voting machines in each state are randomly chosen for testing by representatives of the parties and the OAB. After the machines are selected, party and civil society representatives go to where the machine is located and bring them back to the state election headquarters. The observers can then test whether or not the machines are properly recording the votes being cast. According to the TSE, this parallel vote procedure has never found any irregularities or problems. Some computer scientists have criticized the parallel vote because it occurs a day before Election Day. According to these critics, it would be possible for manipulation of the system to occur between the time of the parallel vote and when Election Day begins.

SECURITY

The Brazilian electronic voting system has several software-based and design-based security safeguards. The EVM is designed to check whether or not the loaded software on each machine has a digital signature (hash) matching the signature provided by the TSE, and only continue to operate if the software verification is successful. Critics have pointed out that this verification process depends on the integrity of the verification software itself and, if this verification code is somehow compromised, then altered code could be loaded onto the machines.

To prevent access to the software and data of the EVMs, the contents of electronic voting machine are encrypted using an AES specification of 256 bits and the same key is used on all electronic voting machines. Critics in the computer science community argue that use of single key is risky because dissemination of the key would compromise all voting machines. The TSE defends the use of a single key because it makes the system less susceptible to a brute force attack. This risk is exacerbated by the fact that the encryption key is recorded in the source code. Since the source code is subject to audits by parties and the OAB prior to each election, the possibility exists that the key could be leaked and thus compromise the machines.

Another feature designed to safeguard the integrity of the vote count is the procedure by which machine vote totals are distributed. At the end of Election Day, the head poll worker ends the voting session and prints out six copies of the machine bulletin (Boletim de Urna). Five of these copies are distributed to the parties and one is posted at the precinct for the public. Theoretically, the parties or candidates could tabulate the totals from the printed machine bulletins and check the vote totals reported by the election authorities. Starting in the mid-2000s, electronic copies of machine bulletins were posted online and available to the public.

VOTER EDUCATION

The TSE hired private firms to conduct voter education for the first implementation of EVMs in 1996 through mass media including television, radio and print media. Local state courts were in charge of local campaigns, which included demonstrations of the new technology, lectures and mock elections. Civil society did not provide any voter education campaigns.

The TSE has continued the use of mass media as a voter education tool prior to all subsequent electoral events. Poll workers are also trained to help/support voters during voting. The machines are designed to facilitate voting for handicapped or marginalized groups. For example, the machines are equipped with earphones for deaf voters and the keypad has Braille. Poll workers are trained to explain the voting process to the voters, if necessary.

Opinion polling since 1996 has shown strong positive evaluations of EVMs. Local polling in 1996 showed high levels of awareness of the change in voting technology. In recent years, the TSE has hired independent polling firms to measure voters' evaluation of the system. According to the TSE, 94 percent of voters polled positively evaluated the electronic voting system.

ELECTION DAY PROCEDURES

Poll workers are responsible for organizing polling on the Election Day. They are responsible for the equipment and reserve equipment. Civil society groups generally do not observe Election Day procedures. Political parties, in contrast, send representatives to polling places. This practice is not universal, as not all parties have the size and organization to observe elections widely. Larger parties are more likely to have widespread observer representation at polling stations.

At 7.30 a.m. on Election Day, the president of the precinct turns on the e-voting machine in front of representatives of the parties, as well as the other poll workers. The e-voting machine prints out a report, called "zeresima," which certifies the ballot box is empty, i.e. that there is no candidate with a pre-assigned number of votes. No other tests at this stage of elections are allowed. Consequently, no reports are made. According to the political parties, their representatives at the polling locations do not have the technical capacity to check the system properly during Election Day.

Close-out procedures for Election Day are as follows:

- At 5:00 p.m. on Election Day, the president of the precinct uses his or her password to close the voting machine and print a voting machine report for the precinct. This report contains: precinct's identification code; voting machine's identification code; number of voters who attended and voted; and total voting results for each candidate.

- Five copies of the report are printed. These five copies are signed by the president of the precinct and representatives and inspectors of political parties. One copy is displayed announcing the results of the precinct. Three copies are sent to the Electoral Committee. The last copy is delivered to the Political Parties Committee. If required, the machine can print out five additional copies that can be distributed to the district attorney of the political parties, representatives of the press and the public prosecution office. The copy delivered to the Political Parties Committee is extremely important, because it allows parties to check whether the data have been modified during transmission. Upon data reception, the TRE and the TSE send an electronic receipt to political parties.

- The voting machine program saves the data on a diskette in an encrypted format to prevent data modification. The diskette is delivered to the local electoral committee.[47]

In case of problems, each polling station has the additional reserve e-voting machines to replace the failed one. If no replacement voting machines are available, a paper ballot is used.

TABULATION

Once the polling is over and the polling place is closed, the data from the e-voting machine is then decrypted and uploaded with what is called a "guiding program." The process varies according to the type of election. In the case of municipal elections, the data is tabulated at the precinct of the municipality and transferred to the local TRE and the TSE. In the case of general elections, the data are read at the precinct that corresponds to the municipality and transmitted to the local TRE and to the TSE. The data on votes for the President of the Republic are added and announced by the TSE.

The entire system is ensured by a security infrastructure, which prevents data from being intentionally or unintentionally modified and/or deleted. The security of the system is comprised of the system audit program, which records

---

47 Interpreting the Trustworthiness of ICT--mediated Government. Lessons from Electronic Voting in Brazil

all transactions performed on the machine, and the system security program, which prevents any tampering with the voting machine, such as the removal of the diskette on which election votes are stored.

CHALLENGES AND RECOUNTS

Since the implementation of electronic voting, no recounts of the results have been carried out due to the lack of a VVPAT. As a consequence, there have been no successful challenges of election results, and there have been no recounts carried out in Brazil. In cases were candidates have challenged results and asked for a comprehensive audit of the vote, the TSE has responded that the candidate would have to pay over $1 million USD to fund such a recount.

DEBATES OVER VVPAT

As discussed, there have been several legislative attempts to introduce VVPAT to voting machines, but each attempt has been strongly opposed by the TSE, and legislation has either been repealed or the courts have suspended implementation. While civil society and political parties are generally supportive of using VVPAT, the TSE's opposition has thus far blocked the introduction of VVPAT. As of late 2012, there is a reform initiative by some deputes on VVPAT is in the Chamber of Deputies but, overall, there are not strong advocates for VVPAT in the legislature. Given the strong opposition of the TSE, this may mean VVPAT will not be implemented in the near term.

There are many reasons for opposition to the VVPAT, including the cost of introducing this mechanism; the damage that might be caused to the paper and printer in the heat and humidity of many places in the country; and the voter secrecy implications, given that the individual and unique number of each voter would be printed.

There is a small movement in support of VVPAT in the social media space. An example of this type of initiative is a movement created by Ana Prudente called "Beyond the Electronic, I Want my Vote Printed" (*Quero Meu Voto Impresso, Além do Eletrônico*). These initiatives are not very influential, but interviews with stakeholders indicate the issue of VVPAT will return to the agenda of the legislature.

POST-ELECTION AUDITS AND EVALUATION OF THE SYSTEM

After each election, the TSE conducts an evaluation of system performance, but they are not conducted by independent bodies. The TSE is responsible for evaluating the system. Stakeholders have no formal role in the evaluation process. No public reports about the evaluation of the system have been issued. Even the political parties are not given reports about the process of elections by the TSE.

LESSONS LEARNED

Key findings and lessons learned from Brazil's experience are summarized here. They are organized according to the key issues and considerations outlined in the Overview of this guidebook.

Legality

- Although Congress formally creates the rules governing elections, the TSE is by far the most powerful actor in designing legislation governing elections. Usually when Congress has passed legislation contrary to the preferences of the TSE, the TSE has successfully convinced Congress to repeal the legislation or convinced the Supreme Court to suspend it.

- The institutional structure of election management in Brazil makes it difficult for external actors to independently influence and evaluate the use electronic voting. This stems from the fact that the TSE both implements elections and adjudicates electoral disputes. This arrangement creates a clear conflict of interest, since the TSE's own actions are often involved in any disputes involving election technology. This problem is further exacerbated by the fact that the only judicial body higher than the TSE, the Supreme Court, is partly composed of ministers of the TSE. As a result of this institutional architecture, it is virtually impossible for outside actors to successfully challenge decisions made by the TSE through the legal system.

Accountability

- While the TSE has taken steps to make electronic voting accountable, these steps have not completely addressed issues of accountability.

- Robust forms of external auditing and evaluations are not provided. Opportunities to examine the source code or other aspects of the system are highly controlled and, given the complexity of the system, insufficient time is given for adequate vetting of the code and related systems.

- There is no practical way for political parties or candidates to dispute election outcomes, primarily due to the lack of VVPAT. Despite repeated attempts of congressional actors to modify the system to include a VVPAT, the TSE has successfully resisted such changes.

- Given these factors, some stakeholders have pointed out that greater access for non-governmental actors to examine or audit source codes would be beneficial for the election process in Brazil, and would enhance accountability of electronic voting.

Security and Secrecy

- In comparison to the paper ballot system, where fraud was relatively widespread, electronic voting has substantially improved the integrity of the vote count. The vast majority of electorate and political elites view the system as reliable and trustworthy, although there are some exceptions, particularly in the academic community.

- However, the limits placed by the TSE on full audits of the source code, equipment, and election outcomes breed distrust amongst academics and civil society groups interested in government transparency.

- Critics of the system have pointed out several potential flaws with the encryption and software verification mechanisms, but the TSE rarely responds to these criticisms directly, which lowers trust in the system among interested parties.

- Most of the TSE's security efforts are aimed at protecting against an external attacker. Critics of the system argue that an internal attacker is also possible and that the TSE has not adequately described safeguards against such an attack.

- The voter verification system is linked to the voting machine, which is against international best practices. Congress attempted to sever this link through a change in the law, but the TSE succeeded in convincing the Supreme Court to suspend the law. The TSE argues the link is necessary to prevent voters from voting multiple times.

Transparency

- While the TSE states it is transparent during some parts of the electoral process, this is not always sufficient in meeting international best practices and gaining the trust and confidence of key stakeholders.

- In some cases, transparency was restricted because of sensitivity and secrecy of information, particularly with regard to access source code.

When external parties have access to the source code, basic tools used to test and search the code are not permitted.

- Most importantly, no independent observers are allowed to observe the electoral processes in Brazil. Civil society organizations have to work through political parties to gain accreditation as observers. Only the OAB has access as an independent organization, but it claims it does not have sufficient expertise to assess the processes fully.

- In the experience of Brazil, there are no challenges and recounts carried out, as there is no VVPAT. Even though the trust of citizens and political parties in the system is very high, this does not guarantee a fully accountable process.

- The vast majority of non-governmental interviewees recognize the need of VVPAT for Brazil elections and there have been legislative attempts to introduce VVPAT.

Sustainability

- Since 1996, Brazil began implementation of electronic voting in a staged manner. Beginning in 2000, all elections have been fully electronic and EVMs are accepted by all stakeholders.

- Since 1996, the country has built over 16 years of experience in electronic voting and, as a result, has very few problems associated with EVMs. Error rates are very low; although some modifications were made, the same basic system adopted in 1996 is still in use.

Inclusiveness

- The development of electronic voting in Brazil was somewhat inclusive in 1996, and involved input from technology experts and vendors; it still lacks sufficient input from non-State actors.

- The voter education in Brazil seems to be effective, as polls show that voters have sufficient levels of information on the electoral system and on usage of electronic voting machines, and electronic voting retains widespread support among Brazilian voters.

- Electronic voting has greatly improved inclusiveness for low literacy voters. After the adoption of electronic voting, the fraction of blank and invalid votes has dropped dramatically, as the new system has proven easier to use than the paper ballot system.

Trust

- Most parties and voters trust the electronic voting system and rate it highly, particularly the fact that it produces results quickly and reduces uncertainty over election outcomes.

- A few political parties, civil society activists and members of academia view the TSE as too closed and unaccountable. This distrust stems mainly from the fact that attempted reforms to introduce voter verifiability have been blocked by the TSE. Highly-restricted access to the electronic voting source code also contributes to this mistrust.

- A range of stakeholders, including civil society activists and academics, contend the TSE would be well-served to open up the electronic voting process for further auditability, and explore ways VVPAT can be introduced in a cost-effective manner.

CASE STUDY REPORT ON ELECTRONIC VOTING IN THE NETHERLANDS

BACKGROUND

Electronic voting has a long history in the Netherlands. In the 1960s, the Secretary of the Electoral Council was fascinated by the mechanical voting machines used in the United States, and convinced the Ministry of Interior (MoI) to allow for their use. On November 25, 1965, a new version of the Electoral Law was implemented that regulated the use of voting machines by the local authority in pre-assigned polling stations.

The MoI and Kingdom Relations (MOIKR)[48] is responsible for the overall framework of elections in the Netherlands, including developing the legislation. At the same time, the Netherlands has a decentralized system and the municipalities (currently over 400) have the responsibility for conduct of elections. Accordingly, while the ministry was responsible for ensuring proper regulation of voting machines, it was at the municipal level that decisions were made on adopting new technology. The Electoral Council also serves as an advisory body to the ministry on election-related issues and conducts vote tabulation in national elections.

---

[48] The name of the ministry used to be "Interior" only; in 1998 "Kingdom Relations" was added.

Thirteen local authorities introduced American mechanical voting machines for provincial elections in March 1966. This did not go well, as there were an abnormal number of blank votes due to the fact that machines were introduced hastily and voters were not made aware of the change.

Subsequently, the Dutch decided to design their own voting machines, and the Minister of Interior requested an Order in Council on rules for the approval of voting machines in 1968. It asked the Dutch Organization for Applied Scientific Research (*Toegepast Natuurwetenschappelijk Onderzoek,* TNO) together with Samson Kantoor Efficiency to develop a design for an electronic voting machine. The Dutch Apparatus Factory (*Nederlandse Apparaten Fabriek* NV, NEDAP) was asked to build a machine based on this design. A few years later, NEDAP began not only producing the voting machines, but also designing and developing them. By the end of the 1980s, 1,200 voting machines were in use in 60 local authorities.

This initial development of the machines set a precedent; TNO and NEDAP were in control of the situation regarding voting machines and made most decisions regarding their development. Neither the Electoral Council nor the MoI set any requirements for them.

In the late 1980s, the first electronic voting machines appeared, and by the mid-1990s their use in Dutch elections was widespread. The machines appealed to local authorities, as they were seen to reduce mistakes in the process, decreased the number of staff needed for the vote count and made the release of results much quicker. There was no public or political debate regarding the early introduction of mechanical or electronic voting machines, and they appeared to be popular with voters. The only concern raised was whether elderly voters might be discouraged from voting as a result of the adoption of technology.

LEGAL FRAMEWORK

From the early introduction of voting machines in the Netherlands, their regulation in law remained limited. In 1989, the Electoral Code was revised thoroughly; however, there were still few references to electronic voting. The code explicitly stated local authorities could decide if voting means other than ballot papers are used, that this was only allowed with technical appliances approved by the MoI, and other rules would be determined in the Electoral Decree, although they were never elaborated.

One paragraph of the code (Article J33, Paragraph 2) listed requirements for the "approved technical appliance," including: secrecy of the vote needed to be guaranteed; the appliance had to be well-made; the voter had to be able to operate it easily; the candidate lists, their assigned number and the name of the political groups needed to be mentioned clearly; and the voter only had the possibility to vote once and had the opportunity to correct a mistake.

Later in 1989, the State Secretary produced a Ministerial Regulation for the Approval of Voting Machines, but the document was process-oriented and did not include any additional requirements or standards for voting machines. The MoI and the Electoral Council lacked technical knowledge to determine clear requirements regarding functionality, integrality and security of the voting machines.

By 1990, the Electoral Council and the MoI realized the regulation of voting machines was not adequate. For the next seven years a working group was convened to discuss new regulation requirements and approval of voting machines. The working group consisted of members of the MoI, the Electoral Council, TNO, representatives of local authorities and the Expertise Centre, which included HEC, a consultancy agency dealing with public administration/ICT issues. The MoI and the Electoral Council depended heavily on TNO and HEC for their technical knowledge.

TNO drafted a final concept of the technical text of the new regulation in September 1990, including requirements for the software to be reliable, clearly written and not changed or influenced. However, while voting machines informally had to comply with the TNO report from its date of publication, it was not until 1997 that the regulation was approved. It still did not require any security features or address the possibility of manipulation. No requirement for a paper trail was included, as the State Secretary explained, "one can assume that the print out of a voting machine with the voting results is the same as the votes that were cast on the voting machine, so that afterwards there is no need to check the votes cast."[49]

During the working group's deliberations, a lengthy discussion opened about the possibility of phased voting – a possible solution for increasing the number of political parties and candidates per party in elections. The Minister sent a letter to Parliament in March 1996 granting permission for the option. NEDAP stood alone in its opposition to phased voting, as its machines at the time did not have the capacity to process votes in this way. This opened the possibility for other suppliers, and was the starting point for the company VUGA (later SDU) to start developing voting computers. However, NEDAP remained the primary supplier, with 95 percent of the market.

CERTIFICATION

In 1997, the Regulation on Requirements and Approval of Voting Machines came into force, which dealt with approval of the use of voting machines by the MoI. The supplier first needed to receive the approval of the Minister on a prototype of the voting machine. Approval was granted on the basis of a statement from an acknowledged certification office, which checked whether the prototype met the requirements as set out in the Electoral Code, the Electoral

---

[49] Staatsblad 1997, pgs. 164 and 297, Besluit tot wijziging van de bepalingen van het Kiesbesluit inzake stemmen door middel van elektronische stemmachines (Decision to amend the regulation on voting by electronic voting machines).

Decree and the appendix to the 1997 regulation. The Minister did not officially receive any certification reports, and they were not publicly available.

To receive approval to actually use the voting machines, the supplier provided the certification office with 10 voting machines (of which the certification office chose one), so it could be determined whether the voting machines resembled the prototype and the conditions under which it was tested. The decision to approve a voting machine was to be published in the *State Gazette*. The supplier was then required to make available, at least once every four years, 10 voting machines, out of which the certification office would choose one, so it could be examined periodically.

The required technical specifications were detailed in an appendix to the regulation. The accreditation office was required to check whether, based on a list from the supplier, the software had been installed in the machines and whether the software did what it was supposed to do. However, NEDAP had successfully lobbied to exclude the part of the software that was used to program the political party lists and the candidates on the voting machine from the certification process. The source code used for all voting machines and computers was closed software owned by the suppliers. No review by other external actors was allowed. Due to these restrictions, it is unclear if a comprehensive check of the complete source code of all software was ever conducted by the certification office.

Not all of the requirements laid down in the Electoral Code, such as secrecy of the vote or readability of the screen, were elaborated in the regulation. Rules regarding storage, transport and security of the voting machines were also lacking. One month after the regulation came into force, TNO (now called *TNO Centrum voor Evaluatie van Instrumentatie en Beveiligingstechniek*), which assisted in the drafting of the Regulation, was appointed by the minister as the only certification office.

Following the regulation's adoption, different ministers conducted research into the possibilities of recounts and certification, due to minor errors in tabulation software and some limited discussions about these two issues in the media. However, no changes were made until the State Secretary Bijleveld-Schouten withdrew the Regulation on Requirements and Approval Voting Machines in February 2008.

The MoI was responsible for the proper conduct of the election process, and the directorate of Constitutional Affairs and Legislation was responsible for overseeing the regulation of voting machines throughout their development. However, these civil servants, whose expertise was in constitutional and electoral law, lacked the knowledge to deal with the technological aspects of the voting machines. No additional personnel with technical background were recruited. As a result, the suppliers played a large role in deciding which equipment was used, how legislation was written and which parts of the electoral process was part of the certification process.

CONCERNS ABOUT ELECTRONIC VOTING

By the late 1990s, 95 percent of voters were using voting machines. Voters were generally familiar with the machines that had been used for many years, so local authorities did not need to provide much additional voter education. Local authorities were responsible for ensuring accessible voting facilities were provided for persons with disabilities. Polling staff (many of whom were from political parties) received training from local authorities on the procedures and functioning of voting machines. Only minor problems were encountered on Election Day – local authorities had spare machines in case of machine break down, as well as batteries in case of power failure. Technical staff was distributed throughout the country with back-up equipment. They could be reached via telephone if their support was needed.

Because the voting machines were widely seen to work well, few questions were ever raised about their security or compliance with international standards. Still, concerns were raised on several occasions, particularly by the Electoral Council and in Parliament.

The Electoral Council's concerns focused on the lack of any kind of testing or certification for the tabulation software, as well as the Integral Voting System (*Integraal Stem Systeem*[50]) that was offered as a package to local authorities by NEDAP/Groendaal. While the Electoral Council advised the responsible minister on several occasions to introduce a certification procedure for the tabulation software, no action was ever taken by the MOIKR, as it was not considered a priority. In March 2003, the Electoral Council wrote a letter to the minister detailing certain mistakes in the tabulation software that had been discovered during elections in 2002 and 2003 and emphasized the lack of control mechanisms.

Questions were first raised in Parliament in March 1998, after some issues had arisen regarding tabulation and recounting during the local elections. Then, the media raised questions during the May 1998 parliamentary election about the lack of a recount using electronic voting machines. The State Secretary requested an opinion of the Electoral Council on the issues of tabulation and recounts, and expressed his concern about the near monopoly position of NEDAP/Groendaal in the tabulation process. The Electoral Council recommended a review, and, as a result, the ministry created a sub-commission, which included representatives of the HEC, the Electoral Council and the MOIKR. The sub-commission published its report, written by the HEC, in May 1999. The report stressed that calculation errors sometimes appeared in the tabulation software and that only the supplier had access to the source code. It recommended that a certification procedure be created for the tabulation software. While the minister

---

50 This system supports the voting machine software and contains a complete set of all political parties and lists of candidates. It also calculates and tabulates the results.

addressed these issues to the Parliament in September 1999, and his proposals received initial support from political parties, no action was taken to follow up on the issues by the Parliament or the MOIKR.

Questions again were raised in 2004 in Parliament because of concerns in Ireland regarding the reliability and security of the NEDAP machines purchased there. The Minister responded that "In the Netherlands, a lot of attention has always been paid to the reliability of these voting machines."[51] The Irish government subsequently decided not to use the machines for the 2004 European Parliamentary elections, but the Dutch Parliament did not take any further action. Questions raised in Parliament in August 2005 regarding the lack of a possibility for a recount were similarly discounted.

OPPOSITION TO ELECTRONIC VOTING

In July 2006, the campaign "We do not Trust Voting Computers" was initiated by Rop Gonggrijp, founder of the first Internet provider in the Netherlands, and a number of other computer experts.[52] The group started its campaign following the March 2006 municipal elections, when electronic voting machines were introduced in Amsterdam for the first time. Although the vast majority of municipalities in the Netherlands used electronic voting machines by this time, Amsterdam had long remained one of the few that still used traditional pencil and paper voting.

The initiators of "We do not Trust Voting Computers" were concerned about the security of the electronic voting machines in use and their lack of auditability. The group sought to publicize their concerns and generate public debate about their use. The campaign set up a website (http://wijvertrouwenstemcomputersniet.nl) and sought to further investigate the use of electronic voting computers through a series of State freedom of information requests.

---

51 TK 2003-2004, Aanhangsel van de Handelingen, nr. 1453
52 The group established itself as a non-partisan foundation on 29 August 2006.

Both the Amsterdam City Council and the MOIKR responded to the freedom of information requests, providing copious documentation about the electronic voting systems, which the campaign posted on their website in late July 2006. The documents revealed several serious security flaws in the systems, as well as demonstrating the extent to which the government had outsourced the election process to equipment suppliers.

Although the campaign generated a certain amount of media interest from the start, the publication of documents and the reaction to it by the technology suppliers brought increased media interest and coverage. SDU accused the campaign of disclosing confidential documents and pursued legal action (ultimately unsuccessful) to remove the documents from the website. NEDAP similarly criticized the actions of the group, accusing it of a conspiracy and assuring the public that voting machines are extensively tested. TNO also protested against the freedom of information request, and, in particular, the publication of its testing reports of the voting machines, which it said contained confidential information.

The first public reaction from the MOIKR came in late September 2006, following the broadcast of an investigative report on the TV channel TROS RADAR, which raised questions about the security of voting machines. The MOIKR released a statement assuring the public of the security of voting machines and announcing that additional safeguards would be put in place prior to the general elections, including sealing of voting machines, extra protection of the software and extra checking of the software by TNO.

In early October, "We do not Trust Voting Computers" released a security analysis,[53] detailing the findings of independent computer experts who bought two NEDAP ESB3 voting machines from a city council and investigated the machines vulnerabilities for five weeks' time. These findings were highlighted and

---

53 Gonggrijp, Rop, et al., "Nedap/Groenendaal ES3B voting computer: a security analysis", available at http://wijvertrouwenstemcomputersniet.nl/English.

widely publicized in an investigative news report broadcast on national Dutch television.[54] The 17-minute broadcast shows how experts were able to replace a memory chip in the voting machine in less than five minutes that allowed them to manipulate the results of an election. The program raised serious questions also about the system's complete lack of security safeguards and the lack of physical security of the machines while in storage and during transport. The program also questioned the testing of the voting machines by TNO, as TNO only tested one voting machine (out of 8,000) every four years, and did no security testing. Finally, the broadcast showed experts playing chess on the voting machine, having reconfigured the computer for this purpose to demonstrate that the voting machine was an ordinary computer.

The accompanying written security analysis demonstrated the security vulnerabilities of the NEDAP ESB3 and detailed several possible ways to attack the system. Such attacks included the ability to compromise secrecy of the vote through the detection of radio emissions outside of a polling station. According to the experts, a relatively simple radio device could be used for this purpose. The analysis concluded that, given the vulnerabilities of the system, the NEDAP ESB3 could not be made to meet any responsible security criteria and should not be used for Dutch elections. It further concluded that the Dutch legal requirements, which the NEDAP ESB3 met, did not consider any security issues and were insufficient for regulating the use of electronic voting machines.

REACTIONS TO CONCERNS

The government responded quickly to the vulnerabilities identified by "We do not Trust Voting Computers." MOIKR Minister Atzo Nicolaï announced a number of ad hoc measures for strengthening the security of voting machines and requested Dutch intelligence service AIVD, the General Intelligence and Security Service, to conduct independent testing of the voting machines.

---

54 Dutch TV-news program EénVandaag, see video clip at: www.veoh.com/watch/v505707dgewqMsB

Short-term measures for strengthening the security of the voting machines prior to the November general elections included replacing memory chips with non-reprogrammable ones, sealing all of the machines and improvements to physical security procedures. These were proposed by the government and approved by the Parliament.

Testing by AIVD discovered the possibility for intercepting radio emissions from the NEDAP machines and compromising secrecy of the vote to be relatively remote, and identified an easy solution – the removal of diacritical marks from the names of political parties. Three out of the four types of the NEDAP voting machines passed the test. Because the fourth type was no longer used, the minister felt it was not necessary to withdraw approval for the NEDAP machines. However, the AIVD also tested the SDU machines and found a more serious problem related to intercepting radio emissions. The voting computer used a different signal per candidates list, which could be recorded at a distance of tens of meters. AIVD determined the SDU machines, therefore, were not adequately secure for use in the elections.

In reaction to the AIVD findings, Minister Nicolaï withdrew his approval for the SDU machines on October 30, just three weeks prior to the elections. One-thousand and two-hundred voting machines were affected by the decision. Several large cities had to either revert to pencil and paper voting, as Amsterdam did, or switch to the NEDAP machines.

At the same time, Parliament requested the government to establish two independent commissions after the elections to consider the past and future of electronic voting.

COMMISSIONS OF INQUIRY

Following the November 2006 general elections, two commissions of independent experts on electronic voting were established by Minister Nicolaï. The first, The Voting Machines Decision-making Commission, was set up on December 19, 2006. Its purpose was to review how decisions on the approval of voting machines had been made in the past, and what lessons could be learned. The second, the Election Process Advisory Commission, was established on January 18, 2007, to examine the current organization of the election process and make proposals for future elections in the Netherlands.

The Voting Machines Decision-making Commission was chaired by a high-level politician of the Liberal Party (VVD) and included a professor of public administration who specialized in public/private issues. The Election Process Advisory Commission was chaired by Honorary Minister F. Korthals Altes and was composed of five additional members drawn from academia, the private sector and public administration.

The Voting Machines Decision-making Commission published its report *Voting Machines: an Orphaned File* on April 16, 2007.[55] The report was critical of the government's past role in electronic voting, concluding that voting machines did not receive the attention they deserved. It found that the MOIKR did not have enough technical knowledge, leading to a situation in which officials became too dependent on external actors for the conduct of elections. In this situation, technology vendors became part of the decision making process and the ministry was not in a position to exercise effective oversight. It also criticized the government for not reacting to signals that should have caused concern, including the critical report on NEDAP voting machines that was released in Ireland in 2004.

---

55 Report available in Dutch at www.rijksoverheid.nl/documenten-enpublicaties/rapporten/2007/04/17/stemmachines-een-verweesd-dossier.html

The Voting Machines Decision-making Commission was also critical of the laboratory TNO's role in the certification and testing process, finding they were certifying and testing the voting machines according to outdated standards that had not been updated to deal with modern IT and security threats. The certification and testing reports were not made public, depriving independent experts the opportunity to verify the analysis. The report was also critical of the legal framework, which did not deal adequately with the specificities of the electronic voting process, particularly the necessary security requirements.

The Election Process Advisory Commission released its report Voting with Confidence on September 23, 2007.[56] The report laid out a number of principles[57] that the commission believed should be safeguarded in the election process, and discussed the various methods of voting used in the Netherlands (i.e. paper ballots, electronic voting, postal voting, Internet voting, voting by telephone and proxy voting) in light of these principles.

The Election Process Advisory Commission noted, with particular concern, that requirements for election-related equipment had not been adequately established and that the security and management of the equipment were not properly regulated. It also noted that electronic voting machines in use were not sufficiently transparent and verifiable, as there is no way to determine that votes have been accurately recorded and/or stored. It further suggested that audits be conducted during elections to detect any errors or incidents related to the results and to learn lessons for the future.

The Election Process Advisory Commission concluded that voting at polling stations should be the main method of voting in the Netherlands, that each municipality should have the same method of voting and that voting by paper

---

56 Report available at http://wijvertrouwenstemcomputersniet.nl/English.
57 Transparency, verifiability, fairness, eligibility to vote, free suffrage, secret suffrage, equal suffrage and accessibility. These principles are enshrined in the Dutch Constitution or in international and European treaties and recommendations.

ballot is the preferable option, on the grounds of transparency and verifiability. However, given the problems caused by manual counting of the ballots, the commission investigated whether other electronic options would be feasible and still safeguard the principles. It suggested that a ballot printer and ballot counter could be feasible, as they would produce a paper ballot that could be checked by the voter. However, no such alternative electronic option has been adopted to date.

DECISION TO END ELECTRONIC VOTING

The government acted quickly in the wake of the release of the Commissions' reports. During the press conference in which the Voting with Confidence report was released on September 27, 2007, the State Secretary for the Interior announced that the 1997 Regulation for Approval of Voting Machines would be withdrawn.

"We do not trust voting computers" had filed an administrative law procedure against the approval of NEDAP machines with the District Court of Amsterdam in March 2007. On October 1, 2007, the District Court decertified all NEDAP computers in use in the Netherlands as a result of the judicial procedure. With the approval of SDU voting machines already withdrawn, this decision left no voting machines certified for use in the Netherlands. On October 21, 2007, the 1997 Regulation for Approval of Voting Machines was officially withdrawn by Parliament, and the Decree of October 19, 1989 was amended, taking out the provisions that gave the minister responsibility for new regulations on approving voting machines. This legislative action removed the possibility to certify any new voting machines.

NEDAP filed an appeal against the decertification order of the District Court and also lodged a complaint with the MOIKR against the withdrawal of the 1997 regulation. However, these appeals were ultimately unsuccessful.

The MOIKR decided, based on the recommendations from the two advisory commissions, that use of paper ballots is preferred. However, several specific groups of society face challenges using paper ballots. Therefore, the MOIKR is currently conducting research into a new ballot design. The purpose of this new design is to facilitate voting by voters who are blind or have visual impairments, assist voters challenged by the Dutch language, provide the possibility to send the ballot electronically to voters living and working abroad and to facilitate counting of the ballots, possibly by the use of technology. At the moment, testing of several new designs of ballot papers is being conducted and new legislation for the use of the new design is being prepared.

LESSONS LEARNED

- The Dutch legal framework was inadequate to effectively regulate the development and use of voting machines, especially regarding security safeguards, the certification process and tabulation software.

- In the absence of a strong regulatory framework, suppliers failed to update technology in line with modern security requirements, making the voting machines vulnerable to internal and external security threats, as well as criticism.

- The MOIKR lacked the technical expertise necessary to fulfill its responsibility to oversee the conduct of elections, and as a result, suppliers had too much control over the process.

- Civil society, media and independent IT experts were absent from the decision making process on voting machines, and virtually no transparency mechanisms were provided at any stage in the process.

- The ministry ignored signs on several occasions that there were problems with the voting machines, including when problems were discovered with similar machines in Ireland and when the Electoral Council raised issues.

- Political parties and other stakeholders did not pay adequate attention to the integrity and security of the voting system, as they had a very high degree of trust in it, as well as in the election authorities.

- With only a few people involved in the effort, "We do not Trust Voting Computers" mounted an extremely effective advocacy campaign using freedom of information legislation and the media. This demonstrates that, in some contexts, civil society activists and other oversight actors can have significant influence if they engage actively, are well-informed, and provide credible, well-supported arguments.

- The Voting Machines Decision-making Commission and the Election Process Advisory Commission provided an objective, prompt review of the election process, which, based on the above lessons learned, should have been conducted much earlier.

CASE STUDY REPORT ON THE PHILIPPINES 2010 ELECTIONS[58]

INTRODUCTION

IFES and NDI conducted case study research in the Philippines to examine the country's experience and lessons learned from the use of electronic counting technologies in its elections.[59] This study focuses primarily on the experiences and processes surrounding the Philippines' May 2010 elections, while the election commission went through the decision making process in moving to electronic technologies prior to 2010. The Philippines began the process of moving toward electronic technologies for elections in the 1990s. After a series of small pilots, electronic counting technology was introduced nationwide for the May 10, 2010 elections. This transition presented an enormous challenge to the country. Approximately 50 million registered voters

---

58 This case study focused on the transition to electronic counting and use these technologies in the 2010 elections. For this reason, and because it was conducted before the May 2013 elections, the study does not take into account the May 13, 2013 general elections, in which voters elected 12 senators (half of the Senate), all 229 district members of the House of Representatives and local and gubernatorial positions.

59 The case study combined desk research of primary source documents and reports with nearly 30 key informant interviews with 45 individuals in Manila from May 21-28, 2012. The interviewees included current and former representatives of electoral management bodies, advisory committees, government, political parties, former candidates, nonpartisan citizen election observation groups, information technology (IT) experts, polling firms and media.

spread over approximately 2,000 inhabited islands had the opportunity to participate in the polls. The elections involved more than 85,000 candidates for more than 17,000 national (President, Vice President, House of Representatives and Senate) and local positions. The lessons drawn from the 2010 experience not only inform future efforts in the Philippines, but are relevant for other countries considering or implementing electronic voting and counting technologies.

CHOOSING TO ADOPT ELECTRONIC TECHNOLOGIES

The transition to electronic technologies in the Philippines' elections was the product of a long and arduous process that started in 1992, but was not fully implemented until 2010. It began when the Commission on Elections (COMELEC)[60] adopted its strategic plan, which called for the modernization of the electoral process. Subsequent studies conducted by two international consultants gave further impetus to automate elections. The primary reason cited for moving to electronic technologies was to reduce the time for counting and tabulation. In previous elections, counting lasted as long as 18 hours in each polling station, and tabulation could take up to 40 days. This caused anxiety among the public and political contestants, increasing the risk of election-related violence and reducing confidence in the electoral process. Other reasons for the change were an intention to reduce fraud and errors in counting and canvassing results.

Within one year from the adoption of its strategic plan, the commission constituted a team to study available technologies, which at that time included optical mark recognition (OMR), punch card and direct recording electronic (DRE) systems. In 1995, the first election automation law was passed, authorizing the

---

60 The COMELEC has authority over virtually every aspect of the electoral process, including creating procedures and regulations; administering all election laws and regulations; regulating campaign finance; registering parties and civil society organizations that seek to participate in elections; and managing the resources of all State institutions assisting in conducting elections.

COMELEC to conduct a nationwide demonstration of an electronic election system and to pilot-test it in the March 1996 regional elections in the Autonomous Region in Muslim Mindanao (ARMM). Following its perceived success, in 1977 Congress enacted the Election Modernization Act that mandated the COMELEC to use an automated election system (AES) for the process of voting, counting votes and canvassing/consolidating the results of the national and local elections.[61]

For various reasons ranging from late allotment of funds and time constraints, to the invalidation of contracts to supply the machines, the 1998, 2001, 2004 and 2007 national elections remained manual. The COMELEC, however, was able to automate the 2008 regional polls in the ARMM using DRE machines in some locations and OMR technology in others, for the purpose of determining the most suitable system for nationwide use in 2010.

BUILDING THE ELECTRONIC COUNTING SYSTEM

National Standards; Legal and Procedural Framework

The Election Modernization Act, which amends certain sections of the Philippines Omnibus Election Code, provides the legislative framework and standards for the use of an automated election system.[62] The legislation was developed with input from relevant civil society organizations, including citizen election observation groups such as the National Citizens' Movement for Free Elections (NAMFREL), which was primarily gathered through technical working groups set up in the two legislative chambers. In practice, there were some elements of the law that were not consistent with the move to automation. However, most stakeholders noted that the law generally provided a solid legal foundation upon which to conduct automated elections.

---

61 Republic Act 8436, Election Modernization Act of 1997.
62 Ibid.

In preparation for the May 2010 elections, the COMELEC issued general instructions (GIs) for its precinct-level poll workers (Board of Election Inspectors, or BEI) on implementing voting and counting processes, as well as the transmission of results.[63] Other procedures, including rules of procedure for resolving disputes arising from automated elections,[64] were promulgated by the COMELEC.

In addition, several governmental bodies were established to provide advice, oversight and technical assistance to COMELEC throughout the development, preparation and conduct of electoral processes.

The COMELEC Advisory Council (CAC) – which consists of nine members from government, academia, the ICT field and civil society – was tasked with recommending the technology, identifying potential issues, participating in the procurement process and conducting an evaluation of the AES after its use. The Technical Evaluation Committee (TEC) – which consisted of leaders from government, industry and civil society – was established to certify categorically that the AES, including its hardware and software components, was operating properly, securely and accurately. Two legislative committees, the House Committee on Suffrage and Electoral Reforms and the Joint Congressional Oversight Committee on the Automated Election System, provided legal oversight for the electronic counting system. The Joint Congressional Oversight Committee is responsible for assessing strengths and weaknesses of electoral technologies and which electoral processes are suitable for such technologies.

Design Requirements and Selection of Technology

Five technologies were considered and evaluated for the nationwide automation of the 2010 general elections: DRE, the OMR-based precinct count optic scan (PCOS), central count optical scan (CCOS), open election system and

---

63 COMELEC Resolution No. 8786
64 COMELEC Resolution No. 8804 -In Re: COMELEC Rules of Procedure on Disputes In An Automated Election System in Connection with the May 10, 2010 Elections.

botong pinoy.[65] They were evaluated based on accuracy, speed, cost, security, transparency, proven technology, auditability, ballot security and as an end-to-end solution. The CAC advised the COMELEC to use either DRE or PCOS, subject to budget considerations, and CCOS technology for all areas not covered by DRE or PCOS technology.

Several civil society groups contended that more independent voices should have been involved in the decision, and that very few people making the decisions had enough familiarity with the technology. Representatives from the IT community on the CAC were not permitted to participate in developing recommendations on the selection of the technology, as it was seen by the COMELEC as a conflict of interest if they were to become bidders. Other IT experts outside the CAC tried to submit their recommendations, but the COMELEC instead encouraged them to submit bids during procurement.

Ultimately, the COMELEC chose PCOS in part to findings from the 2008 pilot of PCOS and DRE machines in the ARMM. Another consideration was cost, which also favored the use of PCOS over DRE machines. The electronic counting system that was implemented for the 2010 elections consisted of an election management system (EMS); PCOS system; and a consolidation/canvassing system (CCS), detailed as follows:

- The EMS is used to create all base components of an election definition. The application makes the needed associations of offices, candidates, parties and contests to create the election. The EMS outputs data files that are used to customize each CCS within the voting system, as well as creating output files that contain the data needed by the election event designer (EED) to create the election's ballot styles, compact flash-memory cards and iButtons with unique digital signatures used by poll workers to access the PCOS machines.

---

65 OES and botong pinoy are locally-developed computerized voting systems.

- The PCOS is the ballot/vote counting device based on OMR technology. Each PCOS is supposed to be customized with a compact flash (memory) card and an iButton, so that only ballots specific to the particular polling place can be successfully scanned. Ballots are scanned through the PCOS, which reads the markings made by the voter onto the ballot and interprets the positions of the markings on the ballot. When the polls close, the PCOS prints reports indicating the number of votes for each candidate on the ballot and transmits the results to the appropriate municipal CCS.

- The CCS is the application that accumulates and tallies the vote data from the individual PCOS devices and generates results reports. The CCS is implemented at the municipal level, the provincial level, the national level and the central server level. At the municipal level, the CCS accumulates the votes and generates results for that level, then creates and transmits provincial and national level results to the provincial level CCS. At the provincial level, the CCS accumulates the votes and generates results for that level, then creates and transmits national results to the national level. At the central level server, the CCS receives all results from the different reporting levels.

Procurement Process

The COMELEC solicited bids for components of the AES, as well as the project management and electronic transmission of results. For developing the terms of reference (TOR) and request for proposals (RFP), the CAC members (with the exception of IT community representatives) submitted their final recommendations, which were incorporated into the final TOR/RFP. For the bidding and selection process, a Special Bids and Awards Committee (SBAC) was created. The CAC participated as nonvoting members of the SBAC, but representatives from the IT community were again not allowed to participate due to conflict of interest.

Seven technology providers/consortia submitted bids. All bidders were initially disqualified by the SBAC. The CAC and several other stakeholders interviewed believed ambiguities in the TOR and the strict interpretation of the RFP by the SBAC nearly caused the process to break down. After reevaluation, three bidders qualified for further evaluation of their proposals. Eventually, the only bid declared compliant with the technical and financial specifications was the joint venture Dutch/Venezuelan company Smartmatic, working in partnership with the Philippine company Total Information Management.

Immediately after the award of the contract, and while preparations were ongoing, cases were filed against the COMELEC and the vendor to enjoin them from implementing the automation project. Although the Supreme Court eventually ruled for the COMELEC, the latter's decision to wait for the court's decision even in the absence of a restraining order, caused a delay of two months, shortening the timeline for preparing for and administering elections.

While many praised the procurement process for its transparency, a number of observers reported shortcomings. Of the 16.5 billion PHP total cost of the 2010 elections, only 7.2 billion PHP were subjected to competitive bidding, while the remainder was procured through negotiated contracts that were less transparent. This included separate contracts issued to Smartmatic for ballot boxes and the transportation of ballots and PCOS machines to all polling centers. Additionally, CenPeg, the Legal Network for Truthful Elections (LENTE), The Carter Center and other election observation groups reported that, despite multiple requests, the COMELEC did not provide access to complete documentation of the contract between COMELEC and Smartmatic.[66] This impeded the ability of stakeholders to assess the contractual obligations between the two entities and whether these obligations were fulfilled, which was later the subject of a Supreme Court case filed by civil society groups.

---

66 Namely, annexes specifying the list of goods and services to be provided by Smartmatic.

Production, Printing and Delivery

Printing of ballots was completed on time, but was an extremely rushed process. According to some interviewees, a two-month delay in the printing process occurred because the COMELEC extended the deadline for filing of certificates of candidacy, and printing could not commence before the deadline had passed. Others noted the vendor belatedly provided the necessary printers to complete the job on time. Due to the need to print ballots at a higher speed, the UV ink security feature was sacrificed to meet the deadline. Election observer groups and parties had the right to observe the printing process, and some took advantage of this right.

The vendor, Smartmatic, was able to deliver all the PCOS machines days before its deadline.

Certification, Source Code Review and Testing

The TEC was responsible for certifying the AES was operating properly, securely and accurately. Certification was to be done through an established international certification entity. SysTest Lab, a Colorado-based independent testing authority, was awarded the certification contract. SysTest audited the source codes of the following: PCOS firmware, election management system applications, CCS applications and other utilities. Because no independent observation groups or parties took part in a source code review, the certification became even more important. SysTest was unable to complete the certificate within the deadline prescribed by law. The certification was eventually issued two months before the elections. SysTest found the system was acceptable to conduct elections in the Philippines, but reported a number of deficiencies. While several election observation groups requested the certification review be made public, copies of the review were made public at a late date, and were released by senatorial candidate Joey de Venecia, not the COMELEC.

The law also mandates the COMELEC to promptly make the source code available and open to any interested political party or group to conduct its own review. The COMELEC, however, regulated access to the source code, citing security and intellectual property rights concerns. It provided a room within its headquarters with two computer terminals where interested parties could inspect the code on a read-only basis with the guidance of a Smartmatic technician. Those reviewing the source code would also need to sign a non-disclosure agreement. IT and civil society groups chose not to evaluate the source code, rejecting these limitations as too restrictive. They also noted the code was only made available in pieces. Political parties did not review the source code. Some parties acknowledged in retrospect that they did not grasp the importance of the review, and may not have had the capacity to review the source code effectively.

Due to the source code restrictions imposed by the COMELEC, a case was filed against it. The Supreme Court issued a ruling after the election directing the COMELEC to provide access to the petitioning civil society group, CenPeg. According to the Supreme Court, COMELEC "has offered no reason not to comply with this requirement of the law." After years of court battles as well as negotiations between the COMELEC and Dominion Voting Systems, which owns the source code, the COMELEC offered the source code for public review on May 9, 2013, just four days before the May 13 general elections. Watchdog groups and some political parties commented that the source code release had come too late for a meaningful review.

Field tests were conducted about 3.5 months before the elections. Field testing was meant to identify and address problems relating to all aspects of the AES that included voting, transmission, counting and consolidation/canvassing. Further, the COMELEC staged mock elections wherein voters simulated the act of actual voting – verification, receipt of ballot, marking of ballot and scanning of ballot. The mock election used the final version of the election software to cover actual voting, counting, transmission of precinct results and consolidation of results from all canvassing levels. Some partisan poll watchers and nonpartisan observers observed field testing and mock elections.

Security

In its bidding documents and in the contract signed with the COMELEC, Smartmatic claimed the AES was equipped with multiple security mechanisms that included ultraviolet (UV) ink to recognize the authenticity of ballots: security marks printed on them; the digital signature of the Board of Inspectors to authenticate election results at each precinct; bar codes; COMELEC markings; and unique precinct-based numbers on the ballots to authenticate ballots. An interviewee from the IT Department of the COMELEC also reported the data on PCOS machines were encrypted with 128-level of encryption. The encryption key is held both by the vendor and the COMELEC. At the same time, he noted there could be a very small possibility to intercept transmitted data.

While a range of security features were initially planned, several of these features were not implemented or did not function as planned. Several election observation groups and IT experts alleged the range of security vulnerabilities exposed the system to possible manipulation, fraud and failure. Before Election Day, it was discovered that the PCOS machines failed to read the UV security marks. To address the problem, the COMELEC decided to disable the UV ink detection function of the PCOS in favor of handheld UV lamps/readers.[67] However, the UV lamps were not used on Election Day, due to a range of reported reasons, including late delivery and a lack of any training for BEIs on how and why to use them.

Similarly, the plan to use digital signatures from three different poll workers to close the polls and canvass and transmit results for a precinct was not implemented. BEIs did not receive a digital signature of their own. Instead,

---

[67] COMELEC incurred additional cost of more than USD $700,000 for purchasing 76,000 handheld UV readers.

the COMELEC decided to rely on the machine's own digital signature. Some groups, however, claimed investigations found PCOS machines did not have internal digital signatures. One interviewee pointed out that, in the absence of digital signatures, it would be difficult to identify and verify the source of transmitted results.

A console port at the back of the PCOS machines was also criticized by election observation groups, saying it was too easily accessible. The vendor claimed it was an output port, but IT experts said it could be used as an input port which, if connected to a gadget, would provide access to the machine and its operating system to someone intending to manipulate the results.

Recruitment and Training of Personnel

The transition to nationwide electronic counting technologies created the need for a range of new skill sets, which the COMELEC lacked at the start of the preparation. Its IT department was understaffed, while its field offices only had contractual IT workers that were assigned to help in voter registration. To address this problem, the vendor provided trainings to the IT Department, while basic trainings on the PCOS machines were given to a group of personnel who served as trainers of the poll workers.

The poll workers are ad hoc election workers, consisting mostly of public school teachers tasked by law to assist the voting process during elections.[68] The amended election automation law requires at least one of the three members of the BEI to be an IT-capable person, as certified by the Department of Science and Technology (DOST).[69] Interviews with COMELEC staff, however, revealed lessons learned from the training process. There were not enough PCOS machines for use during the trainings, so many trainings were conduct-

---

68 The BEI is composed of chairman, poll clerk, and a third member, each having a vital role in the election proceedings.
69 A BEI receives his/her certification after successfully passing the written and practical exams given by the DOST.

ed without hands-on exercises. Trainings and accompanying materials, such as manuals, were delayed due to significant postponements in finalizing general instructions for conducting elections. Training focused heavily – almost exclusively – on the new technology and operating the PCOS machines. BEIs were not trained on how to conduct the electoral process more broadly, such as managing voter flow and authenticating voters. As discussed, this led to disorganization and inefficient processing of voters on Election Day, which contributed to long lines. In addition, several election officers interviewed recommended that future BEI trainings last longer than one day.

The vendor recruited, trained and provided approximately 45,000 PCOS technicians that were deployed in all precincts to assist the BEIs and address problems that might emerge. Most of the election officers that were interviewed, however, criticized technicians for being ineffective.

IMPLEMENTING E-COUNTING

Project and Risk Management

The COMELEC created a project management office (PMO) to manage the implementation of the different components of the AES. It included heads of different departments in the commission, including operations, administrative, human resources, legal, IT and voter education and planning, among others. The Executive Director headed the office.[70] However, there was no concerted attempt to either define its structure or clarify its duties vis-à-vis the organizational set up and regular functions of the commission. While experienced in managing manual elections, members of the PMO lacked experience managing elections involving electronic technologies and could not anticipate the enormous challenges involved in such a task. The PMO did not establish regular meetings; formal reporting and communication process; or project controls, as it was more involved with day-to-day troubleshooting rather than quality

---

70 COMELEC M.R. No. 09-0612.

control and risk management. Although the PMO developed a project management plan and timeline, it was not able to follow it, with deadlines adjusted as original targets were missed. Because of inefficiencies in the way the preparation was managed, the overall cost of the May 2010 national and local elections ballooned to PHP 16.5 billion from the allotted budget of PHP 11.3 billion.

Current and former election officials, parties, IT experts and civil society groups expressed concern that the COMELEC was unable to manage and oversee the vendor, Smartmatic, effectively. Several reasons have been cited, including the relative lack of IT expertise among the COMELEC and the shortened time frame, which required quick decisions and actions by Smartmatic, sometimes without following proper lines of authority.

Voter Education and Public Relations

The COMELEC conducted a nationwide voter education campaign to inform the public about the new technology to help them become comfortable with it and instruct voters how to properly fill out the ballot. The campaign included broadcast and print media, instructional videos, billboards, flyers and a road show to demonstrate the PCOS machines and have people practice on it. Smartmatic provided voter education materials to the COMELEC, and COMELEC adapted these materials, as needed.

The COMELEC's voter education campaign was able to inform a significant percentage of voters. Public opinion research conducted by Social Weather Stations indicated an increase from a baseline October 2009 figure of 38 percent of voters who had either very much or substantial access to information about the new electronic system, to 67 percent just before the May 2010 elections. Given the limitations in resources and staffing, this is a significant achievement. There were also several areas for improvement that COMELEC staff, public opinion research and civil society cited. Most notably, voter education was not conducted in a strategic way and was not informed by public opinion research. As a result, the campaign did not sufficiently target those most in need of information and hardest to reach. Research during the elections showed that those with insufficient information were primarily elderly, rural and less-educated voters. In addition, some observers noted the campaign almost exclusively focused on the new technology at the expense of providing other important voter information.

The COMELEC also put a great deal of emphasis on public relations. Before elections, the public's opinion of the COMELEC was very low. The COMELEC sought to improve this by being proactive and more open about emerging problems. Its policy was to work on a three-hour deadline to publicly address any problems and criticisms raised by others. COMELEC officials sought to build relations with key journalists, and staff attempted to answer all calls from the media. These public relations efforts contributed to a dramatic increase (approximately 30 percentage points) in public confidence in the COMELEC from before to after the elections.

Equipment Delivery

Smartmatic was responsible for and had custody of the PCOS machines and accessories during their transport from the central warehouse to the hubs and polling centers. The delivery of PCOS machines and accessories was a tremendous challenge, given the short timeframe and geography of the Philippines. Smartmatic contracted three logistics forwarders to deliver equipment to the polling stations. Election observer groups criticized this bidding process for a lack of transparency, calling into question the "small size and limited access to networks" of the three companies, none of whom were in the top 10 in market share of freight shipping (by weight).[71]

The majority of the machines were delivered in the last few days before the elections, with some arriving on Election Day and a small number arriving after.

---

71 Final CenPeg Report, Project 30-30.

Custody over the machines shifted to the relevant election officer when the PCOS machines and accessories were given to the BEIs. The guidelines further stated that in no case shall these machines and accessories be left in the polling places without any security. After the elections, BEIs were directed to give the PCOS machines to the technicians of the vendor, which shifted back the custody over the PCOS machines to the vendor. Regional election directors of the COMELEC indicated that this undermined their ability to supervise election preparations. They noted, for example, that they needed to secure the vendor's approval to obtain backup PCOS machines and batteries in precincts that needed them.

Software/Hardware Maintenance and Storage

Instead of an outright purchase, the COMELEC entered into a lease agreement with the vendor for the lease of the PCOS machines used in the 2010 elections, with an option to purchase. Of these, the commission initially bought only 920 units for electoral protest cases. For the remaining machines, the vendor assumed the task of storing and maintaining the machines after the elections. In March 2012, the COMELEC formally decided to exercise its option to purchase all remaining PCOS machines. In 2012, the COMELEC exercised its option to purchase the remaining machines.[72] The Supreme Court eventually upheld the COMELEC on its position that it can exercise its option to purchase the remaining PCOS machines.

Final Sealing and Testing

A final sealing and testing was undertaken seven days before the election, when all PCOS machines had been deployed. During the sealing and testing, the COMELEC and the vendor discovered a problem with the compact flash card caused by the late modification in the ballot design without a corresponding reconfiguration of the software on the compact flash cards. As a result,

---

72 Election observation groups filed four different petitions challenging the COMELEC's decision to purchase the PCOS machines. However, the Supreme Court eventually upheld the COMELEC's decision.

the PCOS machines did not read the ballots properly. This caused a great deal of public uncertainty and calls to postpone the elections. The vendor and COMELEC had to take extraordinary measures to retrieve and replace some 76,000 compact flash cards with newly-configured cards just days before the elections.

After the arrival of the new, compact flash cards, testing and sealing were conducted in some polling stations. Most procedures occurred within two days of the elections. Election observer groups and some COMELEC officials interviewed noted there were a number of polling stations in which testing and sealing did not occur at all. In addition, the confusion and rush surrounding flash card replacement undermined chain-of-custody security procedures, which some pointed to as providing opportunities for tampering with the flash cards.

Election Day – Set-up, Security, Voting Process, Troubleshooting

The general instructions contain specific instructions for BEIs on: preparation for voting; manner of obtaining ballots; manner of voting; procedure in case of shortage of ballots; procedure in case of rejection of ballots by the PCOS machine; procedure for disposing unused ballots; procedure for the counting of ballots and transmission of results; the disposition of election returns; shutting down of the PCOS machine; and the disposal of PCOS, ballot boxes, keys, election returns and other documents.[73] The COMELEC, however, was criticized for its failure to finalize and distribute the general instructions much earlier.

To ensure integrity of the machine and the system, the general instructions outline steps for BEIs to follow before voting starts. These include initializing the automatic printing of a report showing zero votes for each candidate and including geographic information of the precinct.

---

73 Resolution No. 8786, Revised General Instructions for the BEIs on the Voting, Counting, and Transmission of Results in Connection with the 10 May 2010, National and Local Elections.

For the voting process, after authentication, voters were issued a secrecy folder and paper ballot, upon which they used a pen to shade an oval to mark each of their choices. After completing the ballot, the voter inserted it into the feeder slot of the PCOS machine. If the PCOS accepted the ballot, the machine display flashed a confirmation message. Upon acceptance, the PCOS scanned the ballot and saved the image as a TIFF file in the compact flash card, along with data on how the PCOS read the ballot choices. The paper ballot dropped into a secure box under the scanner. After casting their ballots, voters returned to the BEI to have their finger marked with indelible ink (although observers noted that in many polling stations, voters were instead marked when they were handed their ballots).

The PCOS machines returned a ballot out of the feeder slot if: the marks printed along the ballot did not match the assigned precinct; the ballot had already been accepted or rejected; or there were ambiguous marks. Voters had three more opportunities to correct and re-feed the ballot. After four total feeds, the ballot would be considered rejected, and the voter had to return the ballot to the BEI. Observers found that in most instances, ballots were accepted on the initial try.

The issue of whether the AES provided a sufficient voter verified audit trail (VVAT) was debated. COMELEC officials contended that the ballot itself provided sufficient verification to the voter. However, several election observation groups and IT experts pointed out that voters were not able to verify how the PCOS machine interpreted their votes, which was the data transmitted as the official election results.

Nearly 40 percent of BEIs surveyed in a Social Weather Stations survey had problems operating the machines; although, in most cases, the problems were not severe, and were eventually addressed. The most common problem reported was paper jamming during printing. Other problems reported during

Election Day were inadequate real-time technical support for problems, such as running out of thermal paper; missing or drained batteries; and data transmission problems.

To assist the BEIs, PCOS technicians were provided by the vendor, which claimed that over 48,000 technicians were recruited, trained and deployed for on-site support before and during Election Day. Call center agents were also mobilized during Election Day for monitoring the entire process and for remote support to field technicians. Election officers interviewed, however, complained that most of the PCOS technicians did not have the technical skills to assist them. Election observation groups and some IT experts interviewed also expressed strong concerns about the full level of access that the vendor-provided technicians had to the PCOS machines, particularly since most BEIs were completely reliant on technicians to resolve issues with the machines.

One of the most significant problems on Election Day was long lines in the precincts.[74] This may have led to disenfranchisement of voters who could not or decided not to wait in a long line. The lines were primarily caused by the need to cluster of precincts (i.e., the 250,000 precincts in 2007 were reduced to 80,000 precincts in 2010), wherein the number of voters per precinct was increased from 200 to a maximum of 1,000. The need to cluster precincts arose because the budget for the elections only provided for leasing approximately 80,000 PCOS machines. The long lines were compounded by the fact that the COMELEC did not increase the number of BEIs to handle the increase in number of voters per location, and the lack of training for BEIs on how to run the voting process efficiently.

---

[74] In a Social Weather Stations opinion poll, 71 percent of voters reported "very long lines" on Election Day.

ELECTION DAY – OBSERVATION

Nonpartisan Domestic Election Observers

COMELEC accredits one or more groups as "citizens' arms" for each election period. These groups are supposed to serve as civil society observers and simultaneously play a number of supportive roles throughout the electoral process. They also receive certain rights that give them greater access to observe aspects of the process that unaccredited groups do not receive, such as access to the central server that receives the transmitted precinct-level election results and receipt of paper copies of election results in the precincts.

For the 2010 elections, a limited number of civil society groups sought official accreditation as citizens' arms. Controversially, there was only one group accredited – the Parish Pastoral Council for Responsible Voting (PPCRV), which received funding from the COMELEC to conduct voter education, election observation; staff voter education desks; participate in the Special Bids and Awards Committee; and organize the random manual audit.

Many independent civil society groups questioned whether the PPCRV was able to independently monitor the elections, given its dependence on the COMELEC for funding and its dual role to support the electoral management process and simultaneously monitor the process. Several groups conducted observation without accreditation, either because they were denied accreditation or chose not to seek accreditation due to concerns that becoming citizens' arms could undermine their independence. These groups included:

- Procurement: Transparency and Accountability Network
- Technological preparations: Halalang Marangal
- Campaign finance: Pera't Pulitika and Philippines Center for Investigative Journalism
- Overall election preparations and conduct: Bantay Eleksyon, a coalition

of 47 organizations formed by the Consortium on Electoral Reforms
- Overall election preparations and conduct, with a focus on technology: Center for People Power in Governance (CenPEG), as part of the "30-30 Vulnerabilities and Safeguards" project (Project 30-30), which involved consultants and scholars covering computer science; programming and security; mathematics; and law. CenPeg also involved 12 regional coordinators and thousands of poll watchers from at least 50 provinces. CenPeg also conducted a post-election assessment in nine cities and provinces to verify incident reports.
- Polling and canvassing processes: NAMFREL and Consortium on Electoral Reforms (CER); both attempted to obtain election results from precincts and compare them to officially-reported results in thousands of precincts.
- Electoral violence: Vote Peace and National Task Force HOPE
- Legal monitoring and electoral disputes: LENTE and Libertas
- International observation: The Carter Center conducted a limited election observation mission from March through June 2010. It did not issue public statements during the election period, but did issue a final report following the elections.[75] NDI organized an international pre-election delegation, which issued a report on March 13, 2010.[76]

Groups that attempted to observe elections on Election Day reported that they faced significant problems gaining access to polling stations, observing the transmission and obtaining copies of election results. This caused serious concern among observers, who contended that no independent group was able to genuinely observe Election Day conduct.

Given the challenges involved in observing the move to electronic technologies, greater capacity building and coordination among the groups would have

---

[75] http://www.cartercenter.org/resources/pdfs/news/peace_publications/election_reports/philippines-may%202010-elections-finalrpt.pdf.
[76] http://www.ndi.org/files/Statement_of_Pre-Election_Delegaton_to_the_Philippines.pdf

produced a more effective observation of the 2010 elections. In particular, IT groups and traditional election observation groups did not coordinate their resources well enough to take advantage of each other's strengths, knowledge and networks. Citizen observation groups, particularly those who lacked IT capacity prior to 2009, did not sufficiently refine their monitoring methodologies to take into account the new technologies of the 2010 elections. In many cases, they did not have the specific expertise to anticipate where problems could occur. Without official access to many aspects of the process, the groups often had to rely on access to contacts and relationships to gain access to information on COMELEC decisions and processes (insider information), rather than formal opportunities to observe such processes. Finally, several groups noted they should have better trained observers on understanding the new technology and its vulnerabilities.

Partisan Poll Watchers

Most major political parties and candidates organized partisan poll watchers to deploy to polling stations on Election Day. Parties in the Philippines have done this for many years under the manual election system, so the switch to electronic counting technologies presented a challenge. As in previous elections, parties and candidates tended to field poll watchers in locations and regions where they had a stronger ground presence and where they were most concerned about fraud. Some larger parties, such as the Liberal Party, educated campaign managers, candidates, lawyers, branch offices and poll watchers on the new technology, and how the PSCOs machines worked. However, since the general instructions were issued very late, it was difficult for parties to effectively train their poll watchers on how to monitor Election Day procedures. In particular, they recognize they did not adapt their trainings enough to take into account the new technology, where the vulnerabilities were and how to collect credible evidence in case of fraud or manipulation against their candidate/party.

Transmission and Tabulation

Data from the PCOS machines were electronically transmitted to the municipal, national and central consolidation centers immediately after closure of the polls using two transmission methods: cellular transmission through general packet radio service on the global system for mobile communications (GSM); and satellite transmission through Broadband Global Area Network (BGAN). Although the transmission was, in general, fast and efficient, there were reports of transmission failures or the inability of the consolidation centers to receive data. Approximately 85 percent of results were transmitted with direct electronic transmission, and 15 percent through physical delivery of compact flash cards to the municipal level.

Difficulties also emerged because of the COMELEC's prescription that the electronic transmission of results must follow the reporting hierarchy used in manual elections. This system requires that data must be reported from precinct to municipality to province to the central server. Assessments of the AES noted that this system should have been abandoned, particularly since data communications at the main/central canvassing center were more reliable than those in municipalities and provinces. It would have been more cost effective and efficient to transmit results data directly to a central server.

To monitor the transmission process, several election observation groups had planned to collect precinct-level election results and compare them to the precinct-level results posted on the COMELEC's website, which was required by law. This included the accredited PPCRV, and unaccredited efforts, such as the Bantay ng Bayan network, which included NAMFREL and Bantay Eleksyon of the Consortium on Electoral Reforms. Both mobilized thousands of observers on Election Day to collect precinct-level results. However, the comparison of results for a sizeable portion of precincts was not possible, in part because of a number of cases in which BEIs refused to provide observers – even PPCRV's accredited observers – with a copy of the election results. Unaccredited observers had an even more difficult time entering polling stations and obtaining copies of election results. Further, in some precincts, the BEIs closed the PSCOS machines after transmitting results without printing copies of the election results for distribution. Most observer groups attributed these problems to a lack of training among BEIs about the rights of observer access to election results.

After several days, PPCRV was able to gather printed results from many precincts and compare them to results received by the national canvassing server that received results on Election Day. Of the precincts evaluated by PPCRV (which was not a random representative sample), approximately 0.06 percent of results showed discrepancies when compared to the central server.

The law requires that precinct-level election results be posted publicly on COMELEC's website. However, on election night, the public posting of transmission results stopped after approximately 90 percent of the results had been posted. Thus, no results were publicly released for approximately 7,500 PCOS machines. The data was soon taken down by the COMELEC. Before it was taken down, a group of IT experts created a mirror image of the site for data analysis.[77] They found a number of anomalies and missing data. For example, among precincts that did have data, nearly 40 percent had missing data in one or more candidate positions. COMELEC has never explained why full, precinct-level results were not released publicly, nor has it explained the apparent data errors on the website.[78] This has raised serious concerns among some political contestants and civil society members.

---

[77] Mirror website with election data: http://curry.ateneo.net/~ambo/ph2010/electionresults/res_reg0.html

[78] COMELEC and Smartmatic representatives interviewed who had access to the three main servers reported that the data was complete on the main servers, but no one could provide a reason why the data was never posted on the website.

POST-ELECTION PROCESSES

Post-election Audits

There are two methods through which audits were supposed to have been conducted. However, both methods were not implemented sufficiently to allow for a credible check on the publicly-reported voting results. The first was through public positing of precinct-level results on the COMELEC's website, which was not implemented, as explained in the Transmission and Tabulation section.

The second was through a random manual audit (RMA), which by law was required to be conducted in five randomly-selected precincts per congressional district (a total of 1,145 precincts) after the closure of the voting process. The Random Manual Audit Committee, which included members of PPCRV, was responsible for conducting the RMA. In the pre-election period, election observation groups pressed PPCRV and COMELEC to prepare for the RMA early, and provided COMELEC with RMA guidelines prepared by the Management Association of the Philippines. However, COMELEC staff and PPCRV representatives acknowledge that appropriate advance preparations were not made.

The RMA sample drawing was conducted transparently on Election Day in front of the media. However, the sample was not representative, as precincts in difficult-to-reach communities (the least accessible barangays) were excluded from the sample. Many BEIs were not informed they were selected for the RMA until late in the day, in some cases, after the precincts had already moved the ballots to higher-level tabulation centers. BEIs were not well-informed on RMA procedures. The RMA was not completed until more than two months after Election Day. Further, independent observers were not able to monitor the process in most locations. NAMFREL observers noted that in many of the locations it attempted to observe the RMA, no parties or PPCRV representatives were present.

When finally completed, the RMA demonstrated a 99.6 percent accuracy rating of the election results. This fell below the COMELEC's requirement of 99.995 percent accuracy in the RFP for the automated system. This result is subject to questions, given the delayed process, bias in the sample, lack of independent observation and inconsistent implementation.

Challenges and Recounts

Electoral dispute resolution in the Philippines is handled by several different adjudicative bodies, depending on the type of dispute and the type of election. Prior to the May 2010 elections, expectations were that the move to electronic counting technology would reduce the number of electoral complaints filed. However, the opposite occurred. The House of Representatives Electoral Tribunal received a record number of cases, 65, in 2010 – a significant increase from the 35 filed in 2007. The COMELEC also received more cases filed by losing candidates, 98, in 2010 – compared to 73 in the 2007 elections.[79] Some election protests were related to the behavior of candidates, election officials and others, while a portion of the protests were related to the electronic technology used in the elections. Some of the most common technology-related protests were: erroneous counting of votes or misreading of ballots by the PCOS machines; errors in the initialization of PCOS machines; errors in transmission and consolidation of results; erroneous rejection of ballots; non-implementation of security measures; and manipulation of PCOS machines and/or compact flash cards.

In the case of recounts, paper ballots are to be used. Scanned images of the ballots (scanned on Election Day) are only to be used in cases where the integrity of the ballot box has been compromised. This was a hotly-debated issue. One point of controversy was that, unless there was evidence that ballot box integrity was compromised, scanned images could not be used in cases where there was a significant difference between the physical count of the ballots (excluding rejected ballots) and the number of votes cast as reported in the official election results.

---

79 Issues and Challenges to Dispute Resolution under the PSCOS AES, Libertas.

Some party representatives and candidates interviewed noted the courts did not have the IT capacity to effectively rule on technology-related cases. Others noted the full cost of protests increased as a result of the move to electronic technology, since they have to hire more specialized legal and IT expertise; they need to educate themselves in more detail about the technology; and collecting evidence is more difficult under an electronic system.

Evaluation of the System

Several post-election assessments of the AES were conducted by the COMELEC and other stakeholders, including one conducted by IFES for the commission, which involved the commissioners, senior staff, regional directors, election officers and representatives of civil society and political parties. Additionally, the CAC submitted a comprehensive report on the implementation of the AES to the COMELEC, which contained an evaluation and recommendations for improvement. Several civil society organizations also evaluated the AES. Many of these evaluations were presented in final reports, public forums and discussions. In addition, a local survey group, the Social Weather Stations, conducted a survey after the 2010 elections. Approximately 75 percent of respondents rated the results of the May 10 elections to be "satisfactory," a marked improvement compared to the 2004 and 2007 elections, which registered a satisfactory ratings of only 53 percent and 51 percent, respectively.[80]

Media Coverage

Media coverage surrounding the elections focused primarily on the electoral races and results, not as much on the new technology. Journalists and editors interviewed noted the main coverage of the technology focused on a few major problems before Election Day, such as the replacement of compact flash cards, and on the speed with which preliminary results were announced in comparison to past elections. Generally, the media did not cover electoral protests, with the exception of the protest filed by vice presidential candidate

---

80 People's Evaluation of the May 2010 Automated Elections, SWS (10 July 2010).

Manuel "Mar" Roxas III. In interviews, several journalists attributed some of this lack of coverage to the difficulty in discerning whether the claims were credible or not, because editors and journalists were not familiar enough with the technology. Some media organizations had in-house workshops on the AES system, and some civil society groups engaged with media to educate them on the technology or express their concerns. However, media organizations and staff mentioned they were often confused about the technology and felt ill-equipped to report on it.

LESSONS LEARNED

Legality

- The transition from manual to automated elections is a long process. The legality of electronic technologies in the Philippines' elections was addressed over several years and through a structured, mostly-inclusive process. While there were some legal provisions criticized as inconsistent with automated elections or too ambiguous, most stakeholders agreed there is a solid legal foundation upon which to conduct automated elections.

- The Philippines' experience shows the benefits of conducting a careful, thorough revision of legislation well in advance of a nationwide transition to electronic technologies.

Accountability

- In-house capability is crucial for ensuring accountability of the exercise. The COMELEC faced an enormous challenge to remain in control of the relationship with the vendor, Smartmatic, particularly as Election Day approached and urgent problems arose. This was due in part to the COMELEC staff not yet building the in-house capacity to manage the vendor.

- The accountability of the whole automation process could have been enhanced significantly, had the COMELEC properly implemented post-audit mechanisms. The Philippines planned on two different methods for auditing results – a random manual audit and the public posting of precinct-level results on the COMELEC's website. However, both methods were not implemented sufficiently to allow for a credible check on official election results.

- IT groups and election observation groups did not coordinate well enough to take advantage of each other's comparative strengths, knowledge and networks. Better coordination and cooperation among civil society actors could have helped pair IT expertise with election monitoring experience and methodologies to more effective election observation efforts.

- Oversight actors in the Philippines, including advisory bodies, media, parties and civil society, could have better trained core staff, coordinators and observers on understanding how to effectively observe based on the new technologies. They should have also better assessed and adapted their monitoring methodologies to take into account any new technologies used in elections.

Security and Secrecy

- Ensuring the security of electoral processes was a significant challenge during the transition to automated elections. While a range of security features were initially planned, several of these features were not implemented or did not function as planned. Several election observation groups and IT experts alleged that the range of security vulnerabilities exposed the system to possible manipulation, fraud and failure. In most cases, failure to implement planned security features was attributed to a lack of sufficient time.

- Secrecy of the ballot, with respect to the PCOS machines, was not raised as a concern during the 2010 elections. Some critics argued voters should have been able to confirm how the machine recorded their votes by having the machine briefly flash on its screen the voters' choices as recorded, but others contended it could have compromised secrecy.

Transparency

- While the COMELEC appeared to make a genuine attempt to be transparent during some parts of the electoral process, this was not always sufficient to meet international best practice and to gain the trust and confidence of key stakeholders. In some cases, transparency was sacrificed for expediency. In other cases, critics allege that transparency was restricted because of sensitivity to criticism during what was a very challenging transition to automated elections nationwide.

- Most glaringly, independent observers did not have official, accredited access to any part of the process. Only one group, the PPCRV, was accredited, and most believe its independence was questionable. As a result, independent observers often had to rely on informal contacts and relationships or court appeals to gain access to information on COMELEC decisions and processes, rather than formal opportunities to observe such processes. In many instances, by the time to observer groups obtained the information or documents they sought out, it was too late.

Sustainability

- Cost considerations are a major challenge for ensuring sustainability of automated elections. Despite extensive consideration of the full costs of moving toward automation, some challenges did emerge. With the budget allotted, the COMELEC could not lease enough machines to maintain even a fraction of the number of precincts in previous elections. This led to the need to cluster precincts, which was cited as a major cause of the long lines on Election Day.

- Several people interviewed emphasized how much more complex and challenging the automated elections were to conduct compared to manual elections. They noted that electronic technologies should not be seen as a way to address capacity shortcomings in managing elections – they may magnify those shortcomings. The 2010 experience showed the challenges of implementing electronic technologies without having enough leadership and staff with IT expertise and experience, as well as a high degree of project management capacity.

Inclusiveness

- Early engagement is critical for building trust among stakeholders. During the consideration of different technologies and, later, the procurement process, an antagonistic relationship developed between the COMELEC and some civil society and IT groups who felt they were excluded from the process.

- Several interviewees noted that, at times, inclusiveness was sacrificed, at least in part due to the shortened timeframe for implementing the 2010 elections.

- The 2010 voter education efforts were able to inform a significant percentage of voters, which was a notable accomplishment. However, it was not conducted in a strategic, research-informed way, which meant those most in need of information and hardest to reach often did not receive sufficient information.

Trust

- The COMELEC faced a significant challenge in building trust in the election processes. Following the elections, however, overall trust and satisfaction with the elections increased significantly. Many attributed this boost in trust as a result of the speediness of the results and the absence of reported widespread Election Day failures. The fact that more than 90 percent of precinct results were reported on election night was viewed as a significant achievement, and the presidential election results reflected the exit polls almost exactly. These factors helped bolster voter trust and mitigated the potential for post-election violence.

- However, the lack of transparency of certain aspects of the process reduced trust among election observation groups and IT experts, as well as some parties and candidates.

- Several interviewees noted the increased trust in 2010 was partially due to the novelty and pride associated with the Philippines conducting the first nationwide automated elections and the wide margin of victory in the presidential race, which mitigated potential complaints. They cautioned that this trust may not be sustained unless significant efforts are made to address problems and security vulnerabilities before the next major elections in 2013.

IMPLEMENTING AND OVERSEEING ELECTRONIC VOTING AND COUNTING TECHNOLOGIES: RESOURCE ANNEX

RECOMMENDATIONS AND GUIDELINES ON IMPLEMENTING E-VOTING AND COUNTING

Caarls, Susanne: 'E-voting Handbook: Key Steps for Introducing E-voting', Council of Europe, 2010, available at <www.coe.int/t/dgap/democracy/activities/ggis/E-voting/E-voting%20 2010/Biennial_Nov_meeting/ID10322%20GBR%206948%20Evoting%20handbook%20 A5%20HD.pdf>

Council of Europe, 'Certification of E-Voting Systems', 2011, available at <www.regjeringen.no/upload/KRD/Prosjekter/e-valg/vedlegg/Certification_evoting_system_eng.pdf>

Council of Europe, 'Guidelines on Transparency of E-enabled Elections', 2011, available at <www.coe.int/t/dgap/democracy/activities/ggis/e-voting/E-voting%202010/Biennial_ Nov_meeting/Guidelines_transparency_EN.pdf>

Council of Europe, 'Legal, Operational and Technical Standards for E-Voting', 2004, available at <www.coe.int/t/dgap/democracy/activities/key-texts/recommendations/Rec(2004)11_Eng_Evoting_and_Expl_Memo_en.pdf>

EC-UNDP Joint Taskforce on Electoral Assistance, 'Procurement Aspects of Introducing ICTs Solutions in Electoral Processes', 2010, available at <www.ec-undp-electoralassistance.org/images/operational%20paper.pdf>

Goldsmith, Ben, 'Electronic Voting & Counting Technologies: A Guide to Conducting Feasibility Studies', International Foundation for Electoral Systems, 2011, available at <www.ifes.org/Content/Publications/Books/2011/~/media/Files/Publications/Books/2011/Electronic_Voting_and_Counting_Tech_Goldsmith.pdf>

International IDEA, 'Introducing Electronic Voting: Essential Considerations', 2011, available at <www.idea.int/publications/introducing-electronic-voting/upload/PP_e-voting.pdf>

Norden, Lawrence D. and Lazarus, Eric, 'The Machinery of Democracy: Protecting Elections in an Electronic World', Brennan Center for Justice, 2007, available at <www.brennancenter.org/content/resource/the_machinery_of_democracy_protecting_elections_in_an_electronic_world/>

Norwegian Ministry of Local Government and Regional Development, 'Electronic Voting: Challenges and Opportunities', 2006.

US Election Assistance Commission, 'Voting System Testing and Certification Program Manual', 2011, available at <www.eac.gov/assets/1/Documents/Certification%20Program%20Manual.OMB%203265.004.Exp%206.30.2014.pdf>

US Election Assistance Commission, 'Voluntary Voting System Guidelines', 2005, available at <www.eac.gov/testing_and_certification/voluntary_voting_system_guidelines.aspx>

Yard, Michael, 'Direct Democracy: Progress and Pitfalls of Election Technology', International Foundation for Electoral System, 2010, available at <www.ifes.org/Content/Publications/Books/2010/Direct-Democracy-Progress-and-Pitfalls-of-Election-Technology.aspx>

OVERSEEING ELECTRONIC VOTING AND COUNTING

Carter Center, 'Handbook on Observing Electronic Voting', 2012, available at <www.cartercenter.org/resources/pdfs/peace/democracy/des/Carter-Center-E_voting-Handbook.pdf>

International IDEA, Voting from Abroad: The International IDEA Handbook on External Voting (Stockholm: International IDEA, 2007), Chapter 9, 'Observation of External Voting', available at www.idea.int/publications/voting_from_abroad/upload/chap9.pdf>

Organization of American States, 'Observing the Use of Electoral Technologies', 2010, available at <www.oas.org/es/sap/docs/Technology%20English-FINAL-4-27-10.pdf>

Organization for Security and Co-operation in Europe (OSCE) Office for Democratic Institutions and Human Rights (ODIHR), 'In Preparation of Guidelines for the Observation of Electronic Voting', October 2008, available at www.osce.org/odihr/elections/34725

OSCE/ODIHR: Handbook for the Observation of New Voting Technologies. Warsaw, 2013.

Pran, Vladimir and Merloe, Patrick, 'Monitoring Electronic Technologies in Electoral Processes', National Democratic Institute, 2007, available at <www.ndi.org/files/2267_elections_manuals_monitoringtech_0.pdf>

Vollan, Kåre, 'Observing Electronic Voting', Norwegian Centre for Human Rights, 2005, available at <www.jus.uio.no/smr/english/about/programmes/nordem/publications/nordem-report/2005/1505.pdf

INTERNET VOTING AND VOTING FROM ABROAD

International IDEA, Voting from Abroad: The International IDEA Handbook on External Voting (Stockholm: International IDEA, 2007), Chapter 10, 'E-voting and External Voting', available at <www.idea.int/publications/voting_from_abroad/upload/chap10.pdf>

Trechsel, Alexander and Vassil, Kristjan, 'Internet Voting in Estonia: A Comparative Analysis of Four Elections Since 2005', European University Institute, 2010, available at <www.vvk.ee/public/dok/Report_-_E-voting_in_Estonia_2005-2009.pdf>

OTHER RESOURCES ON E-VOTING AND COUNTING

Barrat I Esteve, J, Goldsmith, B. and Turner, J., 'International Experience with E-voting', IFES, 2012, available at www.regjeringen.no/upload/KRD/Prosjekter/e-valg/evaluering/Topic6_Assessment.pdf

Jones, Douglas W., 'Some Problems with End-to-End Voting', University of Iowa, 2009, available at <www.cs.uiowa.edu/~jones/voting/E2E2009.pdf>

McGaley, M. and Gibson, J.P., 'Electronic Voting: A Safety Critical System', National University of Ireland, Maynooth, 2003.

Oostveen, A.-M. and van den Besselaar, P., 'Security as Belief: User's Perceptions on the Security of Electronic Voting Systems', Royal Netherlands Academy of Arts and Sciences, available at <http://subs.emis.de/LNI/Proceedings/Proceedings47/ Proceeding.GI.47-8.pdf>

Zetter, Kim, 'The Cost of E-Voting', Wired Magazine, 2008, available at <www.wired.com/threat-level/2008/04/the-cost-of-e-v>